AF835808

TRADE WITH THE ODDS

Since 1996, Bloomberg Press has published books for financial professionals on investing, economics, and policy affecting investors. Titles are written by leading practitioners and authorities, and have been translated into more than 20 languages.

The Bloomberg Financial Series provides both core reference knowledge and actionable information for financial professionals. The books are written by experts familiar with the work flows, challenges, and demands of investment professionals who trade the markets, manage money, and analyze investments in their capacity of growing and protecting wealth, hedging risk, and generating revenue.

For a list of available titles, please visit our website at www.wiley.com/go/bloombergpress.

TRADE WITH THE ODDS

How to Construct Market-Beating Trading Systems

Anthony Trongone, PhD, CFP, CTA

BLOOMBERG PRESS
An Imprint of
WILEY

Cover image: Background © Fabian Rothe/istockphoto
Cover design: C. Wallace

Copyright © 2012 by Anthony Trongone. All rights reserved.

Published by John Wiley & Sons, Inc., Hoboken, New Jersey.
Published simultaneously in Canada.

No part of this publication may be reproduced, stored in a retrieval system, or transmitted in any form or by any means, electronic, mechanical, photocopying, recording, scanning, or otherwise, except as permitted under Section 107 or 108 of the 1976 United States Copyright Act, without either the prior written permission of the Publisher, or authorization through payment of the appropriate per-copy fee to the Copyright Clearance Center, Inc., 222 Rosewood Drive, Danvers, MA 01923, (978) 750-8400, fax (978) 646-8600, or on the Web at www.copyright.com. Requests to the Publisher for permission should be addressed to the Permissions Department, John Wiley & Sons, Inc., 111 River Street, Hoboken, NJ 07030, (201) 748-6011, fax (201) 748-6008, or online at http://www.wiley.com/go/permissions.

Limit of Liability/Disclaimer of Warranty: While the publisher and author have used their best efforts in preparing this book, they make no representations or warranties with respect to the accuracy or completeness of the contents of this book and specifically disclaim any implied warranties of merchantability or fitness for a particular purpose. No warranty may be created or extended by sales representatives or written sales materials. The advice and strategies contained herein may not be suitable for your situation. You should consult with a professional where appropriate. Neither the publisher nor author shall be liable for any loss of profit or any other commercial damages, including but not limited to special, incidental, consequential, or other damages.

For general information on our other products and services or for technical support, please contact our Customer Care Department within the United States at (800) 762-2974, outside the United States at (317) 572-3993 or fax (317) 572-4002.

Wiley publishes in a variety of print and electronic formats and by print-on-demand. Some material included with standard print versions of this book may not be included in e-books or in print-on-demand. If this book refers to media such as a CD or DVD that is not included in the version you purchased, you may download this material at http://booksupport.wiley.com. For more information about Wiley products, visit www.wiley.com.

Library of Congress Cataloging-in-Publication Data:

Trongone, Anthony, 1949-
Trade with the odds : how to construct market-beating trading systems / Anthony Trongone, PhD, CFP, CTA.
pages cm. — (Bloomberg financial series)
Includes index.
ISBN 978-1-118-16434-1 (cloth); ISBN 978-1-118-22620-9 (ebk);
ISBN 978-1-118-23941-4 (ebk); ISBN 978-1-118-26414-0 (ebk)
1. Investment analysis. 2. Investments. I. Title. II. Title: Trade with odds and website.
HG4529.T755 2012
332.64—dc23

2012032670

Printed in the United States of America.

10 9 8 7 6 5 4 3 2 1

FSC
www.fsc.org
MIX
Paper from
responsible sources
FSC® C005928

To Lynda, my loving wife

Contents

Preface

For those investors who have come to the simple realization that there are no shortcuts to success, this book is for you. Most investment books promise profits, but are unable to deliver. At this point in their trading careers, traders do not want to keep looking for the elusive money maker. What they are ready to do is focus on sharpening their own trading skills. They are willing to do the work, but where do they start? For them, it is not about spending money on another book; it is about not going down another dead end.

You're kidding yourself if you think mastery over the markets comes from finding the perfect system. This is akin to believing that you could become a landscape artist once you've found the perfect setting to paint.

This book is not about learning the perfect system. In this book, you are learning how to uncover a few profitable strategies to apply in today's trading environment. Although systems may function flawlessly over a series of trading days, the success they give you is often fleeting. Don't worry; as soon as their effectiveness wanes, once you begin applying the trading approach found in this book, there will always be others waiting in the wings.

A Workable Approach to Playing the Percentages

Most market participants agree: Putting the percentages on their side is a workable approach. The question is, how do you run the analysis? The thought of integrating statistical analysis into an already complex trading day can be a powerful disincentive for many individuals.

Because I know that crunching numbers elicits tremendous anxiety for some, this book compiles "fantasy" statistics. There is no heavy quantitative lifting, but rather powerful analysis, such as winning percentages and average returns, along with an assortment of performance charts to monitor the timing sequence of your findings.

In order to directly address these issues, this book contains step-by-step examples using clear instructions on how to use the functions within Excel.

By using these assessment functions, you gain advantages: There is no computational work on your part, no cryptic equations to unravel, and besides getting the answers instantly, as long as you write the formulas correctly, you do not have to worry about proofing for errors.

Given these positive factors, this process becomes less daunting, but the most gratifying feature pertains to the capital outlay of buying another expensive program—there is none! There is absolutely no cost to you because you already own Excel.

Using This Book to Supplement Your Existing Programs

Many traders use the latest in electronic trading programs, and many have over 100 technical indicators, but the majority of traders use very few of them. Most indicators give you similar results, because either they play on running with momentum or use some form of trading between the bands. Still one important aspect is missing—you cannot run a statistical analysis of current market conditions.

For example, after absorbing heavy early morning causalities 30 minutes after the ringing of the opening bell, the market claws back, sharply cutting its percentage loss by three-fifths. Given this information, would you take a long position from 10:00 to the closing bell? Most trading programs are not capable of performing an analysis giving you the winning percentage and summary statistics, nor can they produce a scattergram reflecting the past performance of this trading condition.

A charting program cannot give you these statistics, but by using the functions contained in Excel you can quickly produce this information. Furthermore, the indicators in other programs are restrictive because the focus of prediction is on a single variable. Within the pages of this book, most of the studies implement a multiplicative approach. For instance, a moving average may be encouraging you to take a long position, but is its buy signal getting stronger or weaker? Along with this information, a system should be able to factor in other variables such as trading volume.

Each indicator, by itself, is suggestive, but many variables working together offer a more conclusive analysis.

This book supplements what is missing in other trading programs. By using Excel with your existing trading platform, it expands the investor's ability to assess current market conditions. Since my forecasting procedures afford you more flexibility to study market dynamics, they are a more powerful weapon.

Unlike most trading books, which regiment practically every click of your mouse, this one gives you the autonomy to make your own trading decisions. Certainly there are guidelines and discussions on what to do and what not to do, but its value comes from allowing you to use your own aptitude to create the systems that work best for you. After all, the efficacy of even the best systems are questionable if they are incompatible with your risk tolerance, trading experience, emotional disposition, or your ability to follow their guidelines because of your busy schedule and daily demands.

There is always some material basis on which to begin your analysis. This book gives you a working knowledge of the assessment functions in Excel, how to run the analysis, and a discussion on the interpretation of your findings, as well as a discussion on placing orders on the basis of your conclusions, not arbitrary decision making.

Creative Flexibility

Do you want more creative mastery over your trading day? Many of you, because of your creative ability, are already beating the market, but you want more. Similar to squeezing more juice from a lemon, you can always tweak more profits from your intrinsic abilities.

By consistently playing technical indicators, will you become better at trading the equity or commodity markets?

With technical indicators, you are constantly repeating the same process. This repetition does not strengthen your trading skills in comparison to someone who is making an assessment of the market as its price adjusts to the future expectation of the domestic, as well as the worldwide, economic environment.

After all, these indicators are purely subjective. In fact, technicians seldom agree on the basics. When asking them to define the supporting price of an instrument, you are likely to get different opinions. One reason for not forming a consensus is that the basis of support changes according to the interval you choose (e.g., tick, 1, 5, 10, 20 minutes, hours, days, weeks, months, or years).

This book separates itself from most investment books, because it does not make any claims about creating surefire never miss systems. Few, if any, systems perform effectively across all economic conditions; therefore, you should monitor their performance. This way, you can react accordingly and put them aside when they perform poorly, but when they once again begin predicting market direction, you can simply dust them off and return them to service.

If you were outperforming the markets on a regular basis, would you care if your revenue came from purchasing a trading system, which sends the plays of the day to your inbox? This is a question I asked those in attendance at my 2011 Traders Expo New York presentation. Many participants felt these systems were too mechanical, and after several years, without creative flexibility, they saw only minor improvements in their proficiency as traders.

I believe that in trading, you have to represent yourself; you cannot be whatever a system wants you to be. Be the commander of your finances and take responsibility for your trading decisions; this will afford you the opportunity to take on new challenges with each trading day. Seen from this perspective, in the course of a year, meeting these challenges will bring you closer to your goals.

Acknowledgments

The reality of completing this book cohesively could not have been accomplished without the encouragement and support of the people closest to me.

Of course, I begin with my wife Lynda; she has always been the single most important reason for my success. She is the one I turn to and work with to discuss my thoughts and crystallize my ideas. More importantly, she reduces the distractions around me. She is the perfect companion, not only intellectually gifted, but a romantic and caring person with a wonderful sense of humor and a positive outlook on life.

My daughter, Sara Gia, an exceptional student at Cornell University, is already making great strides in her professional career and will undoubtedly be a positive agent for change. She is a constant source of happiness. Watching her mature and develop into her own person has been a positive motivational force in my life.

Andres, my stepson, and above all, my friend, inspires me with an intellectual curiosity that is matched only by his ability to integrate what he learns into the creative process that he thrives on. He balances his tremendous creativity with remarkable maturity as he constantly challenges himself and others to give and to be the best they can be.

And, to my parents Anthony and Phyllis, whose love and affection I carry with me always.

Of course, education, if you are lucky, is a lifelong process. I am grateful for the valuable lessons I have learned from teaching more than 5,000 students throughout the world. Special thanks go to my favorite student and friend, Edna Yang.

Finally, I would like to thank Jayanthi Gopalakrishnan, the editor of *Stocks & Commodities*, who published my first article; Mina Delgado at eSignal, who has been tremendously supportive of my work; and Kevin Commins and Steven Isaacs for their confidence in this book.

TRADE WITH THE ODDS

CHAPTER 1

Invest in Yourself, Not a Trading System

Emotional qualities are antagonistic to clear reasoning.
—Sherlock Holmes

Those individuals with a passion for trading know success comes from within, but are they applying themselves in this direction?

In this book, the operational definition of beating the market begins with making incremental improvements; that is, as you confront the everyday challenges of the market, you become more adept at finding an imbalance between what you can win and what you can lose.

Are You Good at Decrypting Chart Patterns?

Most technicians claim to be good at decrypting chart patterns. Figure 1.1 shows 16 different stocks ready to breakout from a 340-day (October 31, 2007, to March 9, 2009) bear market. If you study these charts, can you pick the four best and four worst stocks from the bunch?

The line charts record the price movements of 16 companies during the bear market. On March 10, 2009, the bear, after being on the run for 340 trading days, finally hibernates as the bull resurfaces. The market charges ahead over the next 562 trading days. With your prowess in reading chart formations, can you actually make a performance distinction among these 16 stocks?

FIGURE 1.1 These 16 line charts are ready to break out from the 340-day bear market. Can you pick the best-performing from the worst-performing companies over the next 562 trading days (March 10, 2009, to May 31, 2011)?

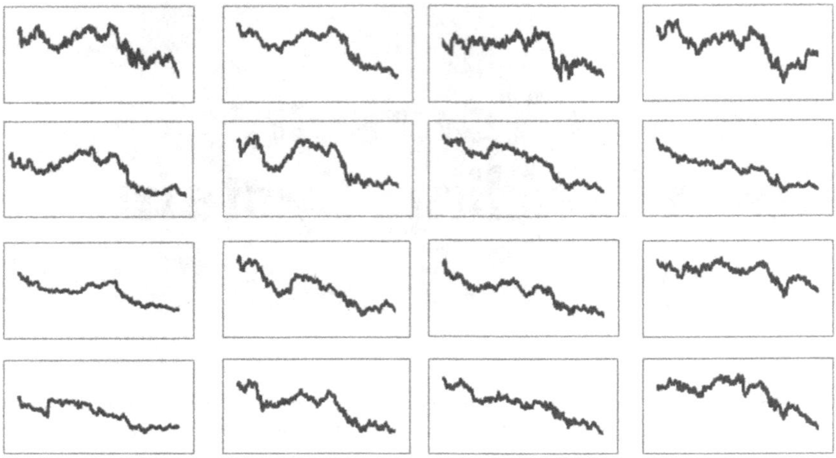

Few investors can spot the best-performing companies, but if you were unable to discern the best from the worst, does it say something about being a chartist? This exercise is not about your current stock-picking acumen, it is about spending all those days, perhaps years, trying to identify future price patterns on the basis of prior results without making a discernible improvement in your trading.

The fundamental question is: Within the year, will your ability at reading chart patterns actually improve, and will you be more profitable because of it?

Beware of Ineffective Solutions

Some technicians, by glancing over candlestick charts, can correctly forecast market direction. Cognitive psychologists would argue as to whether this is something you are born with or a developmental learning process.

Although we want these extraordinary powers, if you do not have them, get over it. The worst thing you can do is to go on deluding yourself.

At any rate, if you do not have this ability after years of trading, can you someday acquire it? This question of whether it continually develops over the years is debatable, but if it is a learning process, does its performance peak? For instance, in running, you can go on improving until you reach your maximum performance, but in trading there are no limitations.

If you are simply maintaining your pace or slowing down, you have to take a different approach in order to make further strides. But where do you turn? Obviously, not every trading system will bring you sustainable success. Some do not complement your ability, emotional disposition, or work schedule. Since everyone runs at a different pace, it is to your advantage to replace a less effective system with something more constructive.

Running in Place

Why would you keep using a system when you are unhappy with its performance? With the market producing a winning performance record, most systems will produce positive results. Since its inception (January 29, 1993, to August 19, 2011), for every 40 trading days, SPDR S&P 500 (SPY)—informally known as the spiders—have had a positive return on 21 of them.[1] Given this uninspiring performance, almost any system will bring us a halfway chance of success; therefore, it elicits a steady sprinkling of positive reinforcement. And with positive feedback coming intermittently, it is more difficult to extinguish.[2]

When any system performs poorly, we attribute our unexceptional performance to external forces by rationalizing our misfortune on bad breaks or transfer the blame directly to ourselves. Still, we believe that if we stay at it, with hard work, someday soon we will put it all together—so we keep trudging along.

Somehow, we never master the chaos, but continually create within it.[3] We constantly toy with minor revisions, which do not alter our unimpressive performance; they do, however, keep us in the game because our occasional wins, along with our attempts to fix things when we have a down day, make it difficult for us to discard our current approach to trading the markets. Recognize the presence of this destructive behavior, and take control over your trading—begin by playing the percentages.

Armed to the teeth with a dazzling array of bells and whistles, your powerful program comes fully packed with every indicator under the sun.

[1]In these 4,675 trading days, the spiders had a 2458-2166-51 daily W-L-T record. See the appendix for a description of the spiders.

[2]According to the principles of operant conditioning, "performance is least persistent after it has been reinforced continuously and most persistent after it has been reinforced intermittently." C. B. Ferster and S. A. Culbertson, *Behavioral Principles*, 3rd ed. (Englewood Cliffs, NJ: Prentice-Hall, 1982), 98.

[3]This is a concept of the venerable existentialist, Simone de Beauvoir. See her *The Ethics of Ambiguity* (New York: Citadel Press, 1948).

Although they give you the illusion of surefire success, it is important to keep them in perspective; more information does not automatically return more revenue.

These bells and whistles are often counterproductive, because when you are using these indicators, they frequently take you in completely opposite directions. Ambiguous distractions adversely affect your analytical powers; when they occur, they often undermine your success because you are likely to fall prey to emotional trading. Certainly, these superfluous indicators are an embellishment of your trading arsenal, but they are not a condition of your success.

Is your program good at crunching numbers? For instance, can it answer this question by giving you the past performance results for this specific trading condition: If the major market indexes close within pennies of their lowest price, can your trading program give you statistics on the performance of the overnight trading session? More specifically, if you are trading the spiders (SPY), can it instantly produce a report of its winning percentage over the previous 300 trading days, its past performance scores, a listing of its outliers, or display a scattergram of the trading days satisfying this requirement?[4]

Supplementing Your Analysis: A Restrictive Trading System

Despite these restrictions, I am not advocating that you replace your powerful programs. In fact, keep your collection of technical indicators, but supplement your analysis by using my statistical techniques.

Crunching Numbers

Following is an analysis of a trading situation lasting 10 years, in which you would take a long position at the closing bell, holding it throughout the night, but sell it when the market opens for trading. It includes a description of the overnight trading sessions (OVS), as well as the regular trading session (RTS). Historical prices showing the specifics of the trading day can be found at popular websites, such as http://finance.yahoo.com.[4]

At the closing bell, the spiders fall to close within ≤ $0.08 of its lowest daily price. What action do you take in response to this information? Given that its price is at the bottom of the trading day, can your trading program produce an analysis of its performance in the overnight session?

[4]Instructions on downloading historical daily prices can be found in the appendix.

TABLE 1.1 Description of overnight trading session.

Date	Open	High	Low	Close	Volume
06/16/2011	127.06	127.97	126.32	127.30	307,830,500
06/15/2011	128.24	129.30	126.68	127.02	300,958,000

OVS: 06/16/2011 (opening price – 06/15/2011 closing price)
OVS: 06/16/2011 (127.06 – 127.02) = .04

TABLE 1.2 Description of regular trading session.

Date	Open	High	Low	Close	Volume
6/16/2011	127.06	127.97	126.32	127.30	307,830,500
6/15/2011	128.24	129.30	126.68	127.02	300,958,000

RTS: 6/16/2011 (closing price 127.30 – opening price 127.06) = .24
RTS: 6/15/2011 (closing price 127.02 – opening price 128.24) = −1.22

Before presenting the findings, Tables 1.1 and 1.2 define the two trading sessions.

Working Hypothesis

If the spiders close within $0.08 of its lowest price, how does it perform in the overnight trading session?[5]

Trading Specifics

When this condition occurs, we want to take a long position at the close of trading but offset it at the ringing of the opening bell. Table 1.3 provides a small sample of this trading condition.

This restrictive system has a winning percentage of 68 percent; it illustrates how we can turn to the percentages to make trading decisions without the emotional distractions, which often are destructive to traders.

Statistical Findings

The analysis for this system looks at the spiders' trading performance over a full 10 years. On December 29, 2000, SPY sat at $131.19; on December 31, 2010, it was at $125.75.

[5]Chapter 4 discusses the reasons for replacing a $ change with a % change when making pricing comparisons.

TABLE 1.3 This is a small sample of seven days from the 10-year analysis. It shows the two days (gray shade) that qualify for this restrictive system because the (close – low) is within $0.08.

Date	Open	High	Low	Close	Volume	(Close – Low)
12/15/2010	124.44	124.93	123.89	124.10	160,823,100	0.21
12/14/2010	124.75	125.23	124.29	124.67	147,249,600	0.38
12/13/2010	125.05	125.20	124.52	124.56	133,812,700	0.04
12/10/2010	124.14	124.60	123.73	124.48	117,571,700	0.75
12/09/2010	123.97	124.02	123.15	123.76	123,705,100	0.61
12/08/2010	122.98	123.38	122.41	123.28	138,019,200	0.87
12/07/2010	123.94	124.01	122.76	122.83	206,581,000	0.07

After 10 years of trading, the spiders had a slight drop in price. This system, which is counting on an overnight recovery, had 119 winning against 55 losing trades. Although we were trading in an unprofitable setting, we were able to construct a system with an attractive winning percentage.[6] In these 175 trades (one tie), it brought in a profit of $22.08 (an average of $12.62). The system affords you one trade in every 14.37 trading days. Occasionally, there was a long respite between trades; however, in trading, patience is often rewarded with profits.

Advances	119
Declines	55
Ties	1
Winning %	68.00%
Sum	$22.08
Average Return	$0.1262

Summary of the System

I refer to this as a restrictive trading system because it is not an everyday play. When constructing these systems, you are generally looking for a high percentage of success; in contrast, we can be profitable if the system has a high

[6]When calculating the winning percentage, a tie is put in the loss column. After all, you do have to pay commissions.

FIGURE 1.2 A snapshot showing the price movement for the spiders (SPY) over 10 years. This SPDR fund replicates the movements of the 500 stocks in this popular index, leaning heavily toward large-capitalization companies.

percentage of failure by playing the downside. The unattractive part of this system comes from having only one play in 14.37 trading days. With experience, however, you will construct a handful of these restrictive systems to complement your trading arsenal.[7]

During these 10 years, the financial markets had two excessive meltdowns. The line chart in Figure 1.2 displays these ugly downturns. Always run an analysis to determine if the systems you are using can weather the storm.

The list below gives the summary results of using this system during the 885 days representing these two sharp downturns shown in the 10-year price chart of the spiders. Despite taking a long position during the 885 trading days comprising the two strong corrections, this has a remarkable 36-19-1 record, returning $8.30 in 56 trades.

Advances	36
Declines	19
Ties	1
Winning %	64.29%
Sum	$8.30
Average Return	$0.1482

[7]Chapter 11 focuses on restrictive trading systems. It contains many more of these gems.

FIGURE 1.3 Performance results of the overnight trading session: By separating the winning from losing days, we can easily spot the outlying score along with the more recent performance scores.

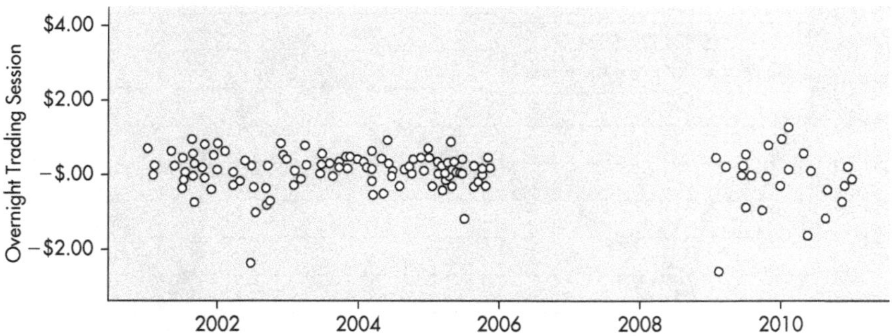

Interestingly, this system was able to stay afloat during two economic recessions. Most often, there is no immunity when taking a long position in a bear market or a short position in a bull market, but it is not uncommon for some of these restrictive systems to still prove profitable, although they are going against momentum.

As we go on, we will uncover more of these anomalies. They certainly deserve our attention.

Next, it is advantageous to display a scattergram (Figure 1.3) showing each one of the 175 trades using this system. Each dot represents a single trade made during this 10-year period.

In these 10 years (2001 to 2010), when the closing bell rang, if the closing price was in the vicinity of its lowest daily price, taking a long position appears to have given us a trading advantage.

Notice that in 2007, the scores in the scattergram begin producing more volatility. Observe the wider spacing between the scores; when this occurs, it often invalidates future performance and therefore is an incentive to reassess our analysis.[8]

Modifying Your Behavior for Better Results

Again, it is important for me to emphasize that this book introduces many of my systems, but unlike most investment books, they are not the primary

[8]Chapter 3 evaluates the ongoing performance of a system; we want to know if it is still performing admirably, or if its performance is starting to fade.

focus. Rather they are a roadmap for enduring success! Think of this book as a tour guide with the express purpose of expanding your imagination so that you can construct your own trading systems. Once you begin experimenting, you will become more self-determining, which promotes a more positive attitude.

Coming from this cognitive perspective, you eventually become less dependent upon external sources for making your trading decisions. This strengthens your self-confidence, and in turn, will give you the conviction that you can execute winning trades despite market adversity.

In addition to taking you through the process of creating a system, there are other discussions within the book, such as designing the worksheet, implementing the assessment functions in Excel, running the analysis, and interpreting your findings. After you amass this information, there is a discussion on how best to place your trades on the basis of your findings.

Always do your homework. Allow your analysis to put you on the correct course. Make your trading decisions only after you discover an obvious advantage. And remember that you are playing the percentages; you may have the advantage, but this does not ensure success. A few trades are not a measure of success or failure. Cultivating a positive learning environment takes you halfway; in order to arrive at your destination, you have to consistently discover new profitable opportunities.

The solution to the earlier problem portraying the 16 charts of companies in the bear market is shown in the appendix at the back of the book.

CHAPTER 2

Playing the Percentages

Man is born free but lives everywhere in chains.

—Jean-Jacques Rousseau

Systems have boundaries, imagination has none. If you release yourself from system constraints, you'll be better able to uncover and utilize your creative ability.

The trading philosophies of most systems disregard your natural resources. And the rigid restrictions they enforce hardly ever take advantage of your own creative powers; this eventually undermines your intrinsic motivation. Without using your inherent ability, your self-confidence as a trader never blossoms, because your success corresponds to the vagaries of the marketplace—bull markets bring success, bear markets bring failure. Consequently, you will eventually achieve only this modest performance expectation.

When you are less bound by conventional restrictions, you can see each new trading day as an opportunity to apply your talents.[1] This is necessary because existentialism encourages you to stop running away from yourself, but these restrictive trading programs never allow you to be yourself. If you are going to make improvements, they are going to arrive within the structure of your individualism.[2]

In managing your own accounts, take responsibility for your actions. This way you are more likely to accept any setback as just a temporary

[1]Abraham Maslow, *Motivation and Personality* (New York: Harper & Row, 1954), 158-167.

[2]The Danish philosopher Søren Kierkegaard wrote in his famous passage, "The thing is to find a truth which is the truth for me." *The Essential Kierkegaard*, ed. Howard and Edna Hong (Princeton, NJ: Princeton Paperbacks, 2002). (Søren Kierkegaard's Journals & Papers IA Gilleleie, 1 August 1835, 35 I, A 75.)

roadblock. When setbacks do occur, be passionate about working through them. Although these obstacles may impede your progress, if you view them as lessons instead of failures you will quickly get yourself back on track.

Nevertheless, one has to work within the framework of making trading decisions on the basis of playing the percentages. For instance, if you were to flip a coin with a 50-50 chance of winning, given 6 to 5 (a chance to win \$6 for every \$5 bet) on a coin landing heads up, would you take this wager if the minimum bet was \$500? The answer is: it depends! If it were only one toss; I would think twice, but probably give this offer a pass.

If, however, there were going to be 20 tosses, with the same 6 to 5 odds on each one, you could expect to win \$1,000; is it therefore worth pursuing?

$$\$600 \times 10 \text{ wins} = \$6{,}000$$
$$\$500 \times 10 \text{ losses} = \$5{,}000$$

I would accept this wager because this is the same mentality as playing the percentages. If they are consistently in your favor, over many trades, you are going to be ahead of the curve.

Will using statistics allow you to attain mastery over the markets?

As long as the markets continuously transform themselves, it puts us in the position of confronting emerging patterns of profitability. If you are capable of devising some material basis to begin your speculations, you can construct an endless array of trading systems, which can give you a significant edge.

A Data Revolution: Fantasy Sports and False Leads

Given the growing popularity of informational sources, many websites allow you to download their numbers directly into Excel. By taking advantage of this program's powerful assortment of statistical functions, you can place more emphasis on number crunching. This data revolution can be seen in fantasy sports, as well as sports teams espousing the merits of using metrics on players and team tendencies.[3]

---

[3]Take the article from the June 17, 2011 *Financial Times*, "A Football Revolution," by Simon Kuper, which begins by telling the story of Manchester City's training ground in the village of Carrington. Besides spending money on players, the team has hired a team of data analysts. "Largely unseen by public and media, data on players have begun driving club's decisions—particularly decisions about which players to buy and sell. At many clubs, obscure statisticians in back-rooms will help shape this summer's transfer market." According to the article, "Football is in the grip of a revolution. Following the model adopted by baseball and basketball in the U.S., the use of statistics to analyze play and players is transforming the world's biggest sport."

Statistics can support, but not govern, the future; therefore, they will not be the determining factor. Nevertheless, by providing a "best guess" estimate of what is likely to happen, statistics often point us in the right direction. When trading the markets, playing the percentages does not underwrite success.

Whenever you have a strong premonition about market direction, it is important to research the accuracy of your assumptions. If this working hypothesis supports your analysis, you have a basis to begin trading.

Investment decisions function in a binary (winning or losing) outcome; however, when a system does not favor a particular outcome, it's best to remain inactive. After putting the percentages on your side, you can expect a more favorable conclusion, but statistics are never perfect.

Statisticians refer to this filtering process as branches on a decision tree, in which we make either a mental or written list of supporting arguments for each column. When one of the branches has a marginal advantage, we go for it!

After developing different systems, you run an analysis to confirm your hypothesis, retaining those that give you a statistical advantage and discarding those that you perceive to be less useful at that particular time (refer to Table 2.1).

Given the following 16 scores, what action would you take?

4	4	3	3	2	2	2	2	1	1	1	1	−2	−2	−6	−8

In fairness, while such a generous winning percentage would suggest taking a long position, some precautionary measures are necessary. Despite this impressive winning percentage, there still is the possibility of sustaining another negative loss. It is helpful to understand what precipitates these

TABLE 2.1 Disregarding the sequence of these 16 scores, does the 75 percent winning percentage give you the basis to begin trading?

N	16
SUM	8
AVERAGE	.5
ADV	12
DEC	4
WIN PERCENTAGE	.750

slides; is there something in the analysis that could reduce our exposure to the two outlying scores?[4]

False Leads

The same interpretation of a percentage score does not apply across every aspect of investing. For instance, if 50 of the 100 companies in PowerShares QQQ (informally known as the cues) increase in price, in four years, the expectation is for most companies to incur two positive versus two negative years. In the first year, a company experiencing a negative return is less likely to bounce back, whereas a company producing a positive return is more likely to duplicate this performance.

A company's performance is not analogous to a coin toss. A company coming off a bad year may not warrant a halfway chance of success, whereas, the results of a coin toss have no influence on the future—despite the results of flipping a coin, the odds for the next three tosses remain 50-50.

Although there is no interdependency in flipping a coin, in investing, earlier price movements frequently affect future performance. For instance, if on the day, the E-mini S&P 500 (ES) contract rallied strongly from midnight to 09:00, does taking a long position give us a statistical advantage?

Exploratory Study

If the ES contract advances or declines 1 percent from midnight until 09:00, how will it trade from 09:00 to 15:00?

If this early morning price condition has no effect on these 360 minutes of trading, our results would demonstrate no trading advantage in either taking a long or short position. In other words, this condition would have the same chance of success as flipping a coin in the air.

In evaluating the ES contract from midnight until 09:00, we are investigating the possibility of three trading conditions: an advance $> +1$ percent, a decline < -1 percent, or a price change falling between these two pricing parameters.

On March 14, 2007, the ES contract began a fresh new day with a midnight price of 1,419.25; after 1,151 trading days, its price stood at 1,148.00, a loss of 271.25 points (multiplier = \$50 per point).

[4]The focus of Chapter 7 is on mitigating risk.

TABLE 2.2 Given the three pricing conditions in the six hours after midnight, these are the results of trading the ES contract from 09:00 to 15:00.

ES Contract 03/13/07–08/26/11	LT −1%	GT +1%	Between
Trades	70	57	1,024
Sum	−57.75	−90.50	−124.25
Average	−0.825	−1.588	−0.121
Advances	32	24	537
Declines	38	33	478
Winning percentage	0.457	0.421	0.529

Given this information, we would expect these three conditions to be unprofitable long plays, but profitable shorts. Despite this reasoning, in running the analysis, we are searching for differences among the conditions. If the three conditions are found to be negative, we want to short those conditions with the best possibility for achieving success (Table 2.2).

Either way, after a percentage gain or loss, the ES contract was unable to deliver a positive return. The one giving us the best opportunity at converting a short position into a profitable play came after a sharp percentage rise (GT +1 percent). With fewer trades (24-33 record), its 90.50 point decline, offers us a powerful incentive to short this commodity contract.

After a percentage decline (LT −1 percent) from midnight to 09:00, the average per trade (APT) loss was .825 points, with 38 declining price moves in 70 attempts; consequently, after a loss in the early morning hours, this ES contract was unable to recover.

There were 1,024 days in which neither of these conditions was present. Despite the 124.25 point cumulative loss, the average decline was not as devastating in comparison to the two outlying brackets.

Summary of the Study

After a negative early morning session, there was less afternoon bleeding (the average 70-day setback was .825 points); whereas, waking up to a solid advance gave us a 90.5 point loss in 57 opportunities (1.588 × $50 multiplier). For those holding an overnight long position in this contract, it is an opportunity to take profits. And, for those who are willing to play the downside, a short position was appealing.[5]

When the Percentages Go Astray

Occasionally there is a random shock to the business community; on hearing the news, a once prosperous trading environment rapidly dissipates as it places the earnings prospect for companies in a negative light. The relevant clues are often found somewhere below the surface. It takes some investigative analysis to unearth them, but when you discover a pattern that will put the percentages on your side—proceed with conviction!

In the mid-nineteenth century, an acceptable treatment for typhoid fever was bleeding. It was seen by the medical profession "as not an unfavorable event and sometimes even an advantage."[6] This practice continued until someone finally put those patients contracting the disease into two groups: one that was bled, the other given nothing but bed rest.

Similarly, in the investment field, fallacious reasoning abounds; that is, until you put the pedal to the metal by running the analysis to confirm or disprove your beliefs about past performance.

In a casino, the probability of winning is always different from the actual payout you receive for winning. For instance, when betting on craps, the probability for rolling snake eyes (both dice = 2) is one in 36 different possibilities (1/36 = .02778), but the payoff on a \$1 bet is \$32 in winnings (1/32 = .03125).

The difference is the vigorish, or "vig," the fee for doing business with the casino. Given many bets this fair value discrepancy is often the reason behind a losing night.

The formula for measuring this "fair value" difference is:

	Losing Side		Winning Side
Wager	\$1	**Payoff**	\$32
Chances of Losing	35	**Chances of Winning**	1
Total Chances	36	**Total Chances**	36

[5]Anthony Trongone, "Catch the Crest of the Wave," *Technical Analysis of Stocks & Commodities* (April 2004): 15–22.

[6]Robert D. Rudolph, "Bleeding in Typhoid Fever," *Journal of Medical Association* 147 (January 1914): 41–61.

$$(-\$1.00 \times 35/36) + (\$32 \times 1/36)$$
$$= -.97222 + .88888$$
$$= -.08333$$

When you consider all the possible (36) outcomes, the profit resulting from rolling snake eyes on a \$1 bet = –.08333; therefore, the overall outcome return has you losing \$0.08333 for each wager on rolling snake eyes.[7]

Most active participants before making a trading decision do not know the percentages for either success or failure; therefore, they cannot make an accurate assessment of fair value. In this book, I demonstrate how to assess the difference between the probability of winning or losing on a single trade.

Developing a Constructive Strategy

In my article "Catch the Crest of the Wave," I discuss the advantages of creating dynamic systems, with a focus on early recognition of possible emerging patterns. Placing the basis for your decisions on analysis may not completely suppress emotionally driven trading, but it does pave the way for a more productive trading environment.

Some readers may be more active, some less, but they are all receptive to making an assessment of current market conditions before taking unnecessary risks with their money.

In this book, the analyses of the systems presented cover a variety of time frames. Some allow you to hold your trade for the entire session; others focus on a particular hour of the day. Some systems are for market participants who want to make a few morning trades, possibly making a few adjustments when they get a break from their hectic day. And there are systems for swing traders, who are willing to hold a position over several days.

When you are capable of producing remarkable effects, it is because you are good at measuring the difference between what you can win in comparison to what you can lose. On those days when your analysis is correct, "you want to swim with the current; however, the force of the wave eventually dissipates, since the crowd is drifting with the current for the better part of

[7]Anthony Trongone, *Quantitative Methods for Finance and Investing* (Singapore: Cengage Learning, 2008).

the price move it is to your advantage to trade with the aggregate until the tide begins to turn."[8]

Summary

In 1927, Carl Rogers, the personality psychologist, took an approach to therapy that was in direct contrast to psychoanalysis. His principle of self-actualization expressed an optimistic outlook on the person's capacity for growth. This regenerative process inspires a continuous movement towards autonomy; that is, the responsibility for taking on new experiences. Seen from this perspective, a winning day is obviously rewarding, and a losing day is not pleasing, but if we accept responsibility for this unprofitable day, it provides more of a learning environment. And, when we gain knowledge about ourselves as well as the instruments in our portfolio, tomorrow gives us more than an even chance of becoming better traders.

[8]Trongone, "Catch the Crest of the Wave."

CHAPTER 3

Performance Measures

If you always do what you've always done, you'll always get what you've always got.

—Mark Twain

This chapter contains instructions on how to produce descriptive statistics, as well as how to apply them. As we progress, the correct interpretation of our statistics will be directly responsible for formulating our trading decisions.

For those readers already familiar with writing equations or using shortcuts to hasten the process of arriving at your answers, you can give these aspects just a cursory review. However, a working knowledge of these statistical functions is necessary, because they are responsible for constructing new strategies and perfecting your understanding of this material.

Measuring Return

Let's begin this chapter with your assessment of return. Three years after investing $1,000 in each of the five stocks shown in Table 3.1, their three-year summary return is 15 percent. Despite this simple arithmetic solution, is the monetary value of these five companies the same after three years?

In reviewing the performance of these five stocks, they all show a return of 15 percent over three years. But when computing the dollar value, which one do you think had the highest/lowest dollar return?

Surprisingly, the best performer was the steadiest; whereas, the worst was the least reliable. Company BBB, with a 5 percent annual return for each of these three years was the best-performing company (returning $1,157.63),

TABLE 3.1 Yearly percentage returns for the five companies.

Year	AAA	BBB	CCC	DDD	XYZ
2012	$1,000	$1,000	$1,000	$1,000	$1,000
2013	15%	5%	0%	–5%	–10%
2014	15%	5%	5%	5%	–5%
2015	–15%	5%	10%	15%	30%
Total	15%	15%	15%	15%	15%

TABLE 3.2 Performance returns by year for each of the five companies.

Return on Investment					
Year	**AAA**	**BBB**	**CCC**	**DDD**	**XYZ**
2013	15%	5%	0%	–5%	–10%
2014	15%	5%	5%	5%	–5%
2015	–15%	5%	10%	15%	30%
Year	**AAA**	**BBB**	**CCC**	**DDD**	**XYZ**
2013	$1,150.00	$1,050.00	$1,000.00	$950.00	$900.00
2014	$1,322.50	$1,102.50	$1,050.00	$997.50	$855.00
2015	$1,124.13	$1,157.63	$1,155.00	$1,147.13	$1,111.50

closely followed by CCC. In third place, but relatively close to the leaders was DDD. Trailing the field, with the poorest performances were the two companies with the most variation in their returns (Table 3.2).

What happens, if we switch the yearly returns within each company, replacing the yearly return of 2013 with 2015, would this change their dollar value after three years? (See Table 3.3.)

Discrepancies When Measuring Return

An average score by itself is a clean measure of performance; however, there are instances when this statement is misleading.

BlackBerry (RIMM), the maker of mobile phones, has some aggressive competition; this has put the stock in a steady decline. In 600 trading days (March 17, 2009, to August 2, 2011), it has fallen $0.03 per session.

TABLE 3.3 After flipping the scores around, surprisingly, the 2015 performance returns yielded the same results.

Percentage Returns by Year for Five Different Stocks

Year	AAA	BBB	CCC	DDD	XYZ
2013	−15%	5%	10%	15%	30%
2014	15%	5%	5%	5%	−5%
2015	15%	5%	0%	−5%	−10%
Year	**AAA**	**BBB**	**CCC**	**DDD**	**XYZ**
2013	$850.00	$1,050.00	$1,100.00	$1,150.00	$1,300.00
2014	$977.50	$1,102.50	$1,155.00	$1,207.50	$1,235.00
2015	$1,124.13	$1,157.63	$1,155.00	$1,147.13	$1,111.50

FIGURE 3.1 The gray dots result in a mean score of 0.00, but how many scores are 0?

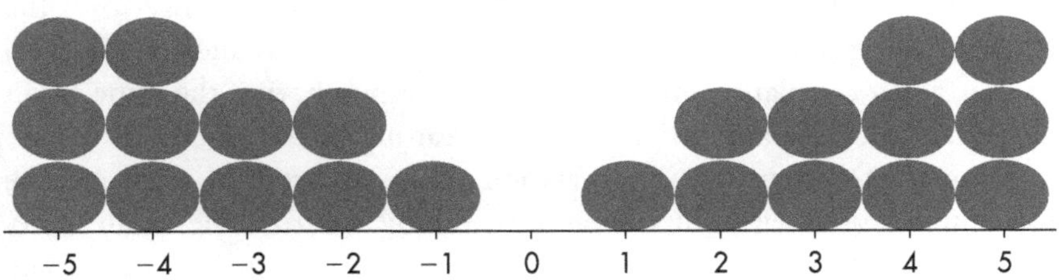

Simple enough, but if you break the trading day down into two sessions, you can better understand how this company behaves. For instance, in those 600 days, this company had a $0.075 average daily profit in the overnight trading session (OVS), but an average loss of $0.105 in the RTS. This additional information changes our thinking about the $0.03 per day average loss.

In many cases, the average score is found at the center of activity; however, this histogram of companies with different performance returns is a hypothetical illustration of how the mean score is not an accurate representation of these 22 scores (Figure 3.1).

Although two stocks can have the same mean score, the one currently increasing in price becomes the more attractive play. For instance, Figure 3.2 displays two stocks going in different directions, although they have the same mean score, which one is the better play?

FIGURE 3.2 While these two stocks went in different directions, they have the same mean score.

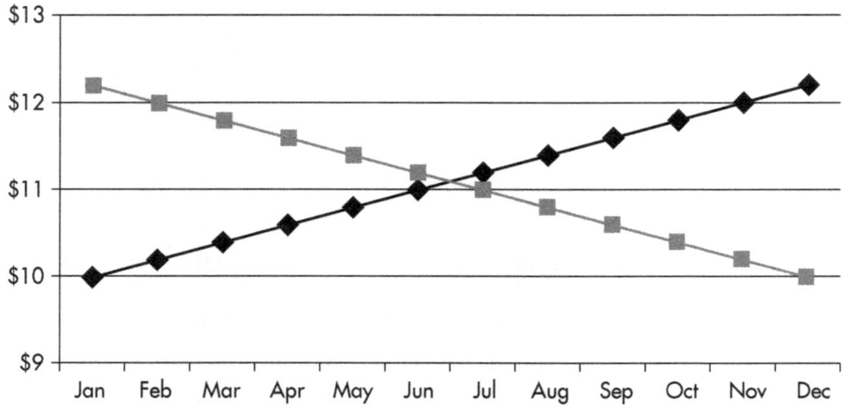

While the mean score is the same for both companies in this yearly line chart, a momentum investor will favor the stock with rising prices over the one with falling prices. The sequence of a stock's price is another factor to consider when calculating an average score. Despite having the same mean score, their price disparity increases as the year unfolds.

Because of outliers, an interpretation of this statistic, by itself, can be misleading. This often occurs because scores fall far from the mean score. These deviations either inflate (an extreme positive score) or deflate (an extreme negative score) the results. For instance, a listing of the daily price change for eight consecutive trading days was 1, 1, 2, 2, 3, 3, 4, and 24.

How many days are above the mean score?

Be cautious when interpreting the mean; assess the entire picture before drawing any conclusions. Carefully inspect how the outlying scores deviate from the mean. Whenever deviation among scores occurs, it becomes more difficult to postulate market direction.

When to Convert a Price Change to Percentage Score

Normally, a simple price change difference gives us a good reading on the market's performance. When comparing these price changes over a series of trading days, especially when the highest-to-lowest (range of scores) widens, a simple price change is deceptive. For instance, once a $10 stock doubles in price, a daily price change of $0.25 no longer has the same significance.

TABLE 3.4 Yearly price change among the four companies.

Stock	AAA	BBB	CCC	XYZ
2013	\$10	\$20	\$50	\$100
2014	\$12	\$22	\$52	\$102

TABLE 3.5 When the price of an instrument varies dramatically, a percentage change score more accurately reflects differences in performance.

Stock	2013	2014	Price Change	Percent Change
AAA	10	12	\$2	20%
BBB	20	24	\$4	20%
CCC	40	48	\$8	20%
DDD	60	72	\$12	20%
EEE	80	96	\$16	20%
XYZ	100	120	\$20	20%

The price change difference among these four companies is \$2.00, but it does not accurately reflect the percentage price change score (Table 3.4).

The calculation of a percentage change score for company AAA is

$$(12 - 10)/10 = .20$$

Since a series of scores generally appreciates or depreciates over the duration of your study, when comparing differences, you can maintain the consistency of these price changes by converting them into a percentage score (Table 3.5).

Frequently daily price changes are small; this requires a four-decimal answer. Since this makes interpretation more difficult, fix this by multiplying the percentage price change score by 100.

Stock price	= \$120
Price change	= \$0.20
Percentage change	= 0.0017
Multiplying by 100	= 0.1667
Percentage change	= (.20/120) × 100

When a stock has a large upside movement, using a percentage score is preferable. Netflix certainly qualifies. This online movie rental subscription company became more attractive once it began down-streaming movies instantly. The company at $39.73 (June 1, 2009) spurted to $304.79 (July 13, 2011); however, on November 25, 2011, its price fell to $63.86. Given these dramatic price swings, when performing this analysis, a percentage score is necessary.

Outlying Scores

Negative outliers are a good representation of fear. Anyone with a long position has the fear of losing on an acute downturn. And, if you are not holding a long position, there is the fear of not participating when the market makes a strong profitable move to the upside.

Before we can report outliers, we have to compute the price change between consecutive trading days (Figure 3.3).

These equations provide the five daily price changes for the SPDR GOLD Shares (ticker: GLD); certainly, this fund was experiencing a meltdown.

"C2" =B2–B3
"C3" =B3–B4
"C4" =B4–B5
"C5" =B5–B6

In order to record the outliers, use the =LARGE for the largest positive outliers, and the =SMALL for the smallest negative outliers.

FIGURE 3.3 This contains the price change along with the written formulas for these six trading days.

	A	B	C	D
1	GLD	close	price change	equation
2	9/26/2011	157.58	-2.22	=B2-B3
3	9/23/2011	159.80	-9.25	=B3-B4
4	9/22/2011	169.05	-4.54	=B4-B5
5	9/21/2011	173.59	-2.19	=B5-B6
6	9/20/2011	175.78	2.47	=B6-B7
7	9/19/2011	173.31		

Statistical Functions

You can produce a function argument dialog box. In doing so, this allows you to plug in the information by typing in the = sign, the function, along with the open parenthesis. In this case =LARGE(will open this dialog box once you click on the f_x symbol (Figure 3.4).

If you prefer to write the equation, the array A1:A5,**1** gives you the largest score; whereas, A1:A5,**2** gives you the second, A1:A5,**3** the third, A1: A5,**4** the fourth, and the fifth largest score is A1:A5,**5** (see Figure 3.5).

Of course, Figure 3.6 shows how you can write the equation:

=LARGE(A1:A5,1)will return the largest score = 18

FIGURE 3.4 Inserting the function.

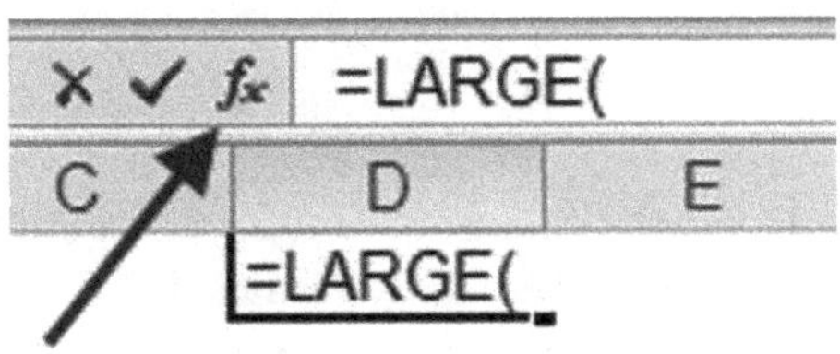

FIGURE 3.5 Writing the equation. This large function includes the range of values and specifies the k-th largest value.

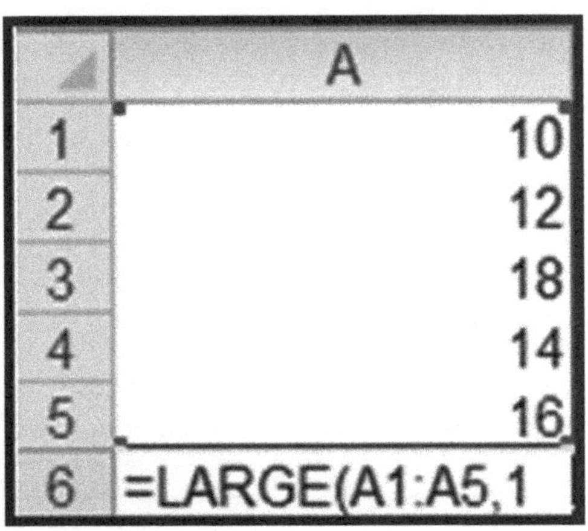

FIGURE 3.6 Opening the dialog box. Inserting the = sign along with the function and providing an open parenthesis "LARGE(" will open the dialog box.

Median Score

The median, put alongside the mean score, can tell us something about the distribution of your dataset. Its calculation is straightforward. If you choose to sort the scores, it is the one in the middle of the pack.

With seven scores, the median, after eliminating the three largest as well as the three smallest numbers, is the one remaining score.

Raw scores:	2	9	7	3	5	8	1

With a median daily price change of \$0.05, you could say half the scores were below and the other half were above a nickel.

When there is an even number of scores, two numbers are left over; their average is the median.

Raw scores:	3	12	8	3	**4**	11	1	**6**

The median is a useful statistic when there are outlying scores. A tilting or, in statistical terms, a skewness of scores occurs when you have an asymmetrical distribution. In this case, the imbalance comes from the two positive 30-plus scores, which create a positive skew.

−2	5	32	−3	−5	3	30

With these two negative outliers, the skew is to the downside. In this case, the mean is negative (−5) and the median is positive (+2).

2	5	−24	3	−5	4	−20

FIGURE 3.7 Netflix: daily price change recording its 25 best/worst trading days.

What are the advantages of using this statistic?

Remarkably, the average daily price change for Netflix, over 500 days (September 8, 2009 to August 31, 2011) was $0.387 per day. Its median score, at $0.19, immediately tells us of a performance discrepancy between its best/worst days. When summing the 25 best/worst days of this entertainment company, there stands a $37 absolute difference. The 25 best days brought in $310, whereas, the 25 worst trading days slid $273. The column chart (Figure 3.7) clearly delineates the difference between these two statistics; therefore, it provides information about its outlying scores.

Risk Is a Moving Target

This comparison chart visually displays the differences of these two statistics; but it is not meant to be a static statistic because prices can move abruptly, especially, for those stocks with inflationary prices. For instance, Netflix, over $300 on July 13, 2011, took a precipitous after-hours fall to an opening price of $74.90 on October 25, 2011. In the 110 trading days (July 13 to December 15, 2011), there were 53 days with a full percentage point loss, including this $43.94 meltdown after the release of a grim earnings report (Figure 3.8).

Since risk can never be fully quantified, it pays to do your homework. Figure 3.8 demonstrates the reality of this statement; particularly when a company with a long string of steady profits confronts strong headwinds, the results can be disastrous.

FIGURE 3.8 The 110 disastrous trading days of NFLX, from \$ 304.79 (July 13, 2011) to \$69.72 (December 15, 2011).

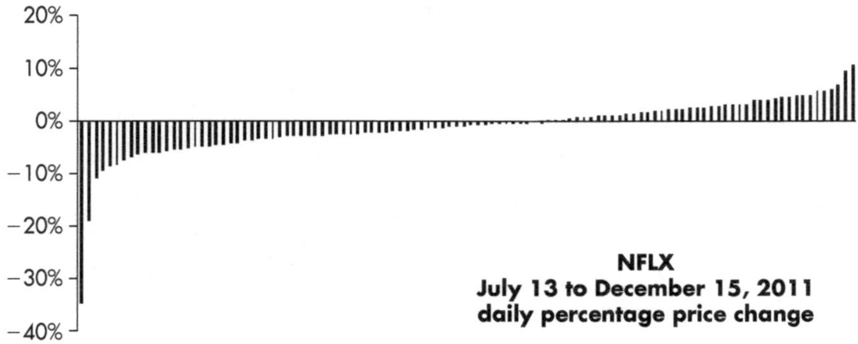

Quartiles

A quartile is one of three quarterly points. Each of the 25th percentiles evenly represent a fourth of the sample population.

=QUARTILE(RANGE,1) = 25th percentile
=QUARTILE(RANGE,2) = 50th percentile or =MEDIAN(RANGE)
=QUARTILE(RANGE,3) = 75th percentile

Percentiles

Although quarterly computations are meaningful, they do not give us the best representation of outlying scores. The percentile function, however, does allow us to numerically classify outliers. This is an especially attractive function for risk-averse investors, who rightfully want to know the downside potential of an investment.

By looking at the past performance of an instrument, it can give us the 5th, 10th, 20th, or any percentile score of your choice. Earlier we looked at NFLX; this company, even with a \$193.53 advance in 500 trading days (September 8, 2009 to August 31, 2011), still had its share of down days. Despite this upward trajectory, the 25 worst days (5 percent of 500) compiled a loss of \$273.58.

Obviously, we want to mitigate some of the undesirable impact of these single-day disasters, but before we can accomplish this, quantifying the downside of any instrument you are actively trading is helpful. The percentage function clarifies this uncertainty.

Table 3.6 is a listing of the 25 worst trading days, on a percentage basis.

TABLE 3.6 The 25 worst-performing days by percentage for Netflix.

Rank	% Loss
1	−13.448
2	−9.044
3	−8.590
4	−6.355
5	−6.064
6	−6.001
7	−5.906
8	−5.877
9	−5.762
10	−5.639
11	−5.564
12	−5.504
13	−5.473
14	−5.467
15	−5.193
16	−4.964
17	−4.693
18	−4.625
19	−4.429
20	−4.366
21	−4.139
22	−4.121
23	−4.081
24	−4.060
25	−4.054

TABLE 3.7 Corresponding to the ranking of the 25 worst scores are the results from the percentile function. Each provides a good representation of the actual loss. The worst approximation is the 3 percentile score of −5.468 against a percentage loss of −5.193 (15th lowest score).

Percentile Score		Actual Score
1%	−6.002	−6.064
2%	−5.639	−5.639
3%	−5.468	−5.193
4%	−4.562	−4.366
5%	−4.121	−4.054

Percentiles offer us a systematic account of the past; however, they are not always an accurate indicator (Table 3.7). Companies with unsustainable price runs often experience excessively large price swings; therefore, the past is often poor at identifying outliers.

Comparison of Two Percentile Functions

Although most statisticians will produce a listing of the maximum/minimum scores, a percentile function allows us to record other possible outcomes. Table 3.8 is a comparison between two different percentile functions in Excel using the following 21 numbers:

The =PERCENTILE.EXC function produces a more realistic account of the extreme scores.

−10	−3	4
−10	−2	5
−8	−1	6
−7	0	7
−6	1	8
−5	2	9
−4	3	10

When replacing the second lowest score (−9) with −10 (gray background), the =PERCENTILE score does not change, but the =PERCENTILE.EXC increases the 10th percentile score from −8.80 to −9.60. This adjustment

TABLE 3.8 A comparison of two percentile functions in Excel offers contrasting results.

−10	−3	4
−9	−2	5
−8	−1	6
−7	0	7
−6	1	8
−5	2	9
−4	3	10
Percentile	**=PERCENTILE**	**=PERCENTILE.EXC**
10%	−8.00	−8.80
20%	−6.00	−6.60
30%	−4.00	−4.40
40%	−2.00	−2.20
50%	0.00	0.00
60%	2.00	2.20
70%	4.00	4.40
80%	6.00	6.60
90%	8.00	8.80

correctly demonstrates more negativity; consequently, in the presence of extreme scores it gives them more weight.[1] (See Table 3.9.)

Correlation

Although this introduces a discussion on correlation among differing instruments, the trading application of these principles occurs when we begin putting together cross-hedging strategies.

What do you think is the correlation between these two companies? In Figure 3.9, STARBUCKS (black line) is in the consumer discretionary sector, whereas COSTCO (gray line) is in the consumer staples sector.[2]

[1]Notice that the scores for the 20th and 30th percentile scores were not affected by changing the second-lowest score.

[2]"Fund Holdings: QQQ," Invesco PowerShares, www.invescopowershares.com/products/holdings.aspx?ticker=QQQ.

TABLE 3.9 After changing the second-lowest score, the 10th percentile score does not reflect this change; whereas, =PERCENTILE.EXC score does make this adjustment.

Percentile	=PERCENTILE	=PERCENTILE.EXC
10%	−8.00	−9.60
20%	−6.00	−6.60
30%	−4.00	−4.40

FIGURE 3.9 With the exception of the divergence in spring of 2011, both these stocks were traveling along in the same direction. In these 300 trading days, both stocks ended significantly above their starting price, SBUX (left axis) closing at $36.73 and COST (right axis) at $81.39 on June 21, 2011.

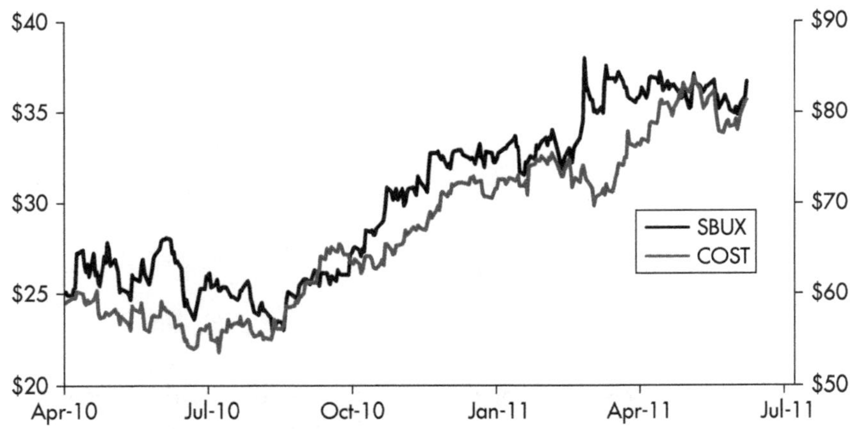

FIGURE 3.10 Fill in the range of scores for these two instruments.

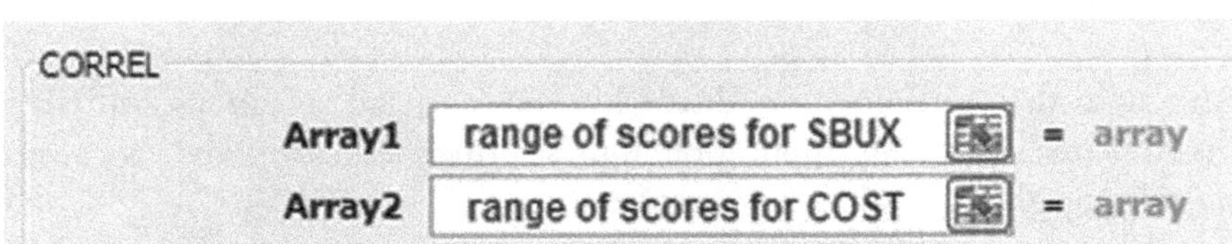

=CORREL (SBUX,COST)

When using the closing price of these two instruments the correlation score is r =.944. (See Figure 3.10.)

When using the $ price change between consecutive trading days, it falls to .4096.

$$\$\text{ price change} = (\text{closing price}_0 - \text{closing price}_1)$$

The significance of this is huge; it tells us something completely different about the relationship of these two consumer stocks. Part of the reason this occurs is because the closing price of an instrument between two consecutive days string closely together. This creates an artificially high correlation; fortunately, the price change between consecutive trading days does not have this restriction.

What do you suppose the closing price correlations of these two companies with the spiders were during these 300 trading days?

=CORREL(SBUX,SPY)	r =.933
=CORREL(COST,SPY)	r =.941

In contrast to these results, when using the closing price change with these two companies their correlation with the spiders over 300 days resulted in less of an association.

=CORREL(SBUX,SPY)	r =.583
=CORREL(COST,SPY)	r =.564

The Basics

Many media "specialists" seem to take pleasure in throwing a correlation score at us. Certainly they have many practical benefits, but as you will see from this discussion, the calculation of the relationship between two variables is often misleading.

When the movement of two variables is going in the same direction the correlation is positive; conversely, when they are moving in opposite directions, it becomes an inverse correlation.

The range of correlation resides between a score of −1.00 to +1.00.

Table 3.10 shows three separate spreadsheets; each one contains five scores for the two variables.

=CORREL(B2:B6,C2:C6)

A positive correlation ($r = 1.00$) occurs because the rank order is the same for both variables (the numbers are descending). An inverse correlation ($r = -1.00$) occurs because the rank order for ABC is highest to lowest, whereas XYZ is from lowest to highest. By switching the scores in the XYZ

TABLE 3.10 In the three correlations, the variable ABC remains constant, but the rank order adjustments in XYZ give us a perfectly positive, perfectly negative, and no correlation score.

	A	B	C		A	B	C		A	B	C
1	Month	ABC	XYZ	1	Month	ABC	XYZ	1	Month	ABC	XYZ
2	Jan	9	5	2	Jan	9	1	2	Jan	9	5
3	Feb	7	4	3	Feb	7	2	3	Feb	7	1
4	Mar	5	3	4	Mar	5	3	4	Mar	5	2
5	Apr	3	2	5	Apr	3	4	5	Apr	3	3
6	May	1	1	6	May	1	5	6	May	1	4
		r = 1.00				r = −1.00				r = .00	

TABLE 3.11 The correlation is strong because the rank order is relatively similar for both variables (highest with highest as well as lowest with lowest scores for the two variables).

	A	B	C
1	Month	ABC	XYZ
2	Jan	12	10
3	Feb	11	9
4	Mar	8	7
5	Apr	10	10
6	May	6	9
7	Jun	8	8
8	Jul	4	6
9	Aug	8	5
10	Sep	3	4
11	Oct	6	3
12	Nov	2	2
13	Dec	4	1

variable from 1,2,3,4,5 to 5,1,2,3,4, no correlation was found between the two variables (Table 3.10).

Table 3.11 shows the correlation between two variables is r = .800; this implies a strong positive relationship (Figure 3.11).

=CORREL(B2:B13, C2:C13) = .800

FIGURE 3.11 Although the scores are trending lower, a positive correlation (r = .800) was found between these two variables.

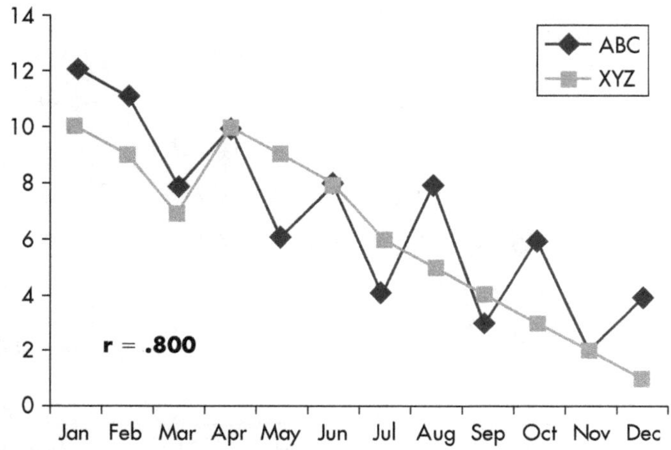

TABLE 3.12 In reversing the scores for both variables (Jan to Dec, Feb to Nov, Mar to Oct, . . .), the correlation remains the same, but the positive correlation is trending upward.

Month	ABC	XYZ
Jan	4	1
Feb	2	2
Mar	6	3
Apr	3	4
May	8	5
Jun	4	6
Jul	8	8
Aug	6	9
Sep	10	10
Oct	8	7
Nov	11	9
Dec	12	10

FIGURE 3.12 Still a positive correlation (r =.800), but the two variables are both moving in an upward direction.

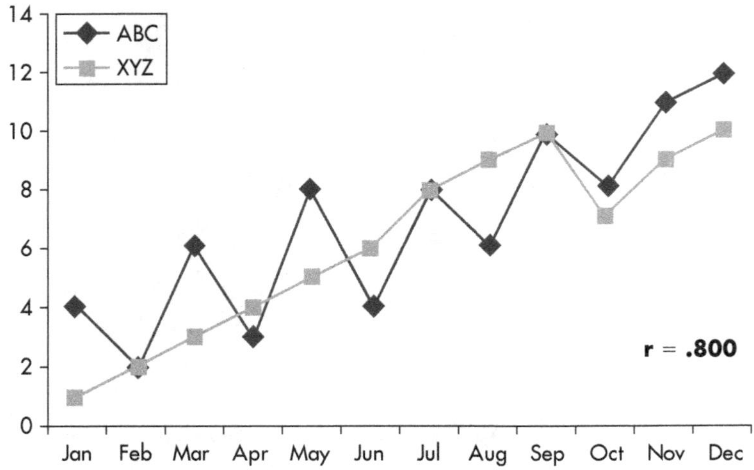

In contrast to a falling trend line, when two instruments have a somewhat strong positive correlation but the lower prices are in the earlier months (Table 3.12), it creates a rising trend line.[3] (See Figure 3.12.)

Switching the scores in Table 3.13 for XYZ (Jan with Dec, Feb with Nov, Mar with Oct, Apr with Sep, May with Aug, Jun with Jul), creates an inverse correlation (Figure 3.13). Compare this with the monthly scores in Table 3.14 and Figure 3.14, in which these two figures have the same correlation (r = –.857) score.

When running a correlation between two stocks, especially when they are in the same sector, it is not uncommon to produce a positive correlation. In Table 3.15, there is no meaningful correlation (r = –.004); in essence, the two variables go in different directions (Figure 3.15).

Drawbacks of Correlation Analysis

In the four examples in Table 3.16, the correlation scores are all perfect (r = 1.00).

[3]Instructions on how to draw a trend line (also known as a *regression line*) can be found in the appendix.

TABLE 3.13 The scores for ABC do not change position, but flipping the scores for XYZ changes the rank order, which in turn, produces an inverse correlation. (See Figure 3.13.)

Month	ABC	XYZ
Jan	4	10
Feb	2	9
Mar	6	7
Apr	3	10
May	8	9
Jun	4	8
Jul	8	6
Aug	6	5
Sep	10	4
Oct	8	3
Nov	11	2
Dec	12	1

FIGURE 3.13 An inverse correlation (r = –.857); notice the change in positioning between the two variables.

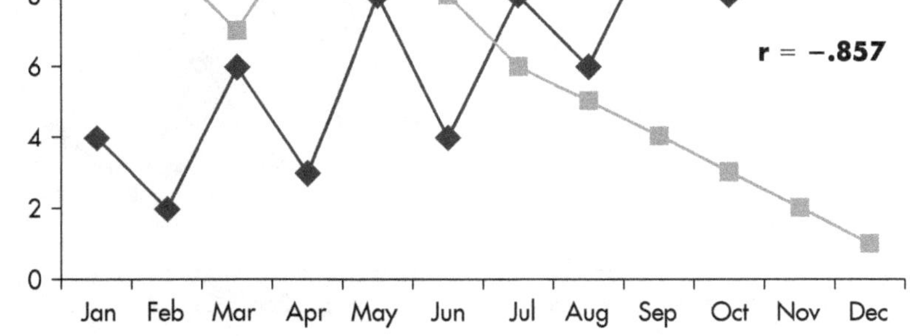

TABLE 3.14 Again, flipping the scores around changes the rank order, which in turn, produces an inverse correlation, but with the same –.857 correlation score.

A	B	C	D
1	Year	ABC	XYZ
2	Jan	12	1
3	Feb	11	2
4	Mar	8	3
5	Apr	10	4
6	May	6	5
7	Jun	8	6
8	Jul	4	8
9	Aug	8	9
10	Sep	3	10
11	Oct	6	7
12	Nov	2	9
13	Dec	4	10

FIGURE 3.14 After switching the variables, it produces the same inverse correlation ($r = -.857$); notice the change in positioning between the two variables.

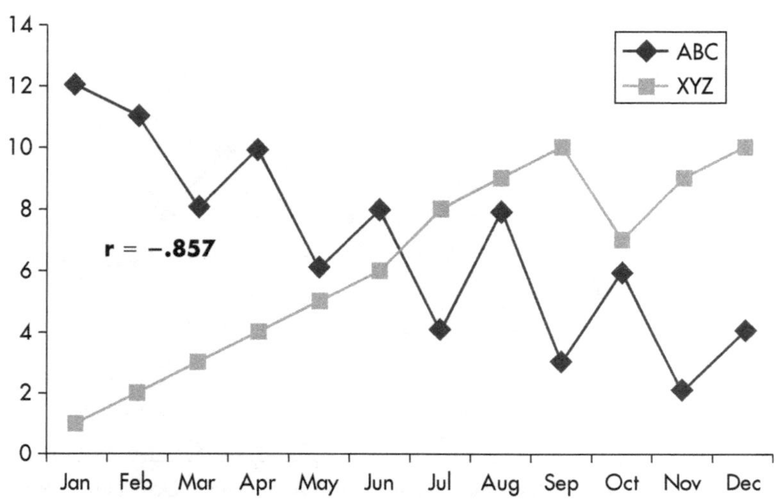

TABLE 3.15 There is no commonality in the rank assessment of these two variables; therefore, no meaningful correlation exists.

Month	ABC	XYZ
Jan	8	10
Feb	4	6
Mar	8	9
Apr	10	5
May	6	6
Jun	12	6
Jul	11	7
Aug	8	3
Sep	3	5
Oct	6	11
Nov	4	8
Dec	2	6

FIGURE 3.15 With the two variables regularly shifting positions, the variables have no pricing relationship (r = .00).

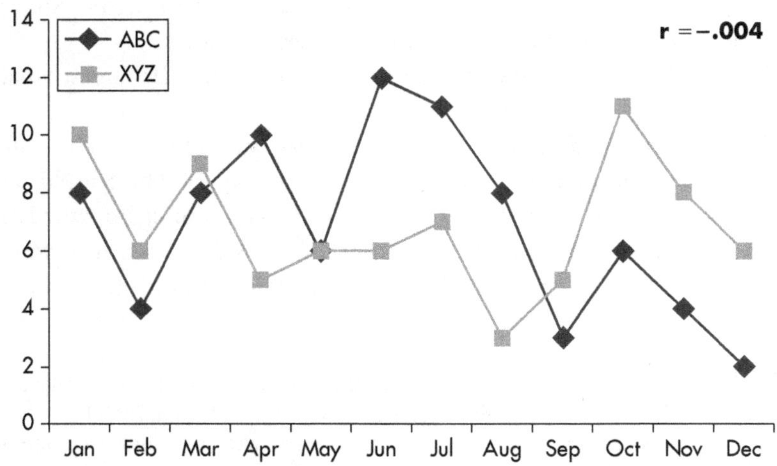

TABLE 3.16 This shows some of the fuzzy math. ABC stays the same, but XYZ increases tenfold. Compare the two tables on the right: the last three numbers (gray shade) are different, but the perfect correlation holds.

Year	ABC	XYZ	ABC	XYZ	ABC	XYZ	ABC	XYZ
2007	1	3	1	30	1	300	1	300
2008	3	6	3	60	3	330	3	330
2009	5	9	5	90	5	360	5	360
2010	7	12	7	120	7	390	7	390
2011	9	15	9	150	9	420	9	420
2012	11	18	11	180	11	450	11	440
2013	13	21	13	210	13	480	13	460
2014	15	24	15	240	15	510	15	490
r =	1.00		1.00		1.00		1.00	

Absolute Shortcut

This shows how to use the absolute $ signs when writing equations. For instance, in the calculation of the 10-largest/smallest price changes within 300 trading days for the SPDR Gold Shares (GLD), these absolute references greatly reduce your workload.[4] Besides demonstrating this procedure, this illustration examines the outlying scores of this fund with an investment in gold bullion.

Since large deviations in price can have a profound effect on the mean score, it is imperative to assess the downside volatility of an instrument. Positive outliers inflate; whereas, negative outliers deflate the mean score. The further back you go in your analysis (such as three years ago versus three days ago), the less relevance given to these aberrant scores.

Table 3.17 shows a side-by-side comparison of the 10 largest/smallest daily price changes in 300 days.

A review of the trading days from April 20, 2010, until June 24, 2011, shows this precious metal fund going from $111.46 to $146.26. The $34.80 profit, in these 300 trading days was slightly ahead of the $28.84 coming from the 10 best trading days. And, if somehow you were able to bypass the 10 worst-performing days, the $34.23 in damages would not have been taken from your account.[5]

[4]Since its launch in 2004, State Street's SPDR GOLD fund (ticker: GLD), with daily trading volume above 24 million shares, is the biggest gold exchange-traded fund (ETF).

[5]Chapter 7 is on risk analysis. It has a lengthy discussion on alternative assessment measures, which will arm you with more ammunition on how to defend against these hefty downturns.

TABLE 3.17 This table generates a listing of the 10 largest/smallest price changes in this gold fund from April 30, 2010, to July 8, 2011.

	Large	Small
1	4.46	−4.64
2	3.40	−4.26
3	3.09	−4.17
4	2.87	−3.97
5	2.82	−3.25
6	2.55	−3.23
7	2.53	−2.86
8	2.40	−2.65
9	2.37	−2.61
10	2.35	−2.59
SUM	28.84	−34.23

For anyone unfamiliar with absolute references, sit tight; this is a demonstration of how to construct this information using these $ signs to increase your efficiency as a programmer.

Since the price for these 20 trading days does not vary, it is perfectly fine to use a daily price change. Once you have your basic information, compute the price change between consecutive trading days. You can accomplish this by subtracting the difference between the two closing prices 146.26 − 148.34 = −2.08 (=B2-B3).[6]

In "C2" of Figure 3.16, write =B2-B3, grasp the handle, and highlight down to AutoFill the remaining cells.

When you want to keep cell references constant, use an absolute reference. By placing a dollar sign ($) in front of the column letter or row number, you freeze the cell reference. Performing this action preserves the structure of the original formula. Once you have your array in the equation, press the F4 function key; it becomes a toggle switch rotating among four possible combinations.[7]

[6]Since the dates are in descending order, the computation is B2-B3.

[7]The appendix contains more of a discussion on the distinction between these two references, along with illustrations showing how to use absolute references.

FIGURE 3.16 This shows how to write the =LARGE function. The absolute $ sign holds the range when you highlight down the column. The 1 (in cell value E2) represents the =LARGE(array,1), which gives us the largest score; whereas =LARGE(array,2), gives us the 2nd largest score in the range.

	A	B	C	D	E	F	G
1	GLD	close	price change			LARGE	SMALL
2	6/24/2011	146.26	–2.08		1	=LARGE($C$2:$C$21,E2)	
3	6/23/2011	148.34	–2.65		2		
4	6/22/2011	150.99	0.23		3		
5	6/21/2011	150.76	0.73		4		
6	6/20/2011	150.03	0.09		5		
7	6/17/2011	149.94	0.97		6		
8	6/16/2011	148.97	-0.15		7		
9	6/15/2011	149.12	0.45		8		
10	6/14/2011	148.67	0.9		9		
11	6/13/2011	147.77	–1.47		10		
12	6/10/2011	149.24	–1.32				
13	6/9/2011	150.56	0.75				
14	6/8/2011	149.81	–0.61				
15	6/7/2011	150.42	–0.06				
16	6/6/2011	150.48	0.26				
17	6/3/2011	150.22	0.72				
18	6/2/2011	149.50	–0.41				
19	6/1/2011	149.91	0.27				
20	5/31/2011	149.64	–0.06				
21	5/27/2011	149.70	1.48				

Ranking

Ranking is a useful way to measure the effectiveness of scores within a variable. The process of ranking a score from an array of scores is similar to sorting the scores; the rank of a number would correspond to its position after sorting the numbers under investigation. After creating an ascending or descending order of scores, this information can make performance comparisons within the same variable or between variables.

When using the =RANK function, it is not always possible to assign rankings uniquely because ties (same values) are given the average score. Therefore, the =RANK.AVG function has an advantage because it automatically makes an adjustment when two or more of the quantities measure equally. Nevertheless, for most trading variables, such as price and volume, this is not a concern because a tie score among these variables rarely occurs.

Why rank scores?

In Figures 3.17 and 3.18, we are looking at a simple moving average. Assume that this indicator is giving you a buy signal, but what is the difference between the following two line charts?

There are two meaningful differences. First, one is above the median and the other is below the median. When you are making a trading decision, knowing if your instrument is at its highest price, lowest price, or somewhere between these two settings is an important distinction.

Second, we have another possibility to consider: Is the momentum of this simple moving average producing an upward or downward trajectory?

FIGURE 3.17 This instrument at a price of $16 is within the upper quartile. Most short-term indicators may indicate a buy signal, but not specify its current position on this line chart. The ranking function puts its current price at the 15th percentile; this information should have an impact on our trading decision.

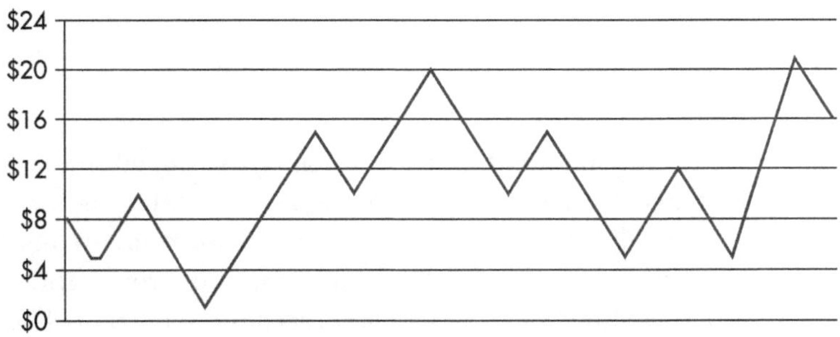

FIGURE 3.18 The instrument at $8 is within the lower quartile. Most momentum indicators (such as a short-term moving average) will give us a buy signal without referencing their positioning on a line chart. In using the ranking function, a price of $8 is in the 79th percentile. Unlike the previous chart, where the $16 price is in the upper quadrant, this chart's closing price is in the bottom quadrant.

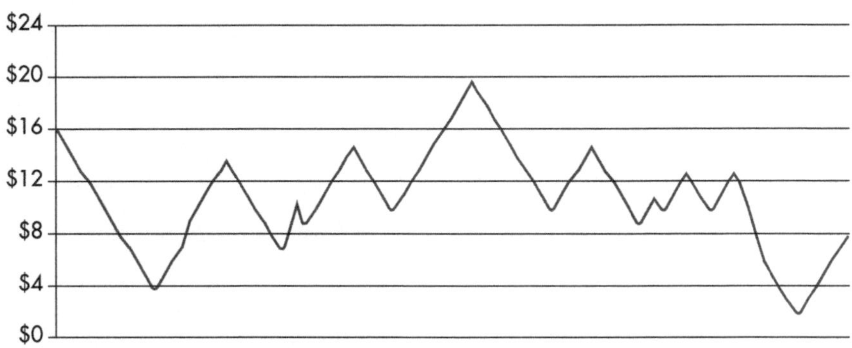

Unfortunately, there is a paucity of research discussing these two aspects of a moving average. Later, we will encounter some studies that specifically focus on these different possibilities. For now, my comments focus on the differences in their rankings.

Given that market sentiment is different for a stock at various stages of its trading cycle, this indicator gives our analysis more substance. For instance, a moving average may produce a buy signal when it is at its upper or lower quadrant. This is an important distinction, which we should consider before placing a buy order.

Throughout the book, I will be showing some interesting studies using these ranking functions. It is particularly instructive when comparing trading activity between two different time frames. For instance, between the hours of 06:00 and 08:30 trading activity is dormant, but it is significantly heavier from 08:30 to 10:00.

Summary

These are some of the building blocks of our analysis; we will revisit these functions in subsequent chapters. If you are not experienced using them, the learning curve is readily achievable because many of them follow the same pattern. With practice, your skill level will show rapid improvement.

Still, most of these functions give us a good account of the past. The next chapter examines logical statements; at first, they may be difficult to conceptualize, but once you grasp them, you will become more adroit at spotting future price movements.

Going forward, we will apply these indicators in other studies; as we progress, their usefulness will become more apparent.

CHAPTER 4

Extracting Performance Results

There are three classes of people: Those who see. Those who see when they are shown. Those who do not see.

—Leonardo da Vinci

In this chapter, we explore two ways to assess the probability of participating in a profitable trading environment. The easiest way to extract statistics from a given worksheet is to use the filter command; however, another alternative is to run the logical functions in Excel. Although the learning process takes longer, its construction furnishes the user with infinitely more possibilities.

Besides providing instruction on how to use these two procedures, this chapter contains some interesting studies. Later in the chapter, we begin to tackle the =IF(AND) function, together with multiple statements. These powerful functions will inspire you to take the appropriate action regarding your earlier suppositions

Still, you can easily perform the analysis for the majority of the studies in this book by using the filtering procedure. This powerful assessment command will satisfy many of your statistical requests. More complex designs, however, can be run by using the =IF(AND) function.

Once you begin the learning process, mastery over these powerful functions will come quickly. As you begin routinely using these statistical procedures, you will expand your investigative skills. More importantly, an assimilation of the complexities of these logical statements will ultimately provide you with the capability to break away from a restrictive trading environment by giving you the autonomy to construct innovative systems that deliver positive results.

This is a two-step process (Figure 4.1), which begins by clicking on one of the columns in your heading row. In order to display the "square" boxes with down arrows you have to click on the filter icon (Figure 4.2).

Once in this screen, select the filter button (Figure 4.3).

When you move your cursor over the filter button it provides the instructions shown in Figure 4.4.

Fortunately, there are many first-rate instructional videos on how to use the AutoFilter command. It is best to start by pressing F1 for the help menu. If you put the filter icon on your quick access toolbar, you can reduce this process to one simple click of your mouse. Figure 4.5 provides the results of this step.

FIGURE 4.1 After selecting the filter icon, the down arrows will appear in your variable headings.

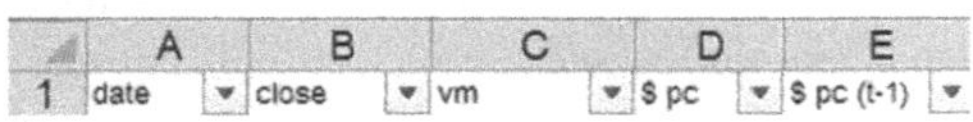

FIGURE 4.2 Access this filter command by selecting Data.

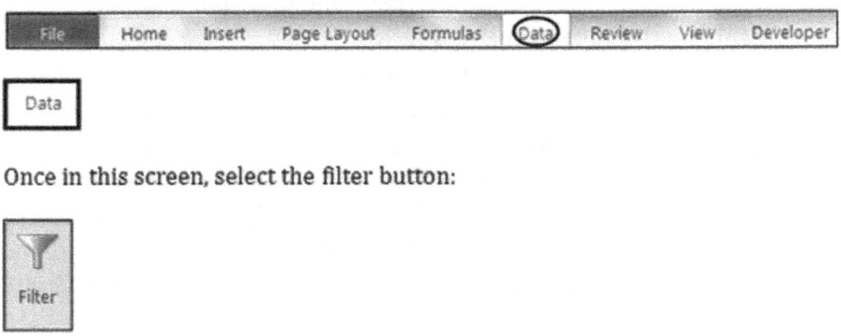

FIGURE 4.3 The filter group for this command.

FIGURE 4.4 Instructions on how to choose a filter for the column you want to investigate.

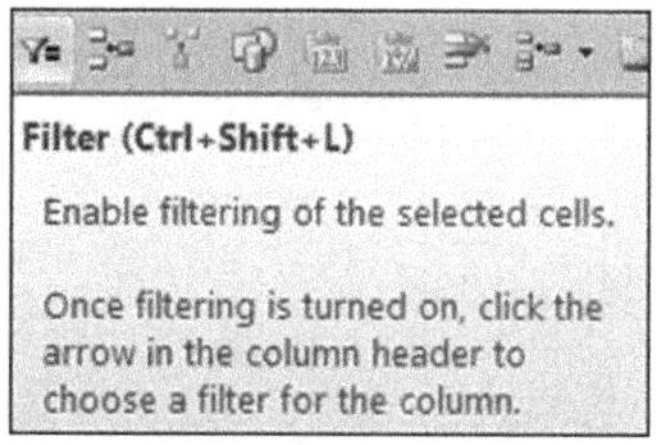

FIGURE 4.5 Putting the filter icon on your quick access toolbar.

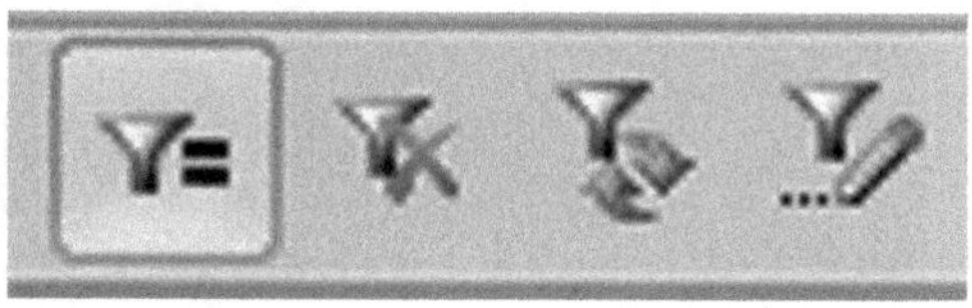

FIGURE 4.6 A worksheet with labels for each column.

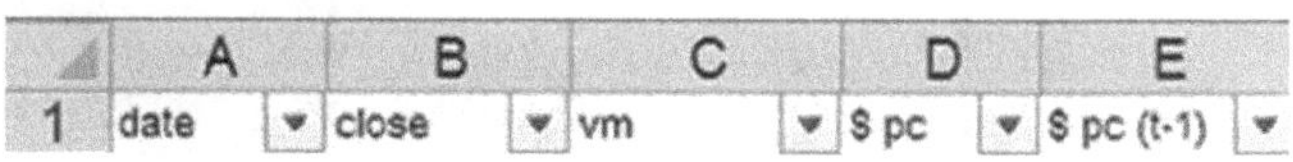

Close = the closing price of the spiders
vm = trading volume
$pc = $ price change between two consecutive closing days
$ pc (t_{-1}) = the (t_{-1}) lag of the spiders closing price

In this case, you still have to position your cursor in the row heading illustrating your descriptive labels; thereafter, by clicking on the filter icon you can easily access your statistics.

In order to show how to use this filter button, it is best to frame a question relating to its usage. For instance, how can we implement this function to measure the following day's performance of the spiders after suffering a daily loss in excess of –$2.00? (See Figure 4.6.)

Begin by clicking on the arrow in the "$ pc" label, the "$ pc (t_{-1})" is the dependent (response) variable.

$$\text{Closing price}\,(t_{-0}) - \text{closing price}\,(t_{-1}) = \text{pc}(t_{-1})$$

Figure 4.7 demonstrates how clicking on the box in the $ pc column will automatically report the worst performing days.

Figure 4.8 shows the results of clicking on the "Number Filters" selection, it opens the custom filtering box.

FIGURE 4.7 Clicking on the box in the $ pc column will automatically report the worst performing days.

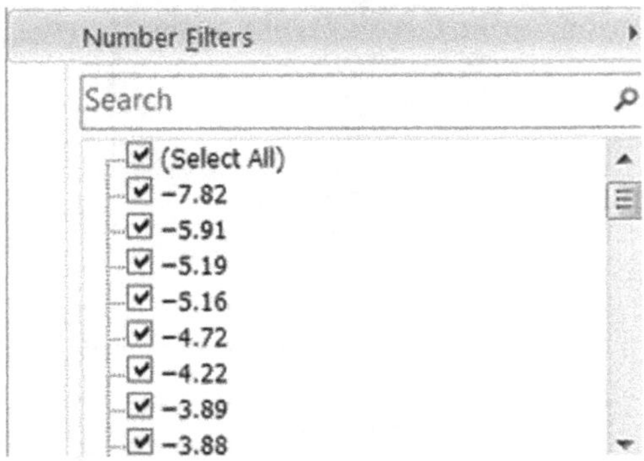

FIGURE 4.8 The AutoFilter box.

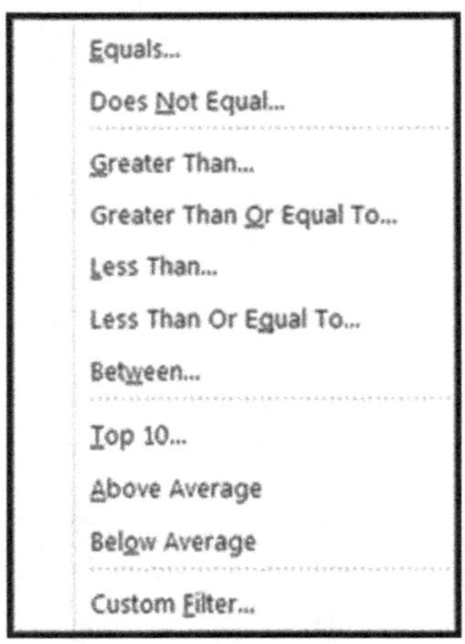

This AutoFilter box (Figure 4.8) contains a very powerful assortment of directional commands. In comparison to the logical statements, they are faster and easier to use; however, the =IF(AND) statements can extract more information.

In order to answer this research question, we have to produce a listing of those qualifying days (that is, a daily loss less than –$2.00 in the spiders).

Figure 4.9 allows us to supply the input information for "is less than."

Figure 4.10 provides a snapshot of 10 days of the 44 days satisfying this requirement.

By highlighting the pc (t_{-1}) field (Figure 4.10), the status bar (Figure 4.11) produces the 44 trading days with a < −$2.00 loss ("C" column).

FIGURE 4.9 Setting the AutoFilter for the "is less than" statement.

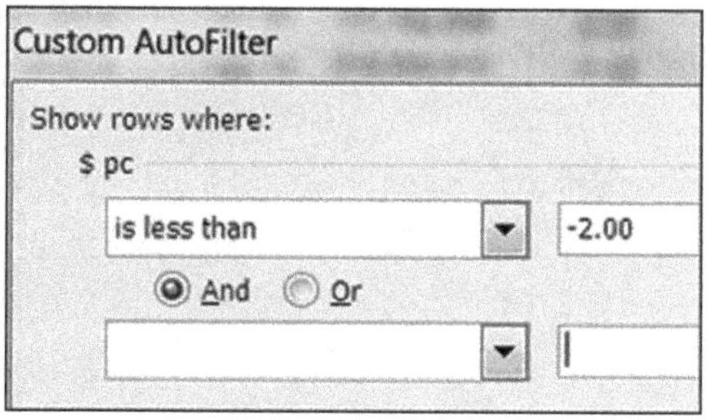

FIGURE 4.10 Snapshot of the pc (t_{-1}) field.

date	close	vm	$ pc	$ pc (t-1)
05/04/12	137.00	193,509,625	−2.25	.10
04/10/12	135.90	235,132,886	−2.32	1.10
12/08/11	123.95	240,189,438	−2.78	2.10
11/23/11	116.56	223,964,569	−2.63	−.22
11/21/11	119.66	228,502,929	−2.32	−.47
11/09/11	123.16	336,967,970	−4.72	1.16
11/01/11	122.00	414,928,250	−3.50	1.99
10/31/11	125.50	227,500,425	−3.10	-3.50
10/25/11	123.05	263,934,604	−2.44	1.25
10/17/11	120.23	201,660,469	−2.34	2.35

FIGURE 4.11 Summary profit of the 44 days with < −$2.00 loss.

Average: .25 Count: 44 Numerical Count: 44 Min: -3.77 Max: 5.22 Sum: 10.82

Figure 4.11 displays a partial listing of the 44 days showing a summary profit of $10.82.

In these 600 trading days (December 23, 2009 to May 25, 2012) there were 44 days with such an excessive daily downturn. So, after a flurry of sell orders, on the following trading day, the spiders came back with an impressive recovery.

FIGURE 4.12 Following-day performance.

date	close	vm	$ pc	$ pc (t-1)
05/04/12	137.00	193,509,625	-2.25	.10
04/10/12	135.90	235,132,886	-2.32	1.10
12/08/11	123.95	240,189,438	-2.78	2.10
11/09/11	123.16	336,967,970	-4.72	1.16
10/31/11	125.50	227,500,425	-3.10	-3.50
10/25/11	123.05	263,934,604	-2.44	1.25
08/02/11	125.49	345,346,540	-3.29	.68
07/27/11	130.60	247,869,769	-2.73	-.38
07/11/11	131.97	195,049,800	-2.43	-.57
06/15/11	127.02	300,389,890	-2.30	-.35
06/01/11	131.87	232,479,465	-3.03	-.14
03/16/11	126.18	465,975,980	-2.38	1.67
03/10/11	129.94	301,230,120	-2.45	.90
03/01/11	130.93	257,726,043	-2.22	.28
02/22/11	131.83	232,808,933	-2.70	-.81
01/28/11	127.72	295,510,330	-2.27	.96

Is there a difference when the analysis applies those scores in the upper region of its price range? We can build on this condition by repeating the process of subfiltering from another directional statement. In this case, we want to access the "close" heading label; once you click the "Above Average" selection, it will automatically filter your scores. That is, after filtering those scores with a $pc loss > −$2.00, you can narrow your search by selecting the filter icon in the close column.

Figure 4.12 records the following-day performance of the spiders after selecting those days with a percentage loss in excess of 2 percent from those days with an above-average closing price.

After highlighting the scores in the pc (t_{-1}) column, Figure 4.13 displays the results on the status bar. When splitting the scores by above average, there is a slight advantage when these conditions are above the mean score.

Fortunately, we can keep on subfiltering these results; this further substantiates our findings.

FIGURE 4.13 Status bar for scores in the pc (t-$_{1}$) column.

Average: .28 Count: 16 Numerical Count: 16 Min: -3.50 Max: 2.10 Sum: 4.45

FIGURE 4.14 Setting the AutoFilter for a "Between . . ." command.

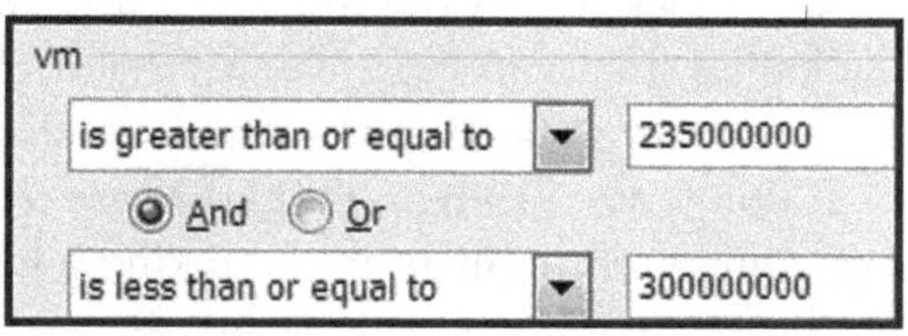

FIGURE 4.15 Results of "Between . . ." command.

date	close	vm	$ pc	$ pc (t-1)
04/10/12	135.90	235,132,886	-2.32	1.10
12/08/11	123.95	240,189,438	-2.78	2.10
10/25/11	123.05	263,934,604	-2.44	1.25
07/27/11	130.60	247,869,769	-2.73	-.38
03/01/11	130.93	257,726,043	-2.22	.28
01/28/11	127.72	295,510,330	-2.27	.96

The "Between . . ." command is a very constructive directional command, because it allows you to pinpoint the performance results between two numbers.

Figure 4.14 displays the "Between . . ." directional command; in this case, we are looking at volume (vm) between 235 to 300 million shares.

Figure 4.15 provides the results of those days with volume between these two numbers.

Although this extra step endorses a long position, subfiltering reduces the samples in your analysis, which makes your findings less robust.

One thing missing with these commands is the W-L record; however, the logical conditional statements in this powerful spreadsheet program provide this information.

IF Statements

This is an indispensable function that allows us to assess one condition (TRUE) against another condition (FALSE). If the first condition is met, it is TRUE; if not, it is FALSE. With it, we can assess an assortment of trading conditions using different variables. As you will discover, a lack of imagination is the biggest stumbling block to constructing innovative research designs.

How will these logical functions empower my trading?

Say you wake up, turn on your computer, and learn that the spiders have rallied. Their price at 06:00 was $130; at 09:00 they are trading at $130.72. You are thinking of going with momentum by taking a long position from 09:00 to 11:00, but before arriving at any conclusion, run an analysis of this condition.

How can we use an IF statement to determine whether this is a prudent decision?

If the spiders produce an advance of > $0.50 between 06:00 and 09:00, in evaluating the previous 300 trading days, how did it perform from 09:00 to 11:00? The dates are May 21, 2010, to July 28, 2011 (300 trading days).

The necessary information for this statement is:

- The instrument is the spiders (SPY).
- The condition is asking for a price change > $0.50 between 06:00 and 09:00.
- When the condition is true, you are asking this function to record its performance between 09:00 and 11:00.
- When this condition is false, do not record any performance response.
- The response variable is the performance of the spiders from 09:00 to 11:00.

=IF(cell with 06:00 to 09:00 price change is > $0.50, record the price change from 09:00 to 11:00).

Since you are not writing anything in the "FALSE" argument, the program will automatically write "FALSE" as its cell value. Table 4.1 shows the results of not providing input in column G.

In this example, the user is working in cell G2. Hence, the true or false statement will appear in this cell value. The result of F2 is false; consequently, G2 is given a default (FALSE) value. (See Figure 4.16.)

When the false (Value_if_false) argument is left blank, "FALSE" is automatically written as the response. (After a discussion on highlighting, this chapter provides a more appropriate response for the false argument.)

TABLE 4.1 If the trading condition is *true* it records the price change, but if it is *false*, it automatically writes "FALSE" as its response.

	A	B	C	D	E	F	G
1	Date	06:00 Price	09:00 Price	11:00 Price	Price Change 06:00 to 09:00	Price Change 09:00 to 11:00	If Statement
2	5-Sep	120.00	119.12	119.40	–.88	.28	FALSE
3	4-Sep	119.00	119.64	120.30	.64	.66	0.66
4	3-Sep	118.00	117.34	117.20	–.66	–.14	FALSE
5	2-Sep	118.00	118.36	118.50	.36	.14	FALSE
6	1-Sep	116.00	116.76	117.12	.76	.36	0.36

FIGURE 4.16 This statement is false; therefore, it records the default response in its cell value.

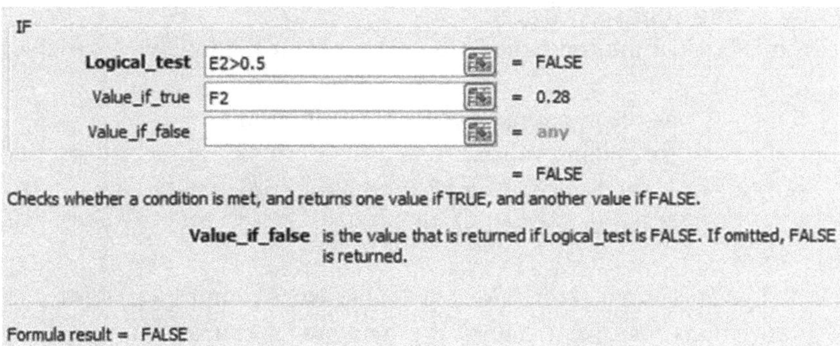

Table 4.2 shows the equations for this logical statement, which calls for a response of either "TRUE" or "FALSE." After writing the conditional statement, this becomes the *true* part of the statement; conversely, the part that does not apply takes on the *false* side of the statement.

Incidentally, with these conditions, from May 21, 2010, to July 28, 2011 (300 trading days), there were 23 trading opportunities resulting in $3.44 in profits ($3.44/23 = $0.15 APT). APT denotes average per trade. In this case the average profit is $0.15 per trade.

Performance Equations

Before we begin using logical statements, the following is a brief overview of how to construct formulas within a spreadsheet. For those with less

TABLE 4.2 Formulas written without including the *false* part of the statement.

	A	B	C	D	E	F	G
1	Date	06:00 Price	09:00 Price	11:00 Price	Price Change 06:00 to 09:00	Price Change 09:00 to 11:00	If Statement
2	5-Sep	120.00	119.12	119.40	=C2-B2	=D2-C2	=IF(E2>.50,F2)
3	4-Sep	119.00	119.64	120.30	=C3-B3	=D3-C3	=IF(E3>.50,F3)
4	3-Sep	118.00	117.34	117.20	=C4-B4	=D4-C4	=IF(E4>.50,F4)
5	2-Sep	118.00	118.36	118.50	=C5-B5	=D5-C5	=IF(E5>.50,F5)
6	1-Sep	116.00	116.76	117.12	=C6-B6	=D6-C6	=IF(E6>.50,F6)

experience using this software program, the discussion shows how to AutoFill the cells within your spreadsheet.

In this book, I use the same letters to represent the following variables:

z	as the opening price for a specific time
v	for trading volume
p or k	is the $price change between two time frames
y	is the dependent variable

Excel gives its users tremendous flexibility when naming variables, with fewer restrictions than most statistical programs. Of course, you can devise your own coding system.

Not everyone wants to be active at their screen making trades throughout the day. If you leave for work at 09:00, you may want to place a few trades before shutting down your computer. This is an example of how you can punch in the early numbers, do the analysis, and make your trading decisions at 09:00. This is a preliminary illustration; as we progress the analysis will contain more variables.

The following is a basic illustration, using fictitious numbers, to produce some simple calculations in the worksheet (Table 4.3).

p06	is the 00:00 to 06:00 price change.
p69	is the 06:00 to 09:00 price change.
y915	represents the response variable (from 09:00 to 15:00).

TABLE 4.3 After writing the equation in cell F2, if written correctly it will return the result of 15 – 12 (C2-B2), giving us a cell value of 3.

	A	B	C	D	E	F	G	I
1	Date	z0	z6	z9	z15	k06	k69	y915
2	9-May	12	15	16	13	3		
3	8-May	13	11	12	15			
4	5-May	11	10	13	11			
5	4-May	12	11	8	12			
6	3-May	15	13	11	10			
7	2-May	12	13	14	11			
8	1-May	10	12	10	12			

Instructions for Automating the Process

These are the primary steps for the process known as drag and drop. They are shortcuts for automatically writing the rest of your equations. Once you get the hang of it, they will increase your efficiency appreciably.

Steps 1 to 7 are illustrated in Figures 4.17 to 4.23.
Step 1: Write an equation in cell F2: =C2-B2. (See Figure 4.17.)
Step 2: Create a crosshatch by pointing your cursor to the bottom right corner of this cell. (See Figure 4.18.)
Step 3: Highlight the cells by dragging the cursor across the row. The row will automatically write the equations (AutoFill). (See Figure 4.19.)

FIGURE 4.17 Begin by writing the equation.

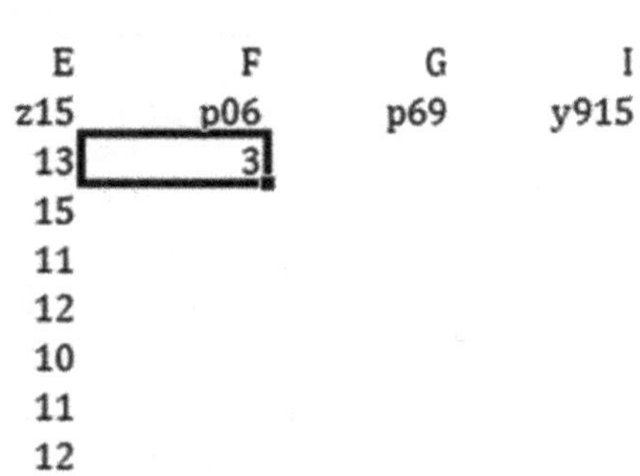

FIGURE 4.18 Create a crosshatch (+ sign) by pointing your cursor at the bottom.

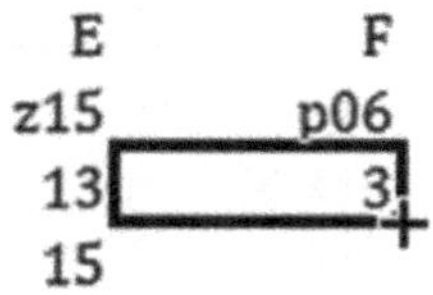

FIGURE 4.19 Once you have a black crosshatch, drag the cursor across the row.

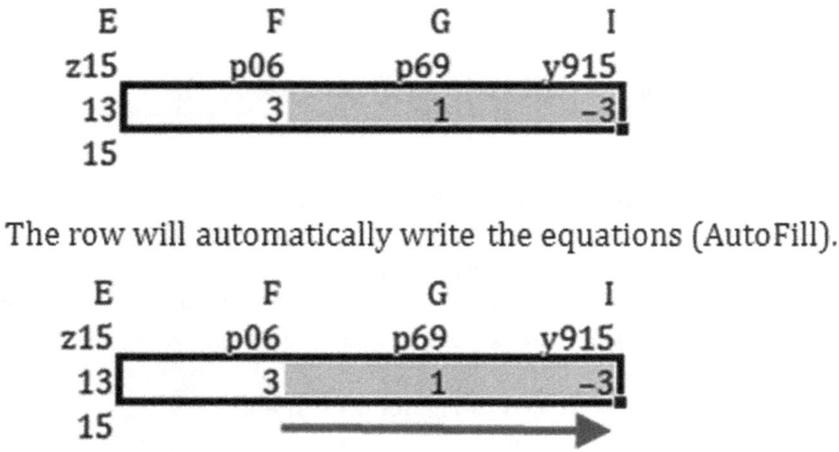

FIGURE 4.20 In order to drag down, repeat the process of creating another crosshatch in the right-most cell.

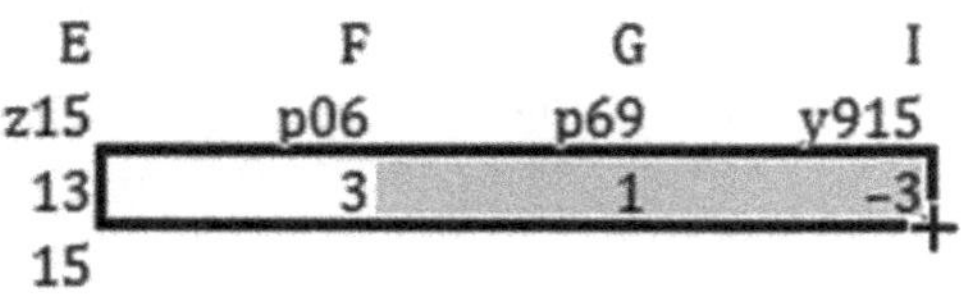

Step 4: Create a crosshatch in the rightmost cell. (See Figure 4.20.)
Step 5: Highlight the cells in the row by dragging the cursor across the rows. (See Figure 4.21.)
Step 6: Drag down, to create this image. (See Figure 4.22.)
Step 7: Release the mouse button. (See Figure 4.23.)

Tables 4.4 and 4.5 show the results of these actions.

FIGURE 4.21 Highlight across the top row (below the heading), and then drag your mouse down the column.

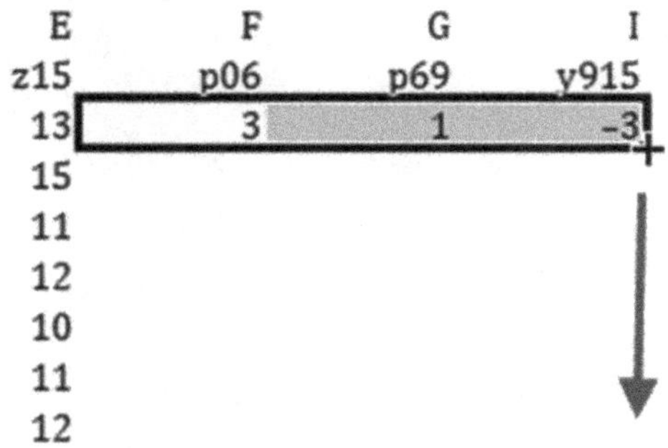

FIGURE 4.22 Create this image.

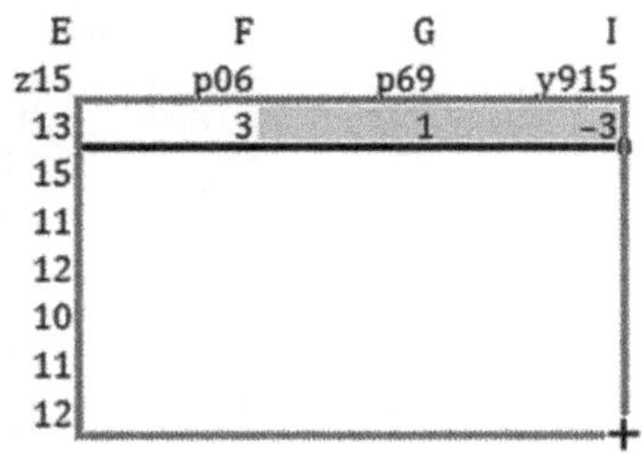

FIGURE 4.23 Release the mouse button.

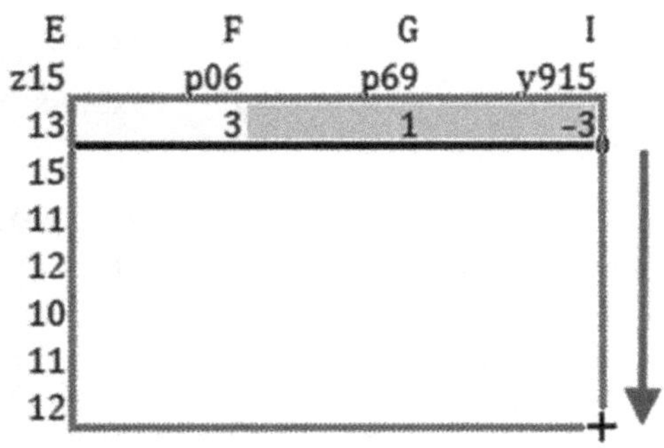

Study: Apple's Performance after Dark

This is an analysis of a remarkable company with a worldwide audience. After showing how to structure the worksheet, there is a discussion pertaining to the specifics of stating a hypothesis. And, of course, at the conclusion of this study, there are the performance results from applying these conditions.

TABLE 4.4 After completing these steps, the table includes the price changes for cells F2:I8.

	A	B	C	D	E	F	G	I
1	Date	z0	z6	z9	z15	p06	p69	y915
2	9-May	12	15	16	13	3	1	−3
3	8-May	13	11	12	15	−2	1	3
4	5-May	11	10	13	11	−1	3	−2
5	4-May	12	11	8	12	−1	−3	4
6	3-May	15	13	11	10	−2	−2	−1
7	2-May	12	13	14	11	1	1	−3
8	1-May	10	12	10	12	2	−2	2

TABLE 4.5 This contains the equations with the correct computations.

	A	B	C	D	E	F	G	I
1	Date	z0	z6	z9	z15	k06	k69	y915
2	9-May	12	15	16	13	=C2-B2	=D2-C2	=E2-D2
3	8-May	13	11	12	15	=C3-B3	=D3-C3	=E3-D3
4	5-May	11	10	13	11	=C4-B4	=D4-C4	=E4-D4
5	4-May	12	11	8	12	=C5-B5	=D5-C5	=E5-D5
6	3-May	15	13	11	10	=C6-B6	=D6-C6	=E6-D6
7	2-May	12	13	14	11	=C7-B7	=D7-C7	=E7-D7
8	1-May	10	12	10	12	=C8-B8	=D8-C8	=E8-D8

In this illustration of how to use the series of logical statements, we are using the =IF function to assess the following conditions:

OVS = overnight trading session
RTS = regular trading session

Condition	=IF statement	Value if true	Value if false
OVS > 0	IF OVS > 0	results of RTS	“”
OVS < 0	IF OVS < 0	results of RTS	“”

Since a “no price change” in the overnight session (OVS = 0) rarely occurs, it seldom makes a difference in your decision-making process. Nevertheless, for the purist checking the findings, you may notice a slight inaccuracy in the summary results because a "no change" is not taken into consideration.[1]

Just how many $0.00 changes were there in 10 years? A review of the spiders in 1,197 days (October 9, 2006, to July 11, 2011) shows that one day (December 19, 2007) had no change, but seven days were within ± one penny. Table 4.6 demonstrates the basics of this system's parameters.

With the exception of a $0.00, this spreadsheet reports the findings of the RTS by placing its results into the appropriate response columns (G or H). The way the equation is written, when the OVS > 0 it resides in column G, otherwise the cell is left empty. When the OVS < 0, it goes in column H as the result of this equation; if it does not qualify, the cell is left blank.

For instance, D2 shows the results of the overnight session. Since it is positive (+$0.14), the results of the regular session (–$5.02) are placed in "G2."

It is not necessary to write the formula in the cell, you have the option of directly typing the values into each of the three arguments in this dialog box (see Figure 4.24).

Why "" as the false argument? If you leave a blank space in the false statement, it returns "FALSE" as the value. You could write =IF(D2>0, E2,"ABC"), but this false statement, returns ABC as its value. So if you put

TABLE 4.6 Given the opening and closing prices for AAPL, we can compute the price change for the regular trading session (RTS). The =IF statement separates the performance of the RTS after an advancing overnight (OVS > 0) along with a declining overnight (OVS < 0) session.

	A	B	C	D	E	F	G	H
1	Date	Open	Close	OVS	RTS	Sum	OVS > 0	OVS < 0
2	6/24/2011	331.37	326.35	0.14	–5.02	–4.88	–5.02	
3	6/23/2011	318.94	331.23	–3.67	12.29	8.62		12.29
4	6/22/2011	325.16	322.61	–0.14	–2.55	–2.69		–2.55
5	6/21/2011	316.68	325.30	1.36	8.62	9.98	8.62	
6	6/20/2011	317.36	315.32	–2.90	–2.04	–4.94		–2.04
7	6/17/2011	328.99	320.26	3.83	–8.73	–4.90	–8.73	
8	6/16/2011	326.90	325.16	0.15	–1.74	–1.59	–1.74	
9	6/15/2011	329.75	326.75	–2.69	–3.00	–5.69		–3.00
10	6/14/2011		332.44					

[1]In most cases, when reporting a W-L record, I put ties ($0.00) in the loss column. After all, a response variable resulting in "no change" in performance, after commissions, becomes a loss.

FIGURE 4.24 This writes the formula by inputting the values for each argument.

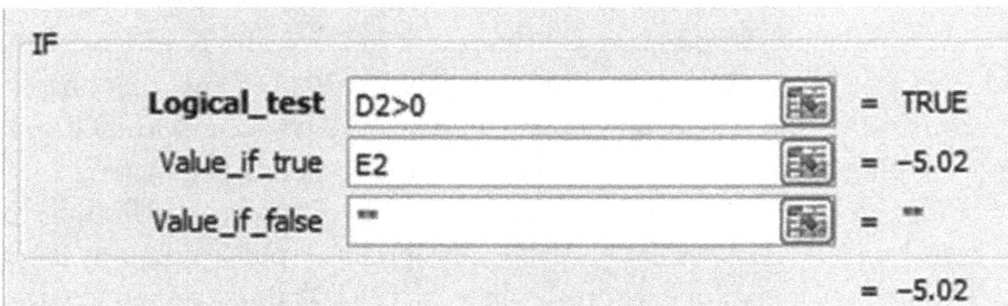

Logical_test The cell "D2" represents the OVS > 0.
Value_if_true If true: "E2" records the performance of the RTS.
Value_if_false If false: "" signifies a blank response for cell "E2."

TABLE 4.7 As you can see, from the two comparisons of a rising overnight session, when the false value records a "0" in the cell, it gives us an inaccurate average score.

Date	OVS > 0	OVS > 0
6/24/2011	–5.02	–5.02
6/23/2011		0
6/22/2011		0
6/21/2011	8.62	8.62
6/20/2011		0
6/17/2011	–8.73	–8.73
6/16/2011	–1.74	–1.74
6/15/2011		0
=AVERAGE	–1.718	–0.859

two parentheses for the false part of the statement, it will leave us with no cell value; that is, it will leave the space empty.

Why not use "0" as the response? By inserting a "0" for the false value, you get a 0. This won't work when trying to compute the average (mean) score, because the "0" is part of the computation (see Table 4.7).

If the overnight session > 0, record the price change of the regular trading session, if this is not a true statement, it is false. This statement puts the user in an either/or situation; if it is not true, then it is false. Be sure to separate all statements with a comma: IF(condition, true, false).

Hypothesis

A theory describes something speculative; it is not accurately tied down to the future; consequently, there are no assurances of its success. What we believe to be reality at the moment may turn out to be error. Of course, fresh developments can always alter the integrity of our findings; that is, they can either support or work against our open positions.

Before running an analysis, it is best to establish a working hypothesis. A hypothesis simply makes a statement about direction, on the assumption a predictor variable or variables will be responsible for controlling this movement. Statisticians refer to this as a cause/effect relationship among variables. The cause (independent variable) will produce a certain response leading to a price change (dependent variable).

In trading, the information has to come before you make your trade. For instance, you cannot use trading volume from 06:00 to 08:00 to make your trading decisions at 06:00 on the same day. In other words, since you are not going to receive information for these two hours of trading volume until after 08:00, there is no way you can go back two hours to fill a position.

The causality among variables begins with the independent variable's action occurring prior to the response of the dependent variable. The cause or independent variable comes before; whereas, the response to this action comes afterwards. The predictor (independent variable), therefore, is the leading variable; whereas, the response (dependent variable) is the lagging variable.

For the purposes of this study the overnight trading session (OVS) is the predictor variable; the regular trading session (RTS) is the dependent (response) variable.

On the basis of recent observations, you suspect the formation of an inverse relationship—that is, if the overnight advances, the regular trading session declines; conversely, if prices decline in the overnight session, they will advance during the day. This becomes our working hypothesis. After framing its construction, perform a statistical analysis to confirm your observations.

Performance of the Regular Session on the Basis of Overnight Direction

Table 4.8 shows the descriptive statistics for trading Apple during the regular session; despite the two different pricing conditions, the winning percentages are similar.[2] The dates are January 3, 2007, to June 30, 2011.

[2]The advancing + declining days do not always total the number of trading days because the ties (no price change) are not reported; 1,133 days – (662 + 465) = 6 ties.

TABLE 4.8 The findings demonstrate the performance of the regular trading session after an advancing (OVS > 0) or declining (OVS < 0) overnight session.

	OVS > 0	OVS < 0
Trading days	662	465
Average	–$0.121	–$0.044
Summary	–$80.42	–$20.44
Advance	339	239
Decline	323	226
Win percentage	.512	.514
Minimum	–$12.18	–$14.36
Maximum	$10.58	$13.02
10 percentile	–$4.37	–$4.12
90 percentile	$3.45	$4.20

In spite of the direction of the overnight session, the $100 plus loss ((−$80.42) + (–$20.44)) in the RTS took a big bite out of Apple. These results were particularly abysmal when you consider the upward flight of this company.[3] Notice the 662 to 465 disproportion between an advancing versus a declining overnight session; this is indicative of a strong overnight performance.

Our assumption pertaining to a price difference in the overnight session was right on target. The 4-to-1 discrepancy, a decline of $80.42 in the RTS after an advancing OVS in comparison to a decline of $20.44 after a declining OVS, was supportive of our hypothesis.

The 1,133 days of summary statistics have a serious flaw in the reporting—it does not show the progression of the statistics. Figure 4.25 is a running summary of the two trading sessions; with this information you become more knowledgeable. (The focus of the next chapter is on tracking your results.)

Clearly, the best strategy was to buy at the closing bell and sell at the opening bell, but will this hold over the next three months? Since January 2010 the OVS < 0 has been in recovery mode; however, the dips have been very strong. The OVS > 0, was a moving average play, because of its sharp downward runs, but in 2009 it did enjoy an impressive yearlong rally.

[3]Apple is one of the few companies that can demand a premium for its products; as the cost of its materials become more expensive, it can easily pass this increase on to its consumers.

FIGURE 4.25 Running summary of the regular session specific to the direction of the overnight trading session. Since January 2010 the OVS < 0 was on the mend, its counterpart appears to make sharp downturns, with one long run to the upside, but, in July 2011, it was back residing at support.

FIGURE 4.26 In order to assess the effect of the RTS on the OVS, the IF statement has to measure the OVS in the row above our predictor variable.

DATE	OP	HI	LW	CL	VM	OVS	RTS
7/20/2011	396.12	396.27	386.00	386.90	33,609,975	19.27	-9.22
7/19/2011	378.00	378.65	373.32	376.85	29,192,429	4.20	-1.15
7/18/2011	365.43	374.65	365.28	373.80	20,440,141		8.37

As you can see, if you break the sessions apart, the chartist can play this stock with a strong international presence, from a different, more interesting, perspective. For instance, the OVS > 0, is displaying a multiple bottom, if its price drops below support, you are not going to take a long position, but if it begins rallying you would be remiss not to take action.

Lagging Ahead

In the last study, the IF statement asked for the true/false part of the statement along the same row in Excel. This study investigates the profitable session; in doing so, we have to look one row ahead for our true/false statement (Figure 4.26).

Condition	IF statement	Value if true	Value if false
RTS >0	IF RTS >0	results of OVS	“”
RTS <0	IF RTS <0	results of OVS	“”

Table 4.9 contains the formulas demonstrating this process.

Notice how the =IF statement, after evaluating the RTS, reaches a cell upwards to capture the result of the OVS.

The Effect of the RTS on the OVS

We know about the overnight sessions superior results, but how does a rising/falling RTS influence its performance?

Unlike the inverse relationship between the two trading sessions, in which a declining was superior to an advancing overnight session, it appears as if a rising regular session contributes more favorably to gains in the night (Table 4.10). After a positive (RTS > 0) session, the average overnight profit was \$0.468; whereas, the average return, after a negative (RTS < 0) session was less commendable (APT \$0.170). The more impressive difference was the 362 – 215 performance record after an advancing RTS.

Why the incredible returns after dark? Of course, there is no single answer, but as daytraders, the more information we have about an instrument the more opportunity for profit. The best way to explain this extraordinary phenomenon is to turn to the graphic features in Excel (see Figure 4.27).

Power at Your Fingertips

The IF(AND) function is definitely one of the most powerful weapons in Excel, because it has the ability to separate a true/false response from two or more

TABLE 4.9 When writing the equation for a difference in the performance of RTS, the results take you into the next trading day.

	A	B	C	D	E	F	G		
1	Date	OP	CL	OVS	RTS	RTS > 0	RTS < 0	Statement	Statement
2	7/20/2011	396.12	386.90	19.27	–9.22				
3	7/19/2011	378.00	376.85	4.20	–1.15		19.27	=IF(E3>0, D2,"")	=IF(E3<0, D2,"")
4	7/18/2011	365.43	373.80		8.37	4.20		=IF(E4>0, D3,"")	=IF(E4<0, D3,"")

TABLE 4.10 Descriptive statistics reporting the effect of the RTS on the Apple overnight trading session, January 3, 2007 to June 30, 2011.

	RTS > 0	RTS < 0
n	578	554
APT	\$0.468	\$0.170
sum	\$270.24	\$94.45
adv	362	299
dec	215	250
win%	.626	.540
min	−\$19.45	−\$17.29
max	\$14.20	\$14.39
10%	–\$1.48	–\$2.21
90%	\$2.81	\$2.41

FIGURE 4.27 Apple trading in the overnight session; the vertical lines represent an overnight return of \$4 or more. Notice the cyclical patterns; there appears to be one of these excessive up days every three months. This often coincides with those after-hours sessions when this company releases its blowout earnings report.

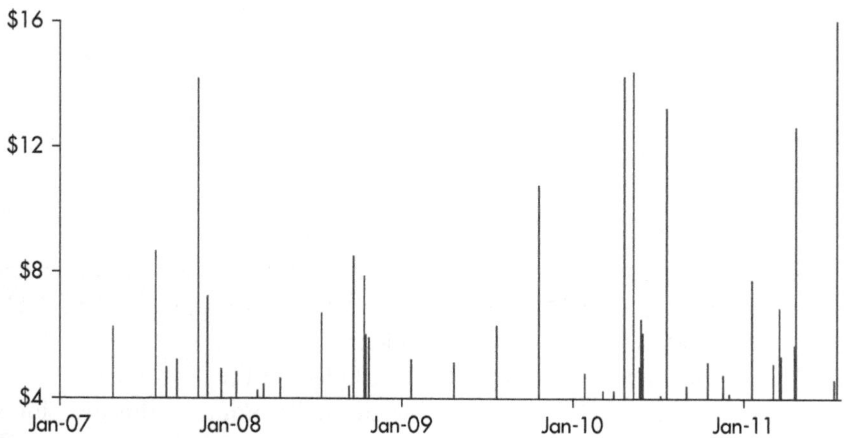

logical statements. This feature increases the complexity of your questions; therefore, it allows you to extract more information from any instrument.

You may not always have an assumption about a particular trading pattern, sometimes a situation surfaces, causing you to be curious about its outcome. In this case, we are examining the financial markets wild ride on the August 1, 2011, trading day. The cues (QQQ) had a Friday close of \$58.00.

After hours, Congress finally came to an agreement on a promise to cut trillions of dollars in fiscal debt along with a decision to raise the debt ceiling. In response to this agreement, the cues ran to an opening price of $58.67, but slid to $57.73 at the closing bell.

This was an uncommon trading day because of the strong (1 percent) advance in the overnight followed by a strong (1 percent) decline in the regular session. Naturally, I was curious about this pricing transformation in the cues. Going back 600 trading days, I found few days with this 1 percent combination.[4]

In this study, after the cues satisfy both conditions, we are looking at taking a long position in the overnight session.

1. > +1% advance in the OVS.
2. < –1% decline in the RTS.

Response Variable: A long overnight position in the cues.

With these two conditions in place, there were seven trading opportunities in which we could take a long position at the closing bell. The sequence of performance results in the overnight session was as follows:

$ change
0.84
0.14
0.62
0.14
0.19
–0.28
–0.02

So, we have a consecutive streak of five days, but can we make a decision from seven trading days? More importantly, how do we apply this IF(AND) function to produce these results? (See Figures 4.28 and 4.29.)

The statement reads =IF(AND(F2>1,G2<–1),D1,“”).[5]

We are not confined to just two conditions. According to this function's description, "up to 64 IF functions can be nested value_if_true and value_if_false arguments to construct more elaborate tests."

[4] Since we are going back 600 days, a percentage price change is our best option.
[5] You can press F2 to see its underlying equation.

FIGURE 4.28 The cues after a 1.155 percent advance, but a −1.621 percent decline. The IF(AND) function gives us the result of the overnight session on the following trading day.

	A	B	C	D	E	F	G	H
1	date	op	cl	ovs	rts	ovs %	rts %	updn
2	8/1/2011	58.67	57.73	.67	−.94	1.155	−1.621	ovs
3	7/29/2011	57.73	58.00	−.46	.27	−.791	.464	
4	7/28/2011	58.10	58.19	.01	.09	.017	.155	
5	7/27/2011	59.25	58.09	−.38	−1.16	−.629	−1.945	

FIGURE 4.29 The two logical statements, along with the true/false inputs.

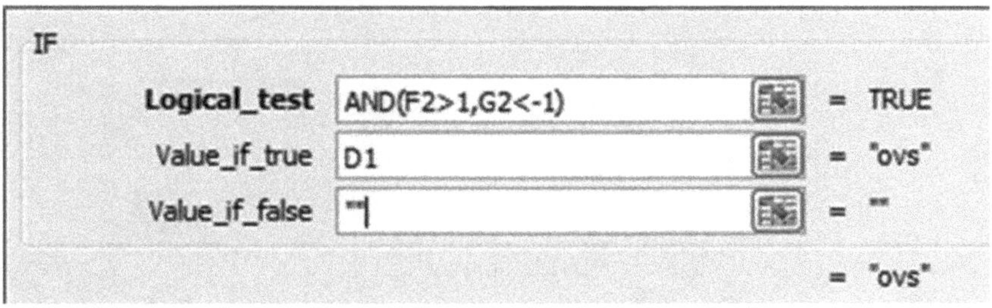

Are seven cases enough to make a decision? The fewer samples you have in your analysis, the less confidence you have in the results. Nevertheless, with overpowering results, taking a position gives you the advantage, but at best, a small position is a sensible approach. Still, in this case, another factor supporting this decision is trading volume. On this day, trading volume was excessively strong, going back 93 trading days; this day had the second-highest volume. A 1.621 percent loss along with strong activity is usually the best indicator of fear; these two factors may produce a toxic mix; therefore, going long may not be a clever decision. Chapter 12 gives us more insight into this question as it looks at relative trading volume.

Summary

These are the building blocks of our analysis. If you are seeking more knowledge, this function offers us many different possibilities. As we go forward, more studies, using this function, will be examined.

CHAPTER 5

Monitoring Performance

Talent hits a target no one else can hit; genius hits a target no one else can see.

—Arthur Schopenhauer, nineteenth-century philosopher

As the days pass, everything changes, and trading systems are no different. A system is not like a bottle of fine wine; it does not improve with age, and you have to adapt it to your trading environment.

Now that we are past the fundamentals, we can begin applying my methods. In this chapter, the emphasis is on monitoring the performance of a trading system; consequently, it begins with splitting the two primary trading sessions.

Tracking Success

Much of your effectiveness at forecasting develops from uncovering emerging price patterns; however, their duration is often fleeting. This makes winning more difficult because it requires the development of two disparate trading abilities. Certainly, early detection of these patterns as they begin to emerge is one, but slowly reducing or completely refraining from trading them once they begin to flatten or turn against you is the other indispensable skill.

By tracking the performance of a system, you are applying a proactive approach. This appeals to many technicians because it offers them the opportunity to make modifications as a trading system adjusts to current economic conditions (see Figure 5.1).

FIGURE 5.1 Tracking the performance of a system.

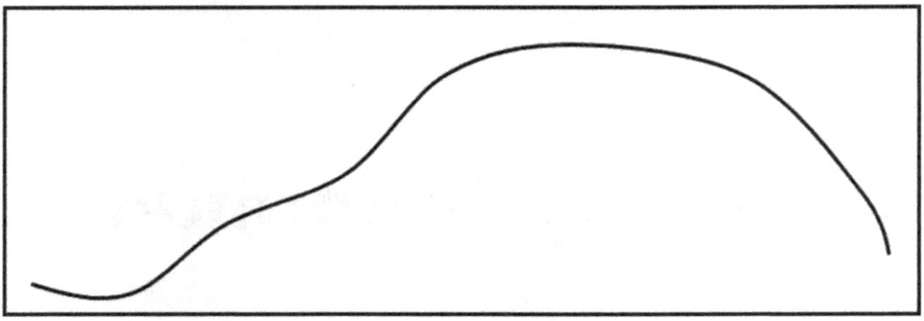

Once you draw a line chart showing the running summary of your system's results, you can accurately assess its performance on a continuous basis. Figure 5.1 is an illustration of a system with a string of positive days; eventually it loses its effectiveness as the steady rise begins to dampen. After reaching its apex, it falls rapidly as it approaches its lowest price. Monitoring this system's performance affords chartists an opportunity to readily apply their technical analysis skills, as they can use a variety of indicators to assess future performance by interpreting the direction of these cumulative line charts.

You may think of charting as following continuous unbroken movements. But often, valuable information can be found by breaking the trading day into smaller components. Without separating the trading day into smaller parts, you may be throwing away priceless information.

Although most individuals are more familiar with the regular daytime hours (09:30 to 16:00 EST), trading is still going on after hours. In fact, some trading platforms have the ability to fill weekday orders until 20:00 EST. Since the commodities market trades on a global basis, prices do not remain stagnant; consequently, the closing price is rarely the next day's opening price.

After briefly closing for a daily maintenance shutdown, the commodities markets resume trading. For instance, the 18:00 to midnight trading session for the ES contract produces approximately 2 percent of the daily trading volume. In spite of this small percentage of activity, it is responsible for a large portion of this contract's profit.[1]

[1]The next chapter discusses the hourly performance of the ES contract.

TABLE 5.1 This is the yearly performance summary of the PowerShares QQQ. After a devastating start this popular ETF has been responding nicely by putting together three winning years.

Year	Trading Days	$ Summary
2001	248	–19.47
2002	252	–14.54
2003	252	12.09
2004	252	3.46
2005	252	0.49
2006	251	2.75
2007	251	8.06
2008	253	–21.48
2009	252	16.01
2010	252	8.71
2011	125	2.59
TOTAL	2,640	–1.33

Since my feature article on the PowerShares QQQ (commonly known as the cues) in January 2004,[2] I became an advocate of splitting the trading sessions into smaller segments. This chapter begins with trading the cues by highlighting the long-term discrepancy between the two trading sessions. My purpose is to stress the importance of tracking the performance of your trading systems.

Table 5.1 shows 10.5 years (January 1, 2001, at $58.38, to June 30, 2011, at $57.05) of trading the cues.[3] This exchange-traded fund (ETF), consisting of the 100 companies in the NASDAQ-100 index, has been unable to return a profit, losing $1.33 in these 2,640 trading days.[4]

[2]Anthony Trongone, "Trading in the Hours of Darkness," *Technical Analysis of Stocks & Commodities* (January 2004).

[3]The complete list of the 100 companies in the index can be found at www.invescopowershares.com/products/holdings.aspx?ticker=QQQ.

[4]The 2011 summary displays the six-month performance of the cues (125 trading days); it extends from the first day of the trading year until June 30.

FIGURE 5.2 The daily price changes of the cues. Without separating the daily performance, this appears easy to play, but this line chart does not reveal the hidden trading opportunities.

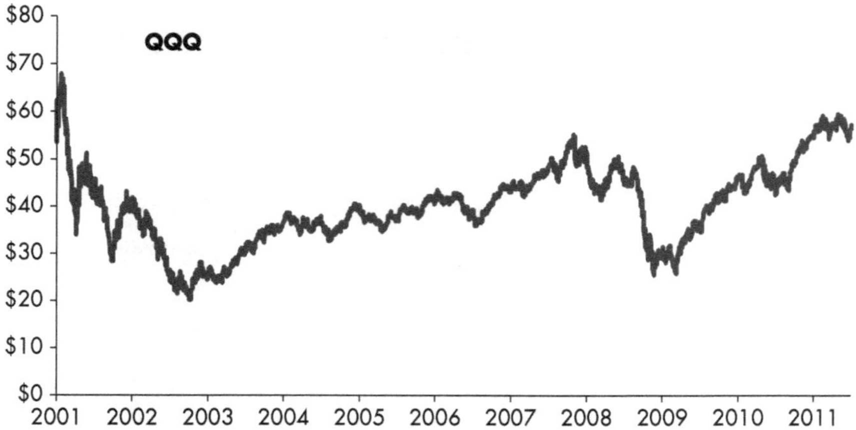

Someone buying the cues back in January 2001 is not going to be satisfied with a loss of $1.33 as a reward for holding fast. Figure 5.2 displays a line chart of its 10.5 year performance.

After each gravitational pull, the cues were able to return to their former glory. Therefore, it gives us the appearance of an easy environment to get the better of by simply selling on the two acute drops, then buying on each of the dramatic upswings. Of course, hindsight is perfect. This is analogous to the horse handicapper who looks back at the previous race, and believes the winner was a sure thing; after all, it is always easy to make money after the fact.

A daily line chart of the cues is informative; however, by extracting its yearly performance for each session, it increases our knowledge about the instrument under investigation. For instance, the overnight had a $30.35 profit, the regular session a $31.68 loss; consequently, there was a tremendous opportunity for anyone willing to take apart the trading day (Table 5.2).

These discrepancies offer incredible opportunities for the savvy investor. As you begin to investigate the performance differences between these two sessions among its 100 companies you will uncover other potentially rewarding possibilities.

Although it has been more than seven years since my article, the overnight session is still delivering attractive profits. Since the bull market, the regular trading session appears to be taking a turn for the better. Figure 5.3 is a bar chart showing the yearly difference between these two trading sessions.

TABLE 5.2 The overnight session was profitable ($30.35); the regular trading session was unprofitable (–$31.68).

Year	Days	OVS	RTS	Sum
2001	248	–2.26	–17.21	–19.47
2002	252	–3.35	–11.19	–14.54
2003	252	7.30	4.79	12.09
2004	252	5.10	–1.64	3.46
2005	252	5.93	–5.44	0.49
2006	251	2.52	0.23	2.75
2007	251	8.61	–0.55	8.06
2008	253	–5.98	–15.50	–21.48
2009	252	4.30	11.71	16.01
2010	252	7.40	1.31	8.71
2011	125	0.78	1.81	2.59
TOTAL	2,640	30.35	–31.68	–1.33

FIGURE 5.3 Splitting the cues into two trading sessions, the after-hours (black) session, with a 9-2 record, was the hands-down winner.

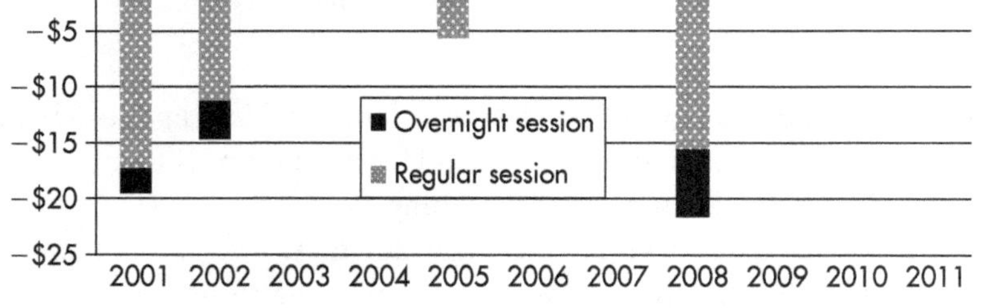

Return back to the column chart showing the yearly performance differences. When making a comparison of the down years (2001, 2002, 2008), the overnight was the performance winner; its losses in these three years were minor in comparison to its counterpart. Still, the day session is gaining traction; in the past 2.5 years, it overtook the night session by a slight margin. But, that is somewhat misleading, since the best years of the regular session appear to surface during bull markets; whereas, the overnight session outperforms its counterpart in bear markets.

Monitoring Performance

You can easily monitor performance in a worksheet by adding the daily price change for each session to its cumulative results. For example, let's assume that over the previous 100 trading days, the summary of the daily price change in the regular trading session is $50. If the stock advances $0.50, this would increase the cumulative price change to $50.50. By maintaining a running summary, you can keep an accurate account of an instrument's ongoing performance. Table 5.3 gives a description of a worksheet; below are the computational equations for the two sessions.

OVS	Equation	RTS	Equation
0.42	=B2-E3	–0.58	=E2-C2
–0.02	=B3-E4	–0.55	=E3-C3
–0.62	=B4-E5	–0.75	=E4-C4
–0.49	=B5-E6	–0.01	=E5-C5
0.43	=B6-E7	–0.17	=E6-C6
–0.06	=B7-E8	–0.10	=E7-C7
0.04	=B8-E9	–0.06	=E8-C8
0.05	=B9-E10	–0.075	=E9-C9

A worthwhile strategy has us taking a long position in the overnight (OVS), with a short position in the regular trading session (RTS). Despite its long-term success, is this pattern still holding fast?

Once you have the daily price changes for these two sessions, the procedural design of arithmetically computing a running summary can be seen in the extension of this worksheet (Table 5.4).

TABLE 5.3 Worksheet depicting the price changes for the two sessions.

	A	B	C	D	E	F	G	H
1	Date	Open	High	Low	Close	Volume	OVS	RTS
2	7/13/2011	57.94	58.34	57.55	57.76	82,366,468	.42	–.18
3	7/12/2011	57.94	58.07	57.46	57.52	83,984,477	–.02	–.42
4	7/11/2011	58.41	58.71	57.76	57.96	52,063,562	–.62	–.45
5	7/08/2011	58.70	59.04	58.37	59.03	69,521,166	–.49	.33
6	7/07/2011	58.82	59.36	58.74	59.19	54,772,823	.43	.37
7	7/06/2011	58.14	58.49	57.94	58.39	49,271,355	–.06	.25
8	7/05/2011	57.95	58.26	57.83	58.20	43,110,623	.04	.25
9	7/01/2011	57.10	57.99	56.92	57.91	53,180,670	.05	.81
10	6/30/2011	56.50	57.09	56.47	57.05	50,472,136		

TABLE 5.4 The cumulative sum (CS) of these two sessions is shown in their respective columns.

	G	H	I	J		
1	OVS	RTS	CS OVS	CS RTS		
2	.42	−.18	−.25	.96	↑	↑
3	−.02	−.42	−.67	1.14	↑	↑
4	−.62	−.45	−.65	1.56	↑	↑
5	−.49	.33	−.03	2.01	↑	↑
6	.43	.37	.46	1.68	↑	↑
7	−.06	.25	.03	1.31	↑	↑
8	.04	.25	.09	1.06	↑	↑
9	.05	.81	.05	.81	=I10+I9	=J10+J9
10			0	0	0	0

After writing the equation in the master cell, use the auto fill handle by selecting the right corner, once the white "+" changes to a black "+"drag the mouse across multiple cells to produce the desired results in these two columns.[5]

After you become familiar with this analytical technique, you will be better at discovering an assortment of profitable patterns throughout the 24-hour trading day. Since you can conceivably separate the 24-hour trading session into a variety of smaller sessions, it encourages the user to experiment freely.

It is instructive to review this session's performance during the bear market. With the financial crisis, the cues took a nasty fall, slipping from \$55.03 (October 31, 2007) to \$25.72 (March 9, 2009). Certainly, such a drop was destructive (Figure 5.4), but the decline in the overnight during these 340 trading days accounted for a small portion of this loss (\$6.01/\$29.29 = 20.52 percent).[6]

---

[5]Once you write the equation in cell I9, drag it across to cell J9. With both cells highlighted, drag the formulas up to the second row. This process provides you with a running summary of an instrument. After producing this information, draw a line chart of these two sessions. A discussion on how to draw a line chart is in the appendix.

[6]Anthony Trongone, "Trading Companies with Split Personalities," *Technical Analysis of Stocks & Commodities* (March 2011).

FIGURE 5.4 After an unimpressive start, the overnight session began its extensive run. Thereafter, the cues had a steady uphill journey until the financial crisis; the overnight session was able to withstand this $29.29 mauling, as the bear went into hibernation in the spring of 2009.

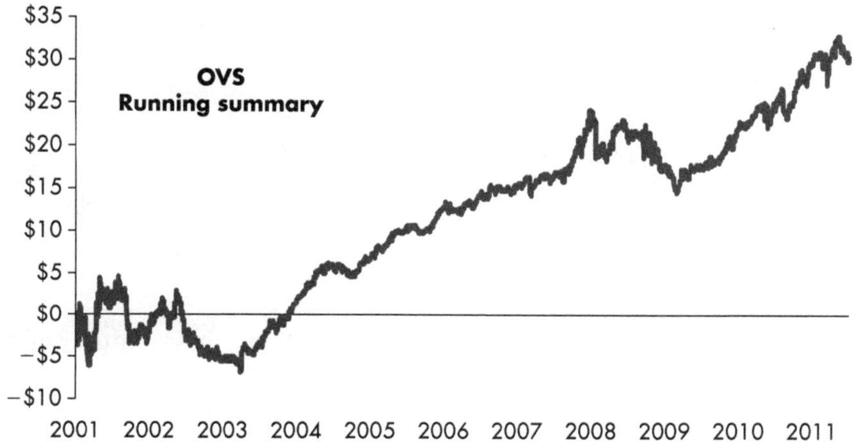

The overnight session takes on significance because its performance reflects postmarket company earnings reports, after-hours economic breaking news with an international perspective, as well as premarket economic reports in the morning (generally at 08:30).

The running summary of the regular trading session (Figure 5.5) shows how this session has taken a different course.

Statistics can be deceptive. Although we are looking at a $31.68 decline, most of it coming in the early years, in the following years (2003 to 2008), the RTS was at a standstill. After being taken down hard by the bear, it made an admirable recovery; however, it appears as if this promising rally is stuck in its previous sideways price range.

With 2,640 trading days, you could say that this system has been through all kinds of weather; therefore, we can begin trading from this information. Referring back to the bar chart (Figure 5.3), a side-by-side yearly forecast between these two sessions gives the early morning a 9-2 record.

A comparison of the unprofitable years demonstrates three losing years for the OVS in comparison to six for the RTS. The biggest came in 2008: $5.98. The RTS, however, suffered three double-digit down years.

You could surely produce remarkable results by taking a long position at the closing bell, replacing it with a short position at the opening bell, and repeating this action; continuously offsetting your current position and

FIGURE 5.5 The regular trading session, after a precipitous fall, has been moving sideways.

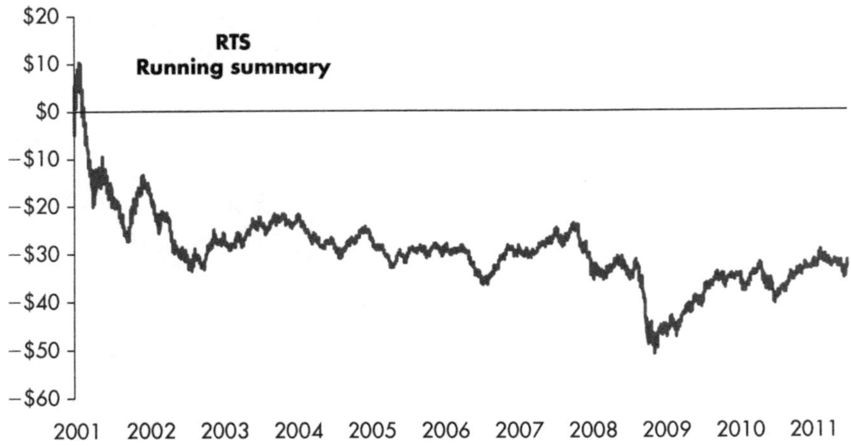

taking an opposite one. This system was profitable for 10+ years, but is it still going strong?

Reasons for Monitoring Performance

Since many of the forces pulling on the market are dynamic entities, they frequently produce pricing abnormalities. Seen from a regressive perspective,[7] they often self-correct. Consequently, the overnight session may eventually begin losing steam, giving the regular session the opportunity to surpass its counterpart. The challenge is to benefit from the early phase of this transformation, but not to chase after the many false moves that often accompany a performance shift between sessions.

Although the cumulative sum of the OVS for the cues has been profitable, when it ceases to be effective, we would simply revise our strategy by either putting it aside until it starts working again or becoming more aggressive by taking a short position.

---

[7] *Regression to the mean* is a statistical term. It plays on the assumption that what goes up is going to come back down; consequently, it is a process that takes us back to the breakeven point. Say you are investigating a series of outlying scores; the process of replicating this phenomenon in the near future is less likely, but if the basis of this performance was not driven by causation, the instrument is more likely to return to the condition of normalcy.

TABLE 5.5 Performance for the two sessions (February 11, 2008 to August 2011); the summary, as well as the August 31, 2011 weighting, of these companies in the cues.

898 Days	OVS	RTS	Sum	% Share	Win Session
AAPL	279.91	–24.53	255.38	14.60	OVS
MSFT	–3.69	2.08	–1.61	8.96	RTS
ORCL	–3.48	12.11	8.63	5.71	RTS
GOOG	406.48	–386.68	19.80	5.54	OVS
INTC	1.57	–2.12	–.55	4.34	OVS
AMZN	.88	139.16	140.04	3.86	RTS
CSCO	–4.45	–3.40	–7.85	3.48	RTS
AMGN	–8.65	17.68	9.03	2.08	RTS
EBAY	–8.23	10.93	2.70	1.63	RTS
COST	–41.74	56.28	14.54	1.38	RTS
SBUX	–15.15	35.25	20.10	1.17	RTS
NFLX	5.20	202.92	208.12	.50	RTS
Sum	608.64	59.68	668.33	53.25	3-9

Historical daily prices come from www.esignal.com.

Performance Differences among Companies

This split personality is not specific to the cues. As I wrote in an earlier article, "By performing a simple analysis in which you separate the performance of these two trading sessions, you can uncover countless examples of stocks manifesting this incongruous trading behavior."[8]

Since the cues appear to have a positive bias in the overnight session, is this a common tendency among stocks in this index? Table 5.5 displays the performance by session, along with the weighting impact it has on the price movement of the cues.[9] The winning session represents the better performer for these 898 trading days. These 12 companies comprise 53.34 percent of

[8] Anthony Trongone, "Monitoring Trading System Performance Day & Night," *Stocks, Futures and Options Magazine* (August 2009), 46–52.

[9] The weightings for this index are constantly shifting. A reporting of daily changes for the 100 companies can be found at www.invescopowershares.com/products/overview.aspx?ticker=QQQ.

the 100 companies in the cues. Apple with a 14.60 percentage share has the biggest influence on the price of this index fund.[10]

Two stocks are primarily responsible for this imbalance; the overnight session took in $608.64 of the $668 in earnings for these 12 companies. A glance back at the bar chart (Figure 5.3) of the cues demonstrates why the overnight dominates with a 9-2 margin of yearly victories with a performance difference of $9.93 OVS versus $1.06 RTS.

In reference to these two sessions, nine of these stocks have split personalities; that is, they were profitable in one, but not the other session. The three stocks with either gains (AMZN + NFLX) or losses (CSCO) in both sessions are the exception. The dominating overnight performers are those primarily creating technology (AAPL + GOOG); whereas, those controlling the day session are the ones using it (AMZN + NFLX).

While some companies appear to have a long-term history with a performance bias toward a particular session, there is always the possibility they will reverse direction. How long they stay on course is not an easy call, but by running a cumulative summary of each session separately, any deviation from an existing pattern becomes easier to recognize.

In order to avert a performance error, always run the following functions after splitting the sessions apart:

=MIN(range of scores)
=MAX(range of scores)

These two functions give you the minimum (the lowest price change) and the maximum (the highest price change) for the session under study. If something is awry, it is probably because of stock splits, which require making the necessary price adjustments. Most stock splits occur after hours; therefore, the overnight session usually contains the measurement error.

Google It!

After writing articles on the cues about differences between these trading sessions, I began writing about this anomaly among companies. Back in March 31, 2006, the focus of my weekly article was the remarkable

[10]Historical daily prices come from www.esignal.com. If you use another website, there are slight pricing differences—mainly minor discrepancies in the opening price of an instrument.

FIGURE 5.6 The first three-year running performance of GOOG in the overnight session shows a straight trajectory to $600. It began trading with a $100 stock price on August 19, 2004.

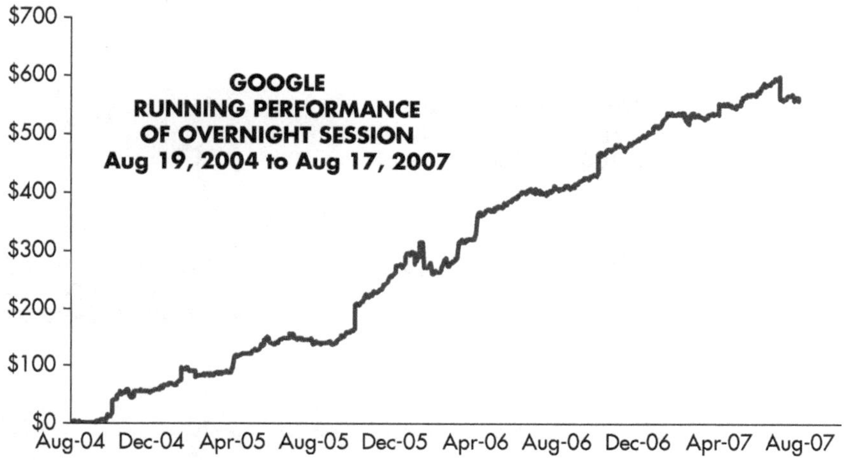

performance of this information provider in the overnight session. Google has certainly been an outstanding breadwinner. On August 19, 2004, it began trading at $100. After three years, its closing price came in at $490.02; however, the overnight session takes the credit for this company's impressive gains.[11] Despite this stellar performance, surprisingly, the regular session remains unprofitable.

But that was then, and this is now—will this pattern still hold? A system with such a steady track record is worth betting on. In spite of this, carefully monitor its performance, because no system can produce a steady stream of profits forever.

What follows is a discussion of a simple strategy with a long run of success by a company with a worldwide presence.[12]

Figure 5.6 runs to Google's $500.04 close on August 17, 2007.

---

[11]Anthony Trongone, "Google's Split Personality: Impersonating Jekyll and Hyde," Interactive Data Corporation, March 31, 2006, www.esignal.com.

[12]The overnight session takes on significance because its performance is reflective of premarket economic reports in the morning (generally at 08:30) as well as after-hours company earnings reports, and the reporting of international economic breaking news, which often take place after the U.S. markets close for the day.

FIGURE 5.7 Performance of the overnight session from Aug 17, 2007 ($500.04) to Aug 19, 2011 ($490.02). Despite its $10.02 loss in these four years, the after-hours session still rises above $1,000.

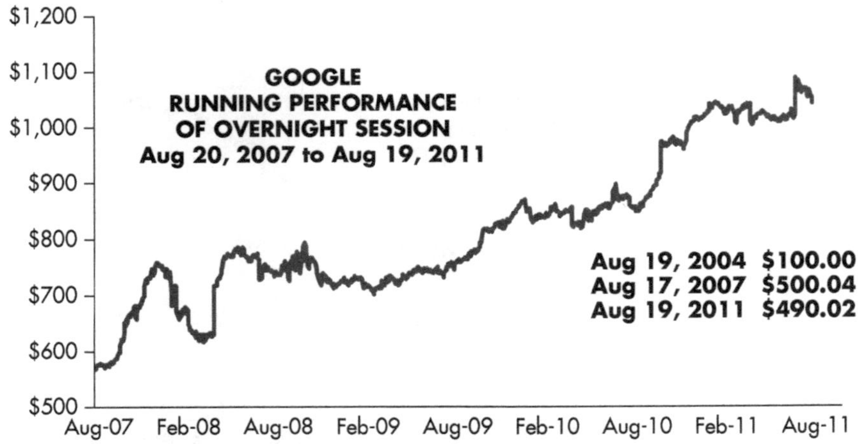

Feast your eyes on the astonishing performance of this innovative company in the aftermarket session.[13] In this three-year performance, its linear run has few deviations. When they do occur; they are minor setbacks with quick recoveries. (See Figure 5.7.)

In response to the vicious attack of the bear market, this performance gets taken down early on, but recovers quickly. Afterwards, it holds at a standstill, taking over 100 trading days to surpass its previous peak. Although its trendline is dampening, it is still pushing toward record performances.

Achieving Mythical Proportions

Most trending patterns have a short shelf life; a streak of this duration occasionally does surface, but is extremely rare. Once a system is working for you, stick with it, until it has played itself out! How long it lasts is not up to you; what is up to you, however, is to consistently monitor its performance and make the necessary adjustments to maximize its benefits and recognize when it has finally run its course.

---

[13] Anthony Trongone, "Some Things Stay the Same," Interactive Data Corporation, November 5, 2010, www.esignal.com.

FIGURE 5.8 The cumulative performance of the spiders after a losing day.

	A	B	C	D	E	F	G	H	I
1	date	op	hi	lw	cl	vm	$change	pc <0	csum
2	10/14/2011	121.91	122.60	121.23	122.57	208205693	2.06	2.06	8.34
3	10/13/2011	120.04	120.87	119.12	120.51	211968551	−0.24	0	6.28
4	10/12/2011	120.60	122.14	120.33	120.75	281302490	1.05	0	6.28
5	10/11/2011	118.87	120.04	118.75	119.70	208809047	0.12	0	6.28
6	10/10/2011	117.68	119.63	117.67	119.58	230116193	3.87	3.87	6.28
7	10/7/2011	117.17	117.25	115.06	115.71	312178510	−0.78	0	2.41
8	10/6/2011	114.36	116.66	113.51	116.49	257358374	2.07	0	2.41
9	10/5/2011	112.62	114.72	111.58	114.42	283515440	2.08	0	2.41
10	10/4/2011	108.35	112.58	107.43	112.34	458247400	2.41	2.41	2.41
11	10/3/2011	112.49	113.95	109.81	109.93	364377200	−3.22	0	0
12	9/30/2011	114.45	115.45	113.07	113.15	288339410			0

You can be long the better-performing session, but when the equity indices are going down, you will still suffer losses in your account.

Tracking a System without Continuous Scores

The two previous charts display a continuous running summary of the cues. When playing a system without steady action, the cumulative sum (CSUM) repeats the previous summary score.

Below is one of the best performance weeks for the spiders. It shows the cumulative sum of a simple system: buy the spiders after a losing day, but do not take a position after a winning day. Although it was profitable, I am not advocating this strategy. My purpose is to demonstrate how to draw a line chart of the running summary of a system when it does not have an everyday play (Figure 5.8).

Since the system does not give us a play on a daily basis, it skips advancing days. When the system is not in play, its running summary holds at its previous score.[14]

[14]Some examples of the formulas for columns H are:

H8 =IF(G9<0,G8,0)

H9 =IF(G10<0,G9,0)

H10 =IF(G11<0,G10,0)

If the error term #VALUE! is written in one of the cumulative sum cell values, write the IF statement with an 0 in the false argument, such as IF(condition, true statement, 0).

FIGURE 5.9 The inactivity of a system. The straight lines indicate when there was no trading action because the system's requirements were not being met.

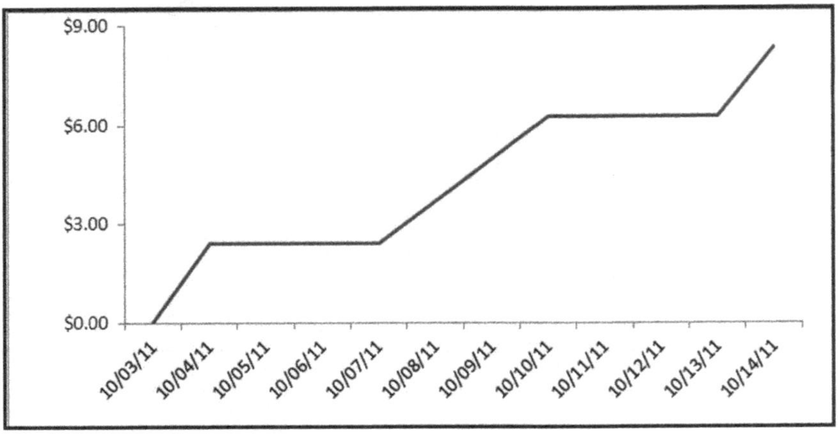

Figure 5.9 shows three upward movements. The flat lines are the days this system is not tradable. Although we are including those days not satisfying our trading conditions (i.e., a price decline in the previous trading day), the cumulative sum (CSUM) is still an effective indicator of the performance of this system.

Three-Day Performance Study

This study measures the performance of the spiders three days after an excessive price change. Although we have been assessing the following days' price change, this response variable takes the summary (t1 + t2 + t3) results of the next three trading days.

In this study there are two research questions:

1. After a +2 percent-plus change in the spiders, how will it perform on the next three trading days?
2. After a −2 percent-plus change in the spiders, how will it perform on the next three trading days?

Hypothesis

The hypothesis is that the effect of an excessive daily gain or loss over 2 percent in the spiders elicits an overreaction from traders; consequently, it gives back a good portion of this single-day price move. See Figures 5.10 and 5.11.

FIGURE 5.10 This is a system with a brief period of success. It begins by hovering around the breakeven line. After a 2 percent daily profit, the spiders could not sustain positive returns over the next three trading days. More importantly, with the exception of a sharp downturn, this system was flat.

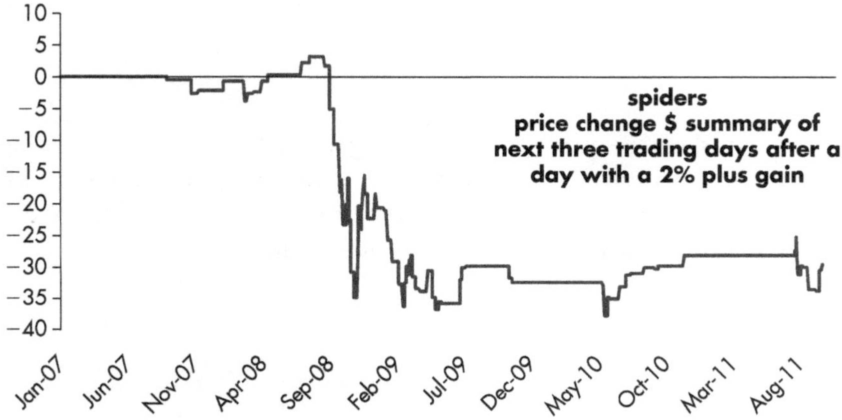

FIGURE 5.11 This part of the system has us taking a long position after a strong loss. After a year of indecisiveness, it rallied, but stayed inactive for a long spell, before making another move to the upside.

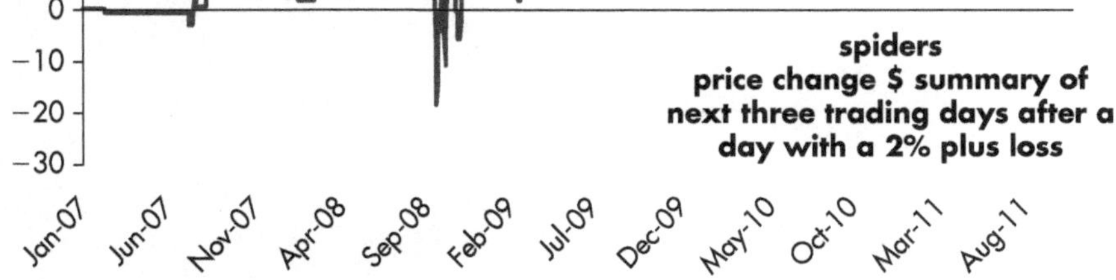

This system, which requires a short position after a 2 percent-plus day, is no longer giving us profitable results; consequently, we would cease trading it, but keep tracking its performance looking for either a recovery or another breakdown.

Holding a long position for three trading days after a strong single-day correction has been a worthwhile play. Despite its success, it was slow generating profits until the beginning of the bull market; thereafter, this strategy had a long respite before working again.

Summary

These results show the importance of tracking the performance of any trading strategy. Unfortunately, it is a skill that many traders never cultivate, but with practice, you will not only be the trader who hits the target others cannot hit, you can be the trader who hits the target others cannot see.

CHAPTER 6

Breaking Down a Stock or Commodity

Know your enemy and know yourself and you can fight a hundred battles without disaster.

—Sun Tzu

In attempting to construct a trading system appropriate for the existing trading environment, you are likely to encounter many false starts. Nevertheless, these exploratory undertakings are a valuable learning process. After researching an assortment of possibilities, you will eventually uncover some attractive candidates. As you narrow the field, you can perform a more extensive examination of those systems offering the most promising opportunities.

This chapter offers a more probing examination into the most tradable equities index commodity, the E-mini S&P 500 (ES) futures contract (multiplier × \$50 with a tick size of .25 index points = \$12.50).[1]

[1] *Hours of operation:*
Sunday 18:00 to 16:15 Monday
Monday 16:30 to 17:30, 18:00 to 16:15 Tuesday
Tuesday 16:30 to 17:30, 18:00 to 16:15 Wednesday
Wednesday 16:30 to 17:30, 18:00 to 16:15 Thursday
Thursday 16:30 to 17:30, 18:00 to 16:15 Friday
(all times Eastern Standard Time).

FIGURE 6.1 The comparison chart displays the closing price of the E-mini S&P 500 commodities continuous contract divided by the closing price of the SPDR SPY 500.

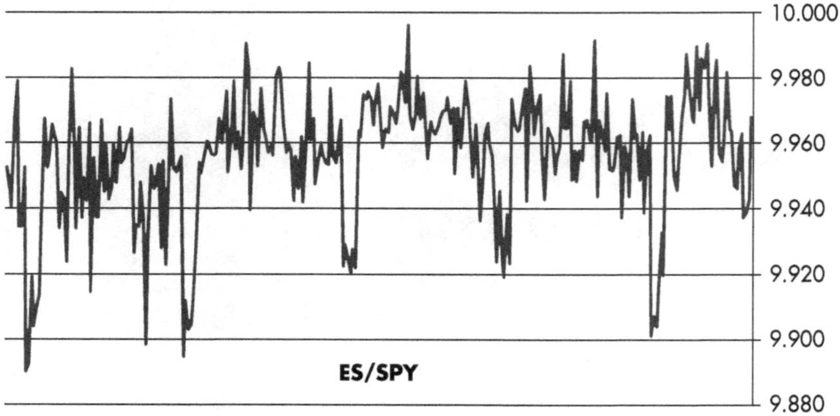

ES Contract versus the Spiders

Although this chapter gives us a description of trading activity for the ES contract, we can apply this information to the spiders when making our trading decisions. With an almost perfect correlation, the price movements of these two instruments stick closely together.

Figure 6.1 shows the minor variations in the closing price movements between the ES contract in comparison to the price movements of the spiders (SPY).

The tight band between these two instruments spans 300 trading days. The comparison chart shows SPY staying within a restrictive 9.88 to 10.00 range. After a ghastly day, August 4, 2011, the ES contract stood at 1,198.75, a single-day loss of 55.75 points; SPY sank $5.91, bringing its price down to $120.26. The proportion between the two instruments is 1,198.75/ $120.26 = 9.968, so you can safely assume a movement of 10 points in the commodity contract is slightly shy of a $1.00 movement in the spiders.

Early Morning Price Swings

This investigation of the ES contract begins on July 11, 2010; its 18:00 price opens at 1,071.50, 300 trading days pass before it closes at 1,138.75.[2] Given a multiplier of $50 per point; this 67.25 advance, registers a tidy sum. This is

[2]This analysis terminates on September 6, 2011; 1,138.75 is the 09:00 morning price.

impressive, but considering 148.25 points came during trading from 18:00 to 06:00, this 12-hour nightly setting should be given more emphasis.

By knowing the statistical characteristics of the instrument you are trading, you can make more informed trading decisions. The investigation provides a postmarket analysis of this ES contract.[3] Although you may not be actively trading after hours, you can take advantage of this information by taking positions either before or after the regular trading session.

Before creating different strategies, we begin with an introspective evaluation of range (i.e., highest to lowest price within the chosen time frame), volume, and price change of this contract within three-hour segments.[4]

Price Range

The price range is the difference between the highest to lowest price within each of the three hours under investigation (Figure 6.2).

The trading range (highest to lowest price), which holds at around $4.00 for the opening nine hours of trading, widens considerably in the early

FIGURE 6.2 Three-hour price range for the 18:00 to 09:00 trading hours for the ES futures contract.

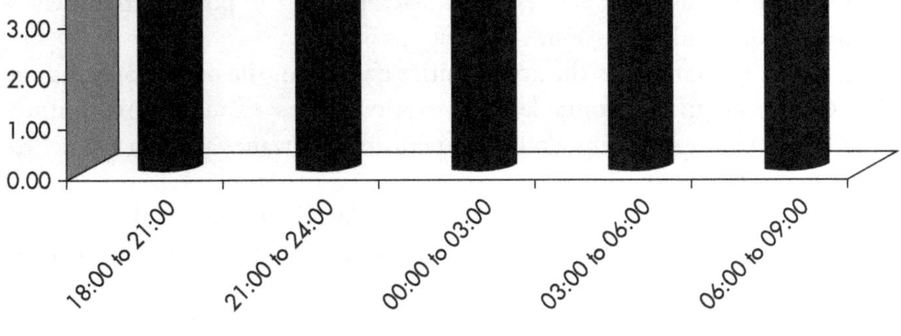

[3]The opening price of this contract begins at 18:00 (EST), its analysis covers 15 hours of trading (18:00 to 09:00).

[4]Excel enables you to do all the analysis in this chapter.

FIGURE 6.3 This bar chart provides the average trading volume (ES contracts) from dusk to dawn. Its activity begins to pick up in the early morning.

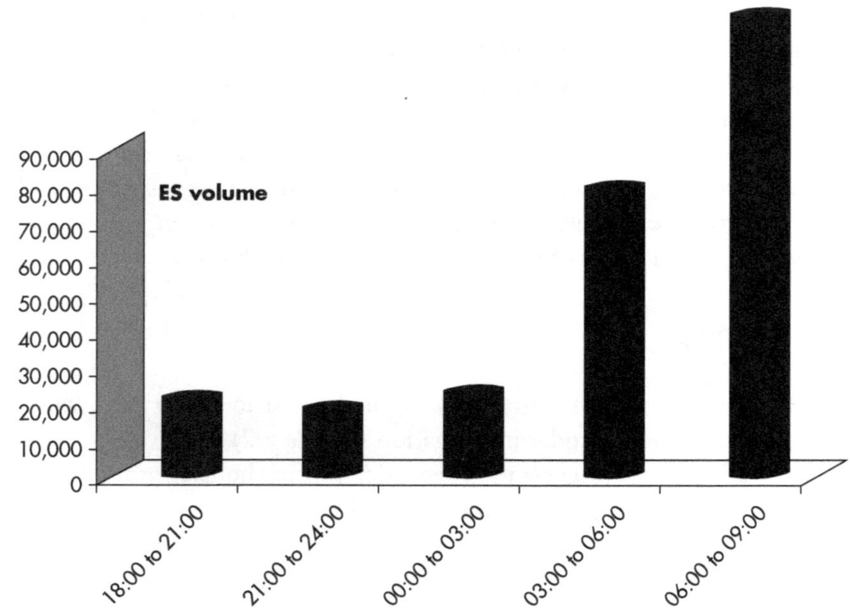

morning hours. Since we have more volatility within 03:00 to 09:00, it offers us some flexibility in placing orders away from its current price.[5]

Volume junkies abound in all corners of the investment world, they predominately are on the lookout for anomalies in activity. After 03:00 the volume increases as more players begin placing orders to position themselves for the regular trading session.[6] (See Figure 6.3.)

Finally, we can review the average price change for the three-hour trading segments. The most profitable opportunity comes from midnight until 06:00, when it appears to peak, but its performance wanes as we get closer to the opening bell of the equities market.

In these 300 days comprising this analysis (Figure 6.4), there was a 67.25-point increase in this contract; however, 148.25 points came within

[5]With knowledge of how a commodity trades in the early morning hours, we have an opportunity to fill our orders at a more advantageous price.

[6]Chapter 12 demonstrates how to make use of trading volume to enhance your predictive powers.

FIGURE 6.4 The ES contract's average performance return by three-hour sessions.

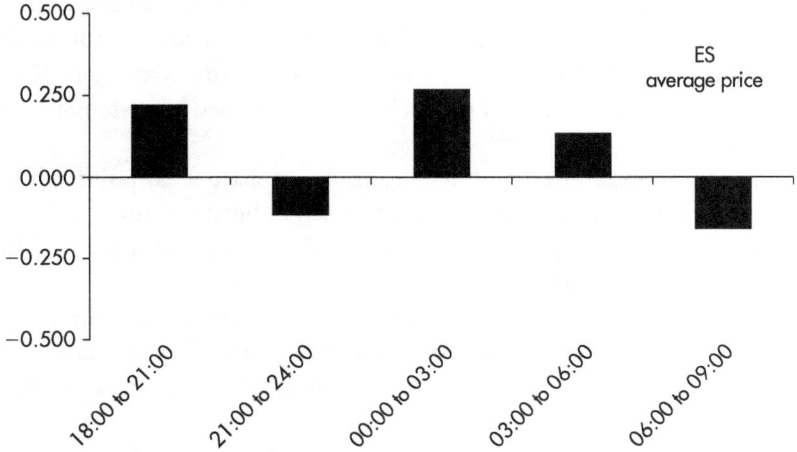

FIGURE 6.5 Running summary of the 18:00 to 21:00 trading session. In these three evening hours, the equities market was able to produce 65.25 points of its entire 300-day output of 67.25 points.

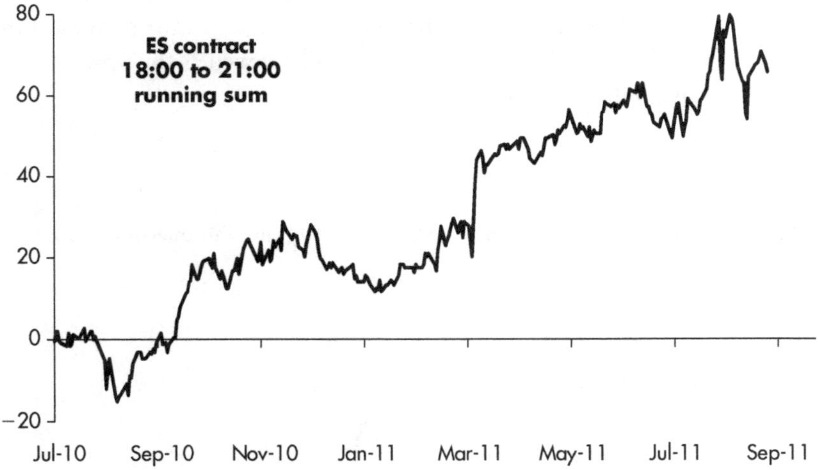

the hours of 18:00 to 06:00. Do not overlook these early hours of trading; they offer clues to the movements of the more traditional hours.

This is an uphill ascent with a few growth spurts (Figure 6.5). There have been some valleys, which may be discouraging, but not reloading when you had the opportunity would have been a mistake.

After soaring some 40 points, was there a way to avoid this frightening March meltdown? And was it a precursor for more disappointment?

Average volume in this three-hour stretch (21:00 to 24:00) is 18.1k, but with the 22.50-point decline (March 14, 2011), it was 168.2k, which is alarming. The three hours before had the third-biggest loss in 300 trading days (a drop of 7.50 points), with volume of 49.6k (the average is 21.4k). The question is how often are these declines accompanied by extremely active trading volume?

The three hours after midnight cannot run past a 20-point advance (Figure 6.7), but after breaking down below earlier bottoms, this commodity generates considerable gains. More importantly, it runs inversely with this contract's previous three hour price direction (Figure 6.6).

After dropping to 1,080, the three white bars—from midnight to 03:00—produce a 46-point advance. Do these three hourly bars, which complete the right side of a "V" bottom, pave the way for a profitable opportunity later in the trading day?

When you see an indication of success, such as the early part of this hourly candlestick chart (Figure 6.8), in which the ES contract turns black (i.e., the closing price is lower than the opening price), it often is a teachable moment. At 22:00 hours, it reaches its bottom, its volatility subsides at 23:00 hours, but it is in the three hours after midnight that this contract comes off its "V" bottom and begins a 46-point rally. The significance of these three hours may be indicative of the early morning rally as well as the upward (long white bar) move, which takes us to 16:00 hours.

FIGURE 6.6 The 22.50 point decline on March 14, 2011, put this three-hour span below breakeven.

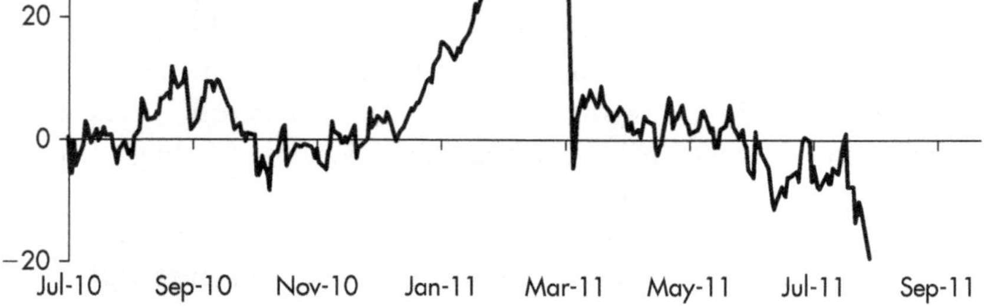

FIGURE 6.7 A spectacular single-day advance rockets these three hours to an attractive long play. What was the catalyst behind this 60-point surge?

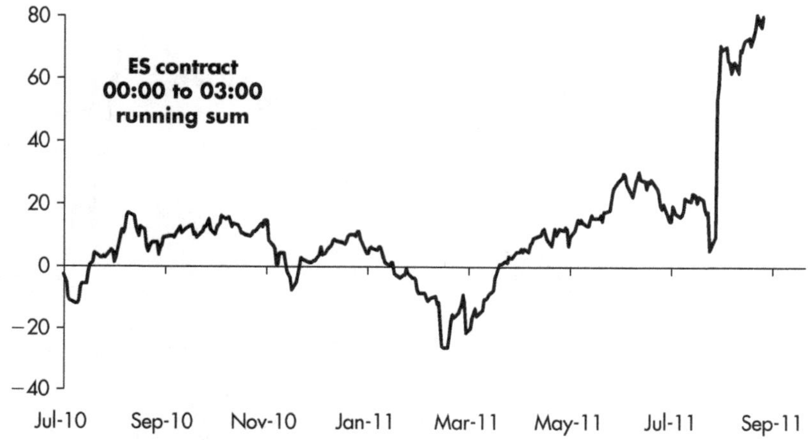

FIGURE 6.8 An hourly candlestick chart showing the meteoric rise of the ES contract on August 9, 2011.

This is what running a cumulative analysis of performance is all about, catching these trending patterns. After all, it would be a shame to miss this 10-month climb to 100 points (Figure 6.9) before it fell off the cliff. Figure 6.10 depicts the 06:00 to 07:00 price movements of the ES contract; it appears to have cyclical growth spurts.

In spite of this optimism, not every chart pattern offers us a trading advantage (Figure 6.11). Some of these hourly breakdowns offer, at best, a spectator's vantage point.

FIGURE 6.9 After a picture perfect progression to 100 plus points, these three hours suddenly implode.

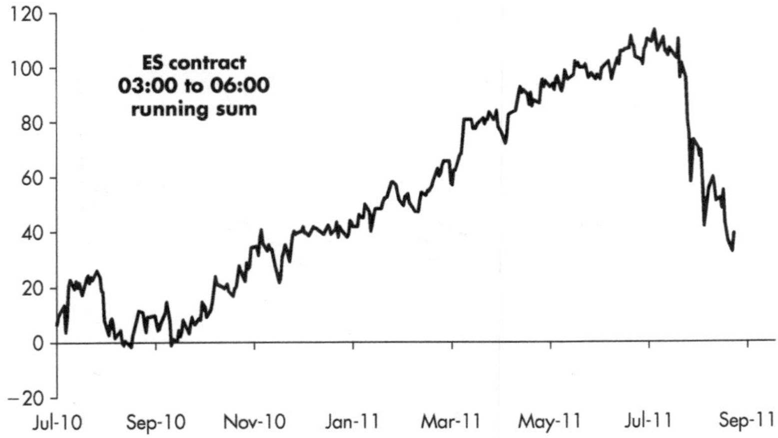

FIGURE 6.10 This is a pattern that appears easy to play, but really wears on your emotions. Nonetheless, if you get it right, it is a very profitable 300 days.

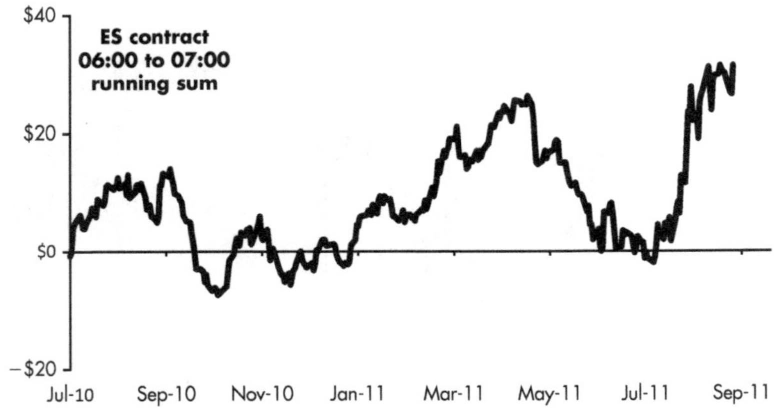

Carefully observe excessive amounts of trading activity; it is often a flashing red light. For instance, the August 11, 2011, decline of 25.25 points had the highest activity in these 300 days (182,126 contracts from an average 32,180). Nevertheless, this knowledge comes during the downturn, which does not give us any insight into preventing this troubling loss. But a warning signal came during the earlier hour; with 95,790 contracts, it had the highest trading activity among these 300 days.

FIGURE 6.11 These fractious movements make this hour extremely challenging; however, some technicians would classify its boundaries as a trading opportunity.

TABLE 6.1 Trouble was certainly brewing in these four trading days before the 25.25-point loss on August 11, 2011, in the hour between 07:00 and 08:00. In the hours between 03:00 and 06:00, there were wide differences in the comparison of these four days with the 300-day study.

Trading the ES Contract from 03:00 to 06:00

Trading Days	Dates of Analysis	Total Points	Average Volume
4 days	08/08/11 to 08/11/11	–43.00	339,497
300 days	07/12/10 to 09/06/11	+39.00	83,800

Early detection of disastrous hourly corrections can come from irregular early morning price swings. For instance, an examination of early morning deviations in trading activity prior to this 25.25-point downward assault was another cautionary indicator. Table 6.1 is a comparison of the trading range between these two daily settings.

Prior to aberrant price swings seen during these four days (August 8 to August 11, 2011), investors often experience tumultuous trading, particularly preceding the hours under investigation. Such a wide deviation in trading range may not give us predictive direction, but it generally acts as a harbinger of more volatility.

Figure 6.12 shows the result of taking a long position in the 08:00 to 09:00 premarket hour. Despite its downward trending pattern, once it sank below the breakeven point, its run was highly predictable.

FIGURE 6.12 Prior to the opening bell of the equities market, this ES contract shows an orderly downward progression of lower prices. Starting with the early symptoms of the sharp descent below the breakeven line, this contract has not been able to offer evidence of a recovery.

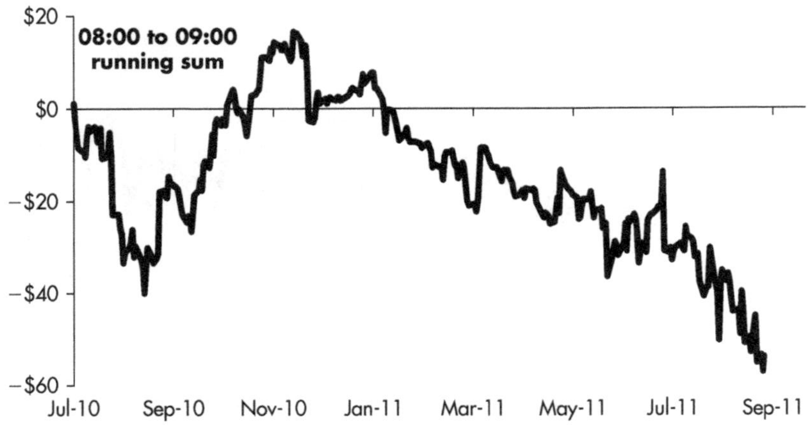

Besides reaching its lowest price, the drop has been more acute. Can we use this information to predict prices from 09:00 to 11:00? More specifically, what is the difference in the 09:00 to 11:00 performance on the basis of the price direction of the 08:00 to 09:00 hour in the previous 200 trading days (November 30, 2010, to September 7, 2011)?

After the sharp downturn, this study contrasts the 08:00 to 09:00 hour by separating the performance of the ES contract into the following two categories:

The 08:00 to 09:00 hour advances (GT $>$ 0).

The 08:00 to 09:00 hour declines (LT $<$ 0).

In this study, we are investigating trading in the ES contract from 09:00 to 11:00. We want to know if the price movement of the ES contract from 08:00 to 09:00 will affect the performance of the next two trading hours (09:00 to 11:00).

An examination of the past 200 trading days (Nov 30, 2010 to Sep 07, 2011) demonstrates an inverse performance difference in these two hours in response to the direction of the ES contract from 08:00 to 09:00 (Table 6.2). When the earlier hour advances, the 09:00 to 11:00 session fell 62.50 points in 87 trading days ($0.7184 APT, with a 44.83 winning percentage).

On the contrary, when the 08:00 to 09:00 hour declines, a long position was the better play. With a 59.41 winning percentage, it resulted in 65.25 points ($0.6460 APT). In either case, taking the opposite position after the 08:00 to 09:00 price change appears to be a safe play.

What is the effect of the ES contract after a sharp loss (< -5 points) between 09:00 to 10:00 on the performance of the 10:00 to 11:00 hour?

TABLE 6.2 The effects of (08:00 to 09:00) price direction on trading from 09:00 to 11:00. It demonstrates an inverse relationship between the earlier hour with the 09:00 to 10:00 hour as well as a continuation of the analysis until 11:00.

	08:00 to 09:00 Price Advances		08:00 to 09:00 Price Declines	
	09:00 to 10:00	09:00 to 11:00	09:00 to 10:00	09:00 to 11:00
n	87	87	101	101
Sum	–21.00	–62.50	36.25	65.25
Average	–0.2414	–0.7184	0.3589	0.6460
Advance	44	39	56	60
Decline	42	46	41	41
Winning %	.5058	.4483	.5545	.5941

FIGURE 6.13 The 09:30 opening hour for the equities market often produces the widest performance range in which there are abrupt price swings, including its drop of nearly 90 points within 6 months.

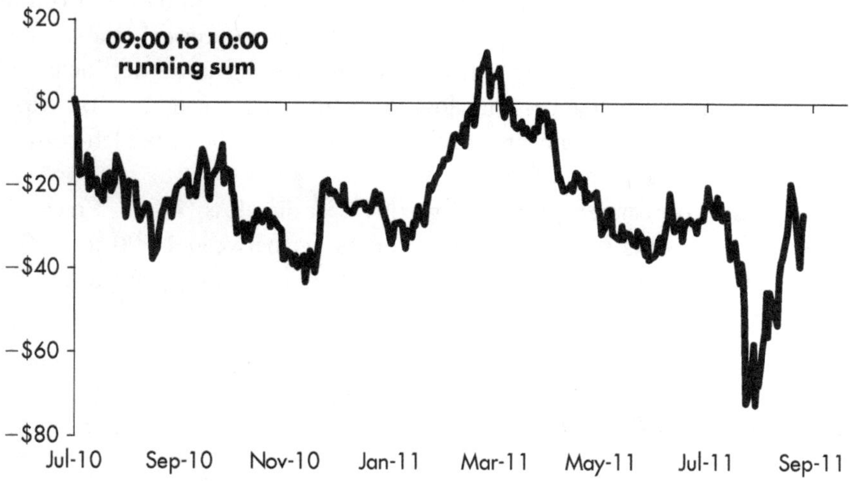

The hour containing the 09:30 market opening bell traditionally displays the sharpest price swings (Figure 6.13).

Unlike the earlier studies, this analysis creates a scatter gram to discern the outlying performance of the earlier 09:00 to 10:00 hour in order to assess the ES contract between 10:00 to 11:00 (Figure 6.14).

After a decline of 5-plus points in the earlier hour, the scatter gram shows how the ES contract performs in the 10:00 to 11:00 hour. With it we can compare two variables simultaneously. This can be seen by looking at how all

FIGURE 6.14 A scattergram of the 09:00 to 10:00 hour provides the performance for the 10:00 to 11:00 hour (y-axis) when the loss in the earlier hour is < −5 points (x-axis).

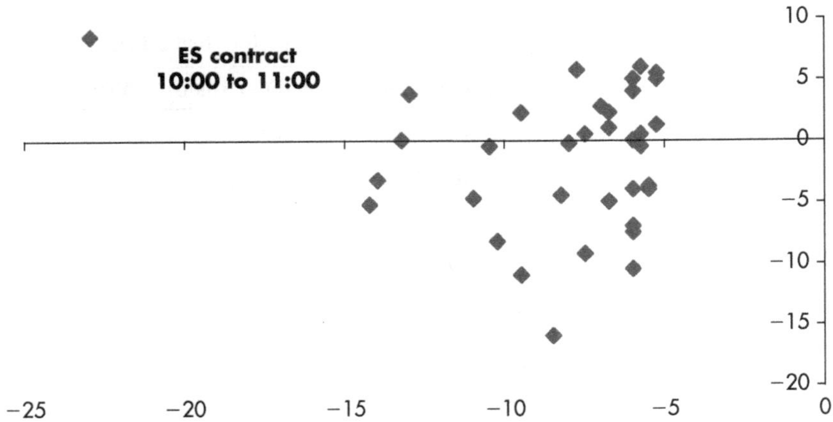

the black diamonds are to the left of a −5-point decline from 09:00 to 10:00; allowing us to pinpoint the performance of our response variable. For instance, the worst loss is at the bottom, it reflects a −8.5-point decline in the earlier hour, along with a 16-point loss in the later hour (–8.5, −16). Most striking, however is how one large decline (single dot in the upper left corner) produces an 8.5-point gain (–23, 8.5).

And as a comparison process of this 51.25-point loss (15-18-2 record), below is the running summary of the ES contract between 10:00 to 11:00. Most technicians are going to quickly spot a long line of support around 50 points. (See Figure 6.15.)

Early Morning Activity

The column chart (Figure 6.16) showing the price (highest to lowest) range is a good snapshot of early morning activity.

Wide price dispersion can play havoc with your emotions. If you fall prey to reckless trading, you can get caught up in a series of reflexive trades. Unless you can make trades specifically conforming to your system's results, it is best to refrain from trading during this unstable setting. (See Figure 6.17.)

Naturally, a large sum of institutional money makes its way into the market at the opening of trading. Providing we have a trading opportunity, it is to our advantage to trade prior to this massive surge in trading volume.

FIGURE 6.15 After a slow start, this hour rockets ahead 80 points, before bouncing around support at about 50 points.

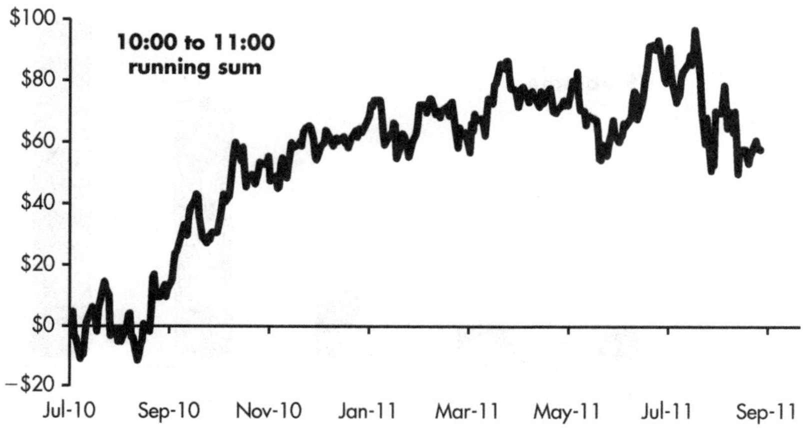

FIGURE 6.16 A cylinder chart of the price range (highest to lowest price) among the five early morning trading hours.

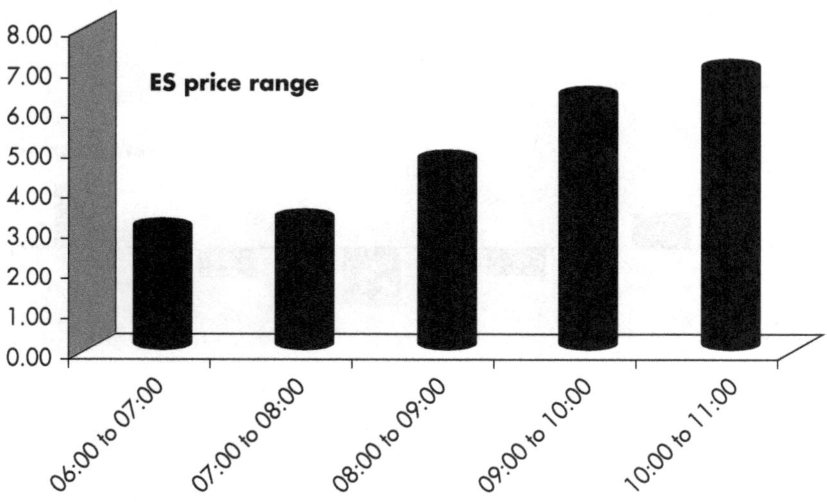

Observing the performance of these five hourly segments gives you the opportunity to conceptualize new strategies (Figure 6.18). In these 300 days, one could consider taking overnight profits before 07:00, together with placing a limit order to buy shares in an equities index fund or commodity below the existing 07:00 price. Before actually taking a position, monitor the accuracy of this statement to be certain this strategy is still working.

FIGURE 6.17 Early morning ES trading volume closely corresponds to this contract's hourly range.

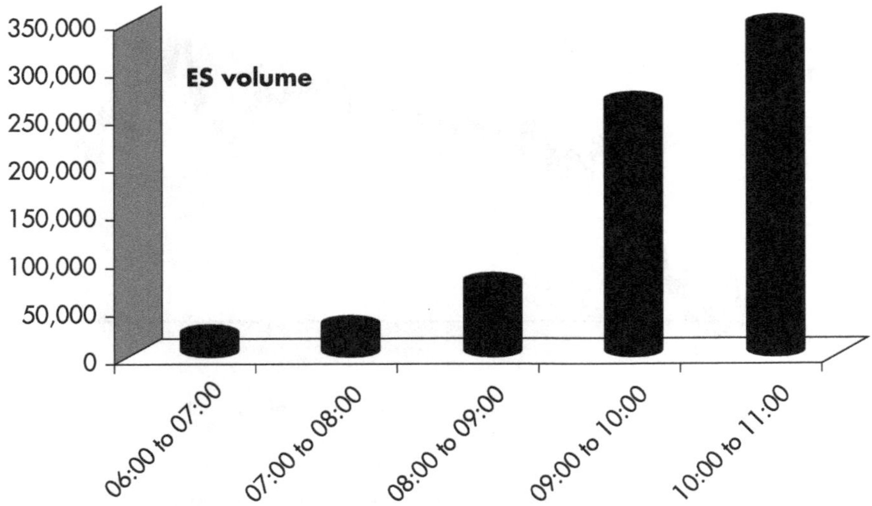

FIGURE 6.18 The hourly performance of these 300 days creates a sagging barbell effect with the inside hourly prices exhibiting declines.

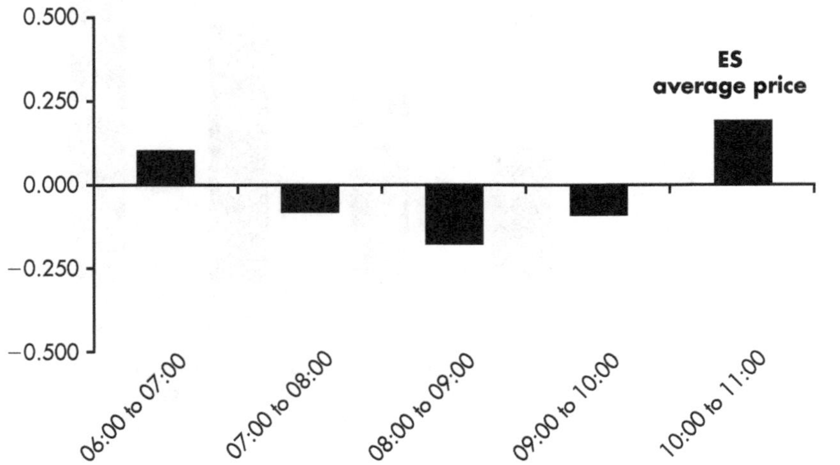

Bear versus Bull Market

An evaluation of the evening session of the ES contract, by itself, is often enlightening, but more information develops from two contrasting directional settings. Consequently, we want to extract information from the previous bear market separately from the more recent bull market by constructing a range (highest to lowest price in the 120 minutes from 18:00 to 20:00).[7]

This study begins on March 13, 2007, with the ES contract at 1392; it completes these 1,198 trading days closing at 1256 on November 3, 2011 (20:00 price). In spite of this 136-point loss, the afterhour session was profitable; however, was there a meaningful performance difference between the two directional settings?[8] In Figure 6.19, the bear, held at −40 point support (gray background), but as the bull market took over, it began by making a jaw-dropping downturn, and then a complete U-turn before charging into positive territory.

Can we capitalize on this otherwise below-average 1,198-day trading setting? Anytime you take a long position in a bear market, you are asking for a wagonload of pressure, but for any trader with risk-taking tendencies, these two hours brought those willing to experiment some advantageous plays.[9]

Sometimes on the surface, an opportunity may not be evident. For instance, if a professional baseball team had 20 wins with 20 losses, no advantage appears to exist. Nevertheless, when you bring more variables into play, they can give you a different perspective. For instance, how does the

FIGURE 6.19 Running summary of this two-hour evening session for the ES contract.

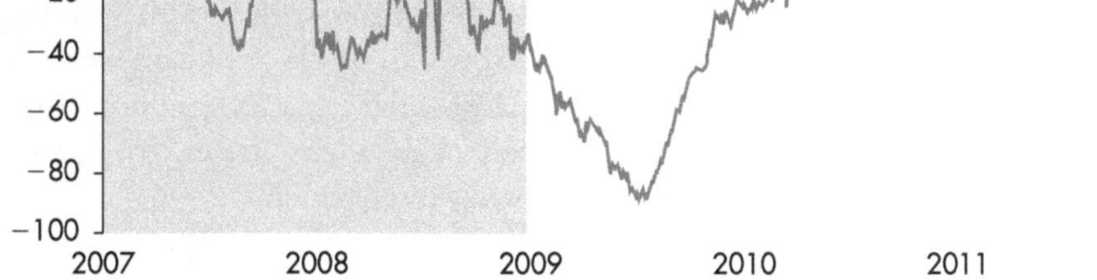

[7]Since most trading platforms allow you to take positions until 20:00 hours, you can actively invest in the spiders, cues, or Russell 2000 because the bid/ask price remains narrow.

[8]eSignal provides intraday commodity numbers going back to 2007.

[9]Channel investing has day traders shorting at resistance, but taking a long position at support. I discuss this in my earlier book; for those without discipline, this topsy-turvy environment can take you on an emotional roller coaster.

TABLE 6.3 Despite the presence of the bear, the evening loss is relatively mild.

ES Market	Dates	Trading Days	Point Sum
Bear	Mar 13, 2007 to Mar 9, 2009	511	–34.75
Bull	Mar 10, 2009 to Nov 4, 2011	687	52.00
	Summary	1,198	17.25

FIGURE 6.20 The 18:00 to midnight performance of the bear market when trading the ES contract. There is an imbalance in the outlying scores with more volatility coming at the conclusion of the bear market.

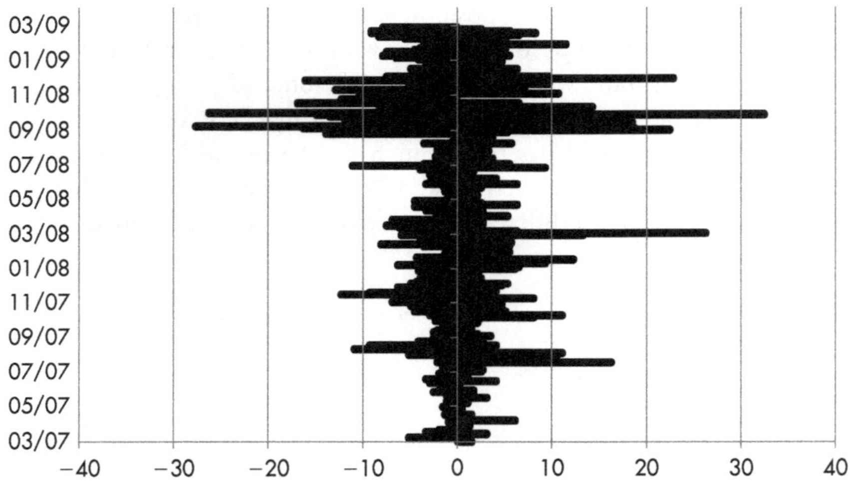

following statement revise your thinking: This team with a .500 winning percentage is playing at home under the lights, facing a lefty pitcher who has never won a game at this stadium. In looking at the statistics, you learn they are 15-5 at home, with a 10-4 record when facing a lefty starter. By digging around, you can often exploit these statistical discrepancies.

Harbinger to a Bull Market

What can you make of this bar chart (Figure 6.20) showing the nightly performance of the 18:00 to 24:00 session?

The bear begins this six-hour session with relatively mild price swings. The volatility of this commodities contract increases dramatically in the fall of 2008; however, the bear, in the winter months, goes into hibernation.

Does this downshift in pricing volatility give us meaningful information about an upcoming change in market sentiment? The important thing is to be aware of any drastic change in market behavior; in this case, it was a precursor to the onset of a long bull market.

Flexible Statements

Excel has some other statistical functions, which are invaluable because they have the ability to compute multiple criteria. In order to unravel the next research question, the analysis utilizes two of these critical functions.

The earlier study, using the six-hour setting, gave us some interesting information, but the results were unremarkable. This analysis, however, uses the information from 18:00 to midnight to make an assessment of its impact on trading the ES contract from midnight to 09:00 hours.

If the six-hour evening market has an explosive gain or loss, does it impact trading in the midnight to 09:00 setting? The dates are June 30, 2009 to July 1, 2011 (517 trading days) and the contributory variables are:

- The price change for the ES contract from 18:00 to midnight sessions is $> +5$ points.
- The price change for the ES contract from 18:00 to midnight sessions is < -5 points.

The response variable is: ES contract's price change from midnight to 09:00 hours.

Table 6.4 displays a worksheet. What function can we use to count the tradable plays in these 517 days?

TABLE 6.4 This is the abbreviated worksheet; these fields allow us to answer this research question.

	A	B	C	D	E	F	G
1	Date	z18:00	Date	z00:00	z09:00	k1824	k0009
2	6/30/2011	1,315.25	7/1/2011	1,313.75	1,315.50	–1.50	1.75
3	6/29/2011	1,304.00	6/30/2011	1,306.75	1,307.75	2.75	1.00
4	6/28/2011	1,294.50	6/29/2011	1,292.00	1,301.50	–2.50	9.50
5	6/27/2011	1,278.00	6/28/2011	1,277.75	1,281.50	–0.25	3.75
6	6/26/2011	1,265.00	6/27/2011	1,262.00	1,264.50	–3.00	2.50
	↓	↓	↓	↓	↓	↓	↓

There are two columns showing dates. One represents the evening hours (18:00 to 24:00), the other shows the results of trading after the midnight hour.

Column A represents the date of the 18:00 price.
Column B is the opening price at 18:00 hours.
Column C represents start of a new day.
Column D is the opening price at 00:00 hours.
Column E is the opening price at 09:00 hours.[10]
Column F is the predictive variable; it is the price change from 18:00 to midnight.
Column G is the response variable; it is the price change from midnight to 09:00.

In this problem we want to know how many days satisfy each of these two requirements. We can count the days meeting any specific trading condition by using the =COUNT function:

=COUNTIF(G2:G518,">5") is a single criteria statement; it is searching in the price change (K1824) column for a price change > +5.
=COUNTIF(G2:G518,"<−5") is a single criteria statement; it is searching in the price change (K1824) column for a price change < −5.

Although this system does not give you many trading opportunities (Table 6.5), both categories outperform the average. Because of the comeback, taking a long position after a decline of 5 points or more was, by far, the better play.

TABLE 6.5 After an excessive evening (18:00 to 24:00) price move (± 5 points), this 517-day analysis reports on the two categories along with the summary results when trading the ES contract from midnight to 09:00.

	GT +5	LT −5	TOTAL
N	31	26	517
AVG	0.427	2.538	0.416
SUM	13.25	66.00	215.00

[10]When you record a price at a particular hour, the price differs slightly because there are two different numbers. For example, in looking at the 08:00 hour, your downloading program will give you the opening 08:00 price as well as its closing price, which, theoretically is at 08:59:59. However, looking at the 09:00 hour, you will receive its opening price; sometimes there is a slight disparity between these two numbers.

Suppose you wanted to make a distinction in trading volume? This would require two more columns (see Table 6.6):

Column B is the opening 18:00 price.
Column C is trading volume in the six-hour evening session of 18:00 to 24:00.
Column E is the price at midnight (00:00).
Column F is the 09:00 opening price.
Column G is the price difference between the 18:00 and 24:00 hours.
Column H is the price difference between the 00:00 and 09:00 hours.
Column I codes the categorical variable. Either a score of 1 is given if trading volume is below 50,000 or a score of 2 if it is above 50,000 contracts.

In order to categorize the trading volume, Table 6.6 uses an =IF statement in cell "I2"; once written AutoFill your formula down to "I518"; since trading volume is in the "C" column, begin by writing this formula in cell "I2": =IF(C2<50,000,1,2).

On June 26, 2011, the trading volume for this ES contract from 18:00 to midnight is > 50,000; consequently, a "2" is put in cell "I6." Of course, an easier way to accomplish this task is by enabling the filter button. Once you access this command, you can click on the box in the volume column (v1824). After selecting the "Number Filters" command, you can choose either one of the directional options. Of course you can keep sub-filtering down by asking more questions (see Chapter 4 for instructions on this filtering command).

TABLE 6.6 With the two extra columns, we are including a categorical variable. In this illustration, it contains a variable distinguishing between volume below 50,000 (a score of 1) or volume above 50,000 (a score of 2).

	A	B	C	D	E	F	G	H	I
1	Date	z18:00	v1824	Date	z00:00	z09:00	k1824	k0009	50,000
2	6/30/2011	1,315.25	24,893	7/1/2011	1,313.75	1,315.50	−1.50	1.75	1
3	6/29/2011	1,304.00	35,551	6/30/2011	1,306.75	1,307.75	2.75	1.00	1
4	6/28/2011	1,294.50	31,395	6/29/2011	1,292.00	1,301.50	−2.50	9.50	1
5	6/27/2011	1,278.00	22,077	6/28/2011	1,277.75	1,281.50	−0.25	3.75	1
6	6/26/2011	1,265.00	61,010	6/27/2011	1,262.00	1,264.50	−3.00	2.50	2
	↓	↓	↓	↓	↓	↓	↓	↓	↓

COUNTIFS

COUNTIF is a statistical function that counts the number of cases in a cell for a given condition. For instance, =COUNTIF(G2:G518,">5") counts the days with a > 5 point advance in the "G" (K1824) column.

Similar to =COUNTIF, adding an S to this statistical function makes it more powerful, because it has the ability to count the number of cases across multiple conditions. The COUNTIFS function (Figure 6.21) is a multiple criteria statement.[11] By using =COUNTIFS, for example, we want to count the cases when the evening price is > 5 AND trading volume is < 50,000.

In this study, there are four COUNTING combinations:

= evening price > 5 AND trading volume < 50,000
= evening price > 5 AND trading volume > 50,000
= evening price < −5 AND trading volume < 50,000
= evening price < −5 AND trading volume > 50,000

Similarly, Figure 6.22 shows how to use the categorical variable for trading volume.

=SUMIFS

With the exception of summing the given conditions, this statistical function (Figure 6.23) works basically the same way as the =COUNTIFS.

The opportunities dwindle, but the ES contract still delivers some attractive prospects. The best-looking results come when prices take a < −5 point decline in the evening hours (18:00 to midnight) with strong activity. (Figures 6.21–6.23).[12]

FIGURE 6.21 The COUNTIFS function is counting the cases for those days with a price change > 5 AND trading volume < 50,000.

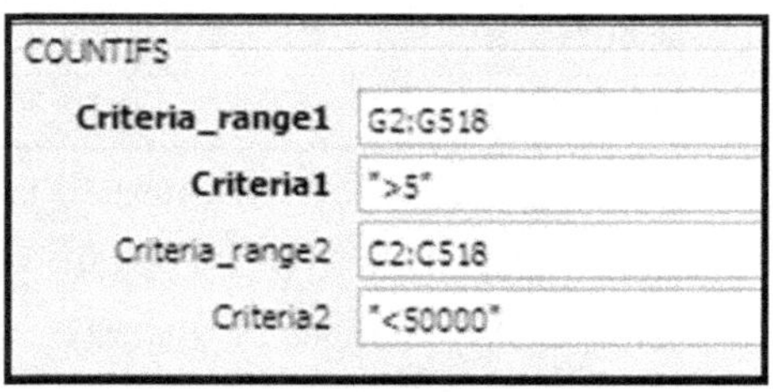

[11]Theoretically, any predictive variable can be applied. Furthermore, Excel allows the user to incorporate additional predictive variables-when using these statistical functions.

[12]This condition consists of > 50,000 contracts, this compares to the 517 trading days average of 32,584 contacts.

FIGURE 6.22 This command is asking for the same information, a > 5 advance AND trading volume with < 50,000 contracts. Notice how Excel creates another criteria range if necessary.

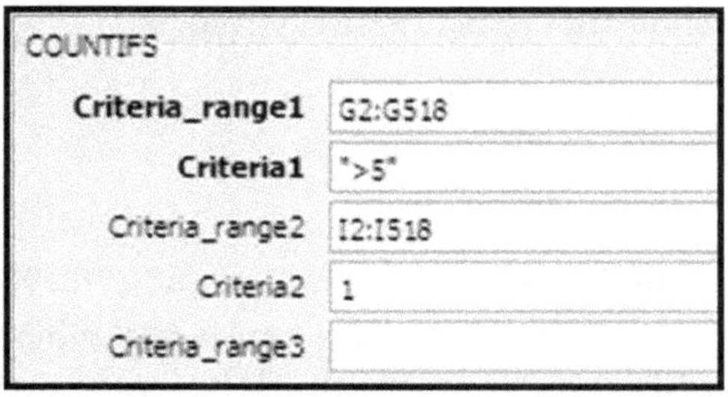

FIGURE 6.23 =SUMIFS begins by summing your response variable. Thereafter, it requests the conditions for your predictor variables.

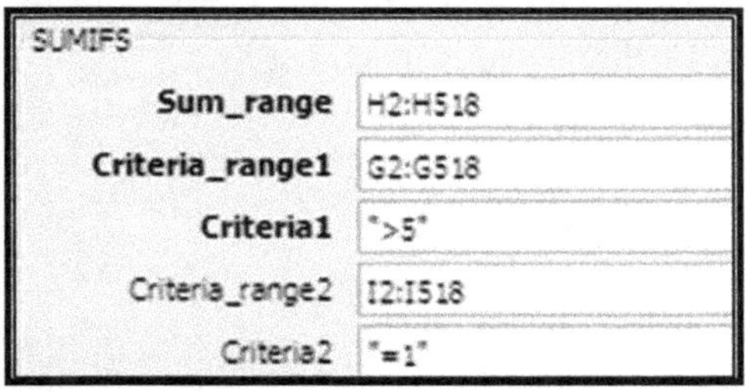

TABLE 6.7 Although the sample is small, the strong increase in activity had an impact on performance.

Category	COUNTIFS	SUMIFS
price > 5 and volume < 50,000	13	–10.50
price > 5 and volume > 50,000	19	24.75
price < –5 and volume < 50,000	14	21.25
price < –5 and volume > 50,000	13	49.00

These two statistical functions offer the investor tremendous flexibility for an extensive examination of the current trading environment. Another one, is =AVERAGEIFS, but this can be easily calculated once you compute the other two functions (COUNTIFS/SUMIFS).

Summary

With years of trading experience, some success is inevitable. Achieving mastery, or the highest stages of success, is similar to climbing a ladder, as you progress; each step takes you to a higher level. But, unlike climbing a ladder, every step you take requires a different set of skills.

With the passing of each trading day, the market transforms itself. This is part of the frustration we encounter as active traders. Although no system works across all economic environments, when one is working, stay with it until its performance fades. How long a system will stay afloat is not something you can control; what is up to you, however, is to consistently monitor its performance and make the necessary adjustments to take full advantage of it until it finally runs its course.

CHAPTER 7

Quantifying Risk

It would cease to be a danger if we could define it.

—Sherlock Holmes

This chapter describes some unconventional measures of risk, which, if applied along with the traditional measures, will vastly strengthen your assessment of this critical aspect of investing.

Active participants know corrections are part of trading; trying to completely avoid them is unrealistic. Therefore, working towards reducing your exposure is a more attainable objective. This is easy to say, but on a steady basis, it is difficult to achieve. Even when putting aside the emotional aspects of trading, sidestepping disaster is never easy because the perception of risk held by most investors is faulty.

Since many investors subscribe to the conventional measures of risk, we begin with a discussion of their shortcomings.

Standard Deviation

It is best to prove this assertion by investigating the downside activity in the daily price change of the spiders from December 27, 2006, to September 30, 2011. Although the most common measure of risk is a standard deviation, this measure does have some disadvantages.

Before attacking this customary measure of risk, a review of the spiders' performance for these 1,200 days portrays a negative landscape as it took a steep $28.43 fall (averaging a loss of $0.0237 per trading day).

By highlighting the range of these 1,200 daily price changes, the =STDEV formula gives us a standard deviation of \$1.7768. Many investors think of risk as a loss of assets, but in arriving at this statistic, its calculation includes the daily price change of both positive as well as negative trading days.

One standard deviation ± this average price change (–\$0.0237) accounts for 68.3 percent and two standard deviations capture 95.4 percent; 99.7 percent of the 1,200 scores lie within three standard deviations. Following are the calculations for this 1,200-day study, which estimates the standard deviation scores below the mean.

Since these numbers contain those days inside the outliers, the percentage of prices outside 95.4 percent would consist of (100 – 95.4) 4.6 percent of the remaining scores. Since our interest usually lies in the negative side of this distribution, it is necessary to split these percentages (4.6 percent/2 = 2.3 percent). With 1,200 days, we expect to have 27.6 (1,200 days × 2.3 percent) cases lying in the negative tail.

In comparison, two standard deviations below the mean score of the spiders calculate to –\$3.58 (–\$0.0237 + (\$1.7768 + \$1.7768)), but there were 41 days with a single-day decline below –\$3.58. This creates a 41 to 27.6 difference; however, this does not characterize the entire problem.

The calculation of a standard deviation score for each of the 1,200 trading days is given the same weighting; however, most investors want to place greater emphasis on the more recent trading days. That is, the sequence of closing prices is not taken into account. Since the most recent observations of price are given no preference over earlier ones, the calculation of risk is often misleading.

Tumbling Prices

How do you differentiate the early observations from the more recent ones? A better description of risk can be seen from charting these corrections across their 1,200-day sequence.

Apparently, once the wound is open, the bleeding becomes heavy. Notice the density of these corrections prior to 2009. The large respite of inactivity (in the vicinity of 2011) offers the active trader the best opportunity for more return with less risk.

One can resolve the problem of identifying the sequence of these excessive down days by drawing a column chart. These vertical lines clearly show an abundance of 2 percent corrections prior to 2009; besides clustering together, they produce some of the steepest drops.

FIGURE 7.1 The 100 days with a daily loss of ≥ −2 percent when trading the spiders over these 1,200 days.

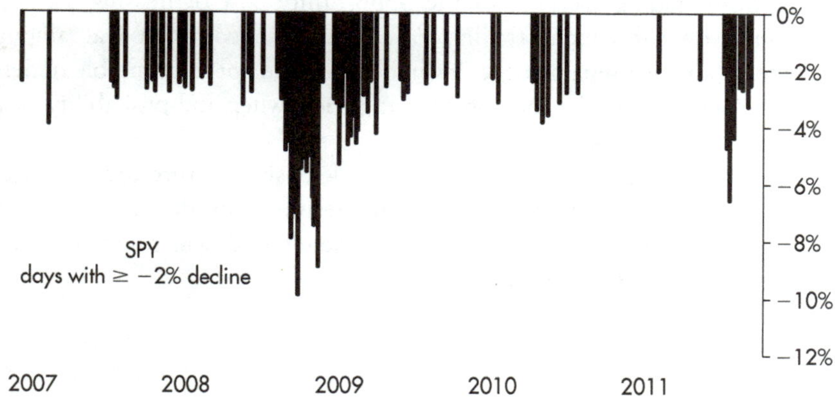

Another way of defining risk is to perform a calculation of the probability of confronting one of these nasty corrections. With 100 corrections in 1,200 trading days, the spiders suffer one correction every 12 days. The chart (Figure 7.1) clearly shows that the spacing of these 2 percent corrections does not occur at regular intervals. Evidently, taking the attitude that there is 1 in every 12 days is a correct statistical assumption, but unless you produce a chronicity of these breakdowns, it is difficult to anticipate unforeseen price dips.

Nevertheless, these results still show us the cage, but no bird—that is, they are incomplete. In spite of this information, we do not have a trading strategy that will directly confront risk as it appears.

When trading a stock with long-term bullish prospects, it is not uncommon to keep or slowly increase your shares, but how do you react when the probability of a correction increases?

When given this information, you can take one of the following steps:

1. You react by buying more shares.
2. You completely disregard the information; that is, you take no action.
3. You act on the information by reducing your position as the impending risk of a correction becomes more imminent.
4. You completely offset your long position.
5. After unloading your existing position, you take a short position to capture profits from the possibility of falling prices.

Although cowering in foxholes until the volatility dissipates may not be appealing, this preserves capital; nevertheless, it is not easy to completely abstain from trading, because of the opportunity cost of missing a sharp turnaround on subsequent trading days. This is a common fear among daytraders, but what separates the profitable from the not so profitable traders is their reluctance to take the appropriate action when the probability of a correction is at its peak.

The astute investor would take a more defensive posture until the frequency—as well as the intensity—of these declines subsides. Once corrections begin to abate (such as the absence of these meltdowns prior to 2011), take a more aggressive position.

Beta Scores

Beta is a measure of systematic risk (i.e., the risk from a market downturn). It is a comparative measure of a security's responsiveness to price movements in a market index (S&P 500). The beta for the market index is 1.00. When a stock has a beta score of 1.00, its downside loss is essentially the same, but if it has a beta score of 2.00 it is twice as risky as the index. An asset with a beta scoring above 1.00 is riskier, making it a more satisfying investment for the aggressive investor; conversely, a score below 1.00 better serves the emotional disposition of the more conservative investor.[1]

The =SLOPE function computes the beta score. The independent variable is the market index; whereas, the dependent variable is the stock or commodity under investigation.

Table 7.1 is a hypothetical account of two instruments alongside the index. Very often, beta is an inexact measure of risk. In general, an insignificant correlation between the asset and the market index can misrepresent the beta estimates. For instance, consider the yearly price movements of the market index (S&P 500) and stock funds (AAA and ZZZ) as seen in Table 7.1.

Using beta scores as a measure of comparative risk can give you a false impression. Despite the smaller price movement, the beta scores of the two stock funds are the same. A standard deviation score, along with these beta scores, paints a more accurate picture of price dispersion, but these statistics

[1]Anthony Trongone, *Quantitative Methods for Finance and Investing* (Singapore: Cengage Learning, 2008).

TABLE 7.1 Comparative Analysis: Despite the difference in the price dispersion between the two stock funds (AAA and ZZZ), the beta scores = 0.000.

Month	S&P 500	AAA	ZZZ
2010	6	3	1
2011	5	3	8
2012	4	2	1
2013	3	2	7
2014	2	3	1
2015	1	3	4
STDEV	1.871	0.516	3.204
Correlation		0.000	0.000
Beta scores		0.000	0.000

If you experiment with these scores in Excel, you will see that switching the numbers around will bring similar results. For instance, reversing the order of the S&P 500 index from 6,5,4,3,2,1, to 1,2,3,4,5,6, does not change the beta scores for either of these two funds.

are often misleading, because some of the weaknesses of measuring risk are not brought into focus.

Applying Risk Metrics to Construct a Trading System

This investigation attempts to define risk as participating in the downside loss of a single-day correction in the GC (gold) contract.

Within this study, the operational definition of a correction is a daily loss in the GC contract in excess of $10. March 19, 2008, begins this study with a $59 loss; it continues until September 30, 2011. After the $59 correction, the closing price of this contract stood at 945.30, in these 895 trading days it rallied to an October 3, 2011, closing price of 1,657.70.

Note that this study uses a $10 correction; however, with the dramatic price rise of this GC contract, in using a daily percentage loss we cannot retain the proportional weighting of the response variable over these 894 trading days. Nevertheless, for the investor trying to confine his or her loss to under $10, this method is preferable.

After a correction, the probability of producing another one on the following trading day was 23.6 percent, whereas the chance of another $10 decline within two days was 42.1 percent (see Table 7.2 for more information).

TABLE 7.2 After a decline in excess of $10 for this GC contract, how many days does it take before there is another correction? For instance, after producing one, the cumulative probability of experiencing another one within three days is 56.2 percent.

Days after Correction	Number of Corrections	Probability	Cumulative Probability
1	42	23.6%	23.6%
2	33	18.5%	42.1%
3	25	14.0%	56.2%
4 to 5	27	15.2%	71.3%
6 to 7	16	9.0%	80.3%
8 to 9	14	7.9%	88.2%
10 to 11	5	2.8%	91.0%
12 to 13	4	2.2%	93.3%
14 to 15	4	2.2%	95.5%
16 to 23	4	2.2%	97.8%
24 to 31	3	1.7%	99.4%
32+	1	0.6%	100.0%
Sum	178	100%	

Starting on the day after a $59 decline on March 19, 2007, there were 177 days in which the daily loss of this GC contract was in excess of $10. The area chart (Figure 7.2) reports the probability of incurring another one on subsequent days following this meltdown.

The research hypothesis is as follows: After a $10-plus decline, what are the past performance results of taking a long position in gold on the following trading days?[2]

[2]There are many ways to take a long position in gold. In this study, we use the GC contract, but you can take a futures position in a contract with a smaller multiplier (such as E-mini Gold and E-micro Gold). Two commodity alternatives to this GC contract have differences in trading volume (September 7, 2010, to November 10, 2011), the average 300-day trading volume is 166k for the GC contract 6.371k for the YG, and 707k for the MGC commodity contract. And the two active ETFs, which mimic the price movements of gold, the most active, GLD (17.3m) at a price of $171.14, is about 10 times that of IAU (6.8m) at $17.17 (both prices on 11/11/11). Another advantage is that the correlation of these byproducts is nearly perfect with the GC contract.

FIGURE 7.2 Once there is a $10-plus correction, how many days does it take before there is another one? As the area chart shows, after experiencing one of these meltdowns, 42 of these corrections occurred on the very next day.

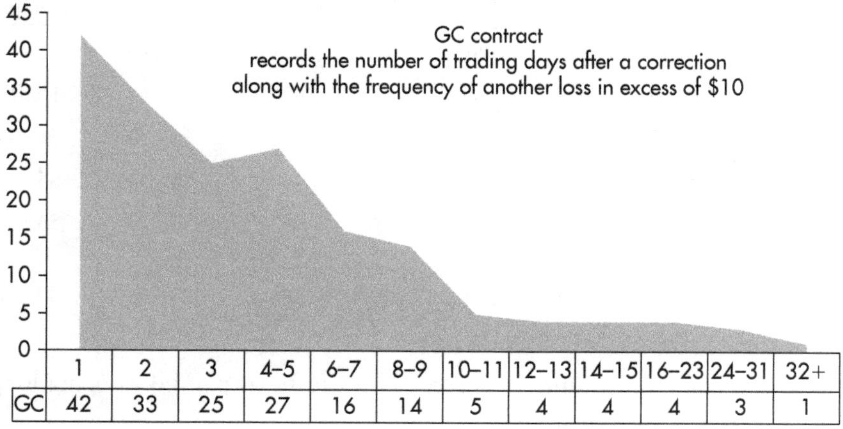

TABLE 7.3 The past performance results of the GC contract by the number of days after a correction.

Number of Days After a Correction	Count	Sum	Average
1 to 3	419	$57.30	$0.128
4 to 9	299	$296.40	$0.991
10 to 19	117	$114.70	$0.980
20 to 29	37	$185.10	$5.003
30 to 51	22	$87.80	$3.991

Table 7.3 includes the 894 days in the investigation; it demonstrates a performance difference specific to the number of trading days after a correction.

Without encountering a correction for 30-plus days, this seems to be a safe environment; the profit from these 22 plays was $87.80. After this many days, investors do not appear to panic. Although there were eight losing trades, the biggest drawdown was –$12.70.

After a correction, we are less willing to participate in another painful encounter, but we do not want to be left sitting on the sidelines when this

TABLE 7.4 The performance results after a decline in the daily price of the GC contract. In the 29 days with a decline in excess of −$30, this contract fell $130.70.

$ Amount of Daily Decline	Count	Adv	Dec	Win %	Sum	Average
−$00.01 to −$09.99	210	120	90	.571	$233.10	$1.11
−$10.00 to −$19.99	105	64	41	.610	$84.60	$0.81
−$20.00 to −$29.99	45	23	22	.511	$64.80	$1.44
−$30.00 to −$39.99	18	8	10	.444	−$91.30	−$5.07
≥ −$40.00	11	5	6	.455	−$39.40	−$3.58
Summary:						
Price decline	389	220	169	.566	$251.80	$0.647

precious metal has a shining recovery. This can be as painful as being long during a full-blown downturn.[3]

Aggressive Selling Pressure

The next research question is: Does aggressive selling pressure produce more negativity on the following trading day? That is, would taking a long position after a $50 decline be more profitable in comparison to a $20 decline in the price of the gold futures contract?

By breaking these meltdowns into five categories, we can make an assessment of the 389 days following a daily loss in the GC contract (Table 7.4).

In the 389 trading days in which there was a decline, on the following day, there were 220 advances and 169 declines, with $251.80 in profits ($0.65 APT). A single-digit setback was responsible for capturing most of these profits, as these tiny declines brought the savvy investor a $233.10 return in 210 days with a 120–90 record ($1.11 APT). This propitious pattern remains for daily losses under –$30.00, but profits fade quickly when they sink below this –$30 benchmark.

A small decline appears to be a good blueprint for success, but before arriving at a hasty decision consider the clustering of these corrections. Taken together, a long position after a strong single-day collapse within a setting with a continuous wave of recent selling appears to be an imprudent decision.

[3]When another correction occurs on the next day, the performance of the best 20 scores ($607 summary return) in comparison to the worst 20 scores (–$688 summary return) were excessive.

FIGURE 7.3 Shows the results of the GC contract in the absence of a correction for ≥ 30 trading days.

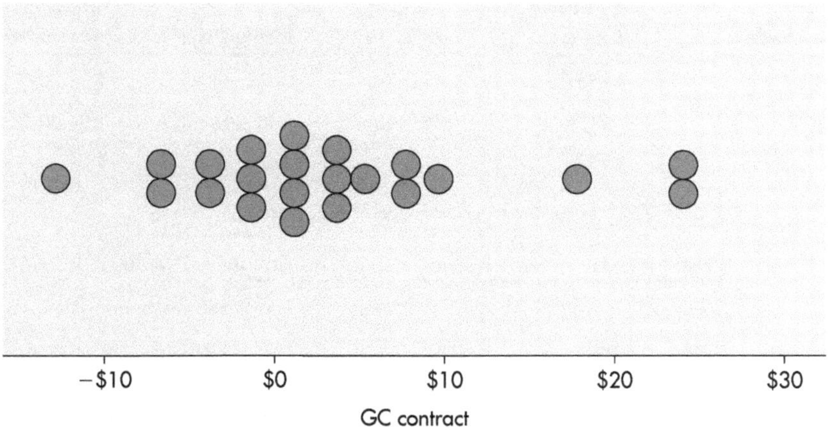

When there is a long absence of single-day meltdowns, it creates a false sense of security. Once investors perceive less risk, they increase their exposure by adding to their long positions. And, with more riding on a long position in this precious metal, once prices take a beating, investors reflexively start unloading their positions before doing their homework. An interpretation of the earlier dot chart (Figure 7.3) shows that investors are not in a hurry; it takes another setback or an aggressively strong single-day loss before they begin acting rashly.

Relief Rally

Another consideration for these 29 days with a $30-plus correction is their ability or inability to finish the trading day with some aspect of a relief rally.

The research question here is: In evaluating those 29 days with a $30-plus correction, do the days with or without separation between the lowest price minus the closing price of the daily trading session make a discernible difference in taking a position on the following trading day? (See Table 7.5.)

The largest correction (AAA) has more spacing between the two intraday prices ($34); the smallest comeback (BBB) has $4 separating them. Going forward, which one offers us the best percentage for success? Table 7.6 shows three categories with different spacing between these two intraday prices with their performance on the following trading day.

TABLE 7.5 This is a hypothetical example of two $32 daily declines. My purpose is to demonstrate the difference between two comebacks.

Comebacks	Daily Price Change	Lowest Price	Closing Price	Difference Close to Low
AAA	–$32.00	$1,700	$1,734	$34.00
BBB	–$32.00	$1,700	$1,704	$4.00

TABLE 7.6 Next day's performance of GC contract.

Price Spreads	Summary Results
10 largest	–$86.80
9 days in between	–$70.10
10 smallest	$26.20

The results shown in Table 7.6 are a comparison of those days with the closing price finishing in the vicinity of its lowest price. During the 10 days with the largest price spread, the GC contract fell $86.80; however, the 10 days with the smallest difference between the two intraday prices, were able to put together a modest recovery ($26.20).

Earlier, a $10 price change was applied as the response variable; however, when encountering rising prices a percentage change score provides more accuracy. The dates are: October 13, 2009, to February 29, 2012 (600 trading days).

This contract starting at $1,055 on October 13, 2009, ran to a price of $1,900 before backing down. On the day after it finally opened above the $1,900 mark, it fell $104 (August 24, 2011). Figure 7.4 shows the vertical moves down. This $104 correction began a series of percentage plus losses, finally ending this study on February 29, 2012 with a $77.10 decline.

Spotting the Cage, but No Bird

Once a financial crisis surfaces, the ramifications can worsen. A tiny leak in the dam, if caught early, can be repaired with minimum effort; however, if ignored, the problem seldom fixes itself. Over time, it gets bigger and more costly to mend.[4]

[4]Anthony Trongone, *Quantitative Methods for Finance and Investing* (Singapore: Cengage Learning, 2008).

FIGURE 7.4 A daily percentage correction of the GC contract. In these 600 days there were 80 corrections with a 1 percent-plus loss, and 29 days with a 2 percent-plus loss.

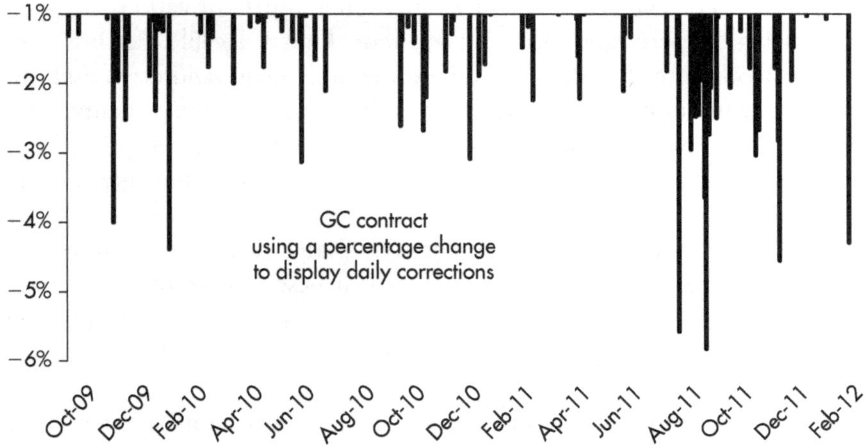

Certainly, when the markets collapse, the news always seems to be a reasonable justification for a string of daily downturns, but how do you actually measure the ramifications of the news? After all, prices don't correct without bad news, so it is best to strictly focus on the percentages and leave the soothsaying to the economists. Particularly because of their outstanding record; "it has been said that the only purpose of economic forecasts is to make astrology look respectable."[5]

Anytime the markets begin trading as if they were a house of cards, the economic pundits immediately begin dramatizing the current ailments, exaggerating the severity of the problems. In response to this, market participants often react by taking the market down beyond "fair value."

When trading the markets on a daily basis, nothing is completely obvious; one is forever coping with the uncertainty of a moving target. Risk metrics by themselves are unquantifiable because the psychological reaction of the crowd does not reside in any model; it does not contain the unquantifiable measure of group fear. Although mathematical models facilitate judgment, they are not a foolproof solution.

When trading, you are always putting your capital at risk. Since we cannot reliably pinpoint market direction on a consistent basis, the best we

[5]Derek Scott, "Switchback Ride Puts Premium on Resilient Stocks," *Financial Times* (August 2, 2011).

can do is put our portfolio in a position where the rewards outweigh risk. Unlike most studies, the focus of this one was not on price, but on using probability to defend against getting caught in another correction.

Playing the percentages can make us more knowledgeable. For instance, when corrections occur, they often flood the investment landscape. Still, no strategy is without its flaws because market direction is never a certainty. One fact remains, however; our investment decisions ought not to spring from arbitrary feelings regarding the possibility of a storm brewing in the background.

Stock bubbles and other troubles will always negatively sway equity markets; after the market stumbles, when is it best to raise the white flag? After experiencing some dreadful losses, we become less willing to put our money to work, but we simply cannot go on rejecting bargains because of our fear of losing.

After surviving a brush with disaster, it should make us smarter as we start preparations for another correction. As you become better at spotting risk, there still remains the problem of putting your theories to work for "it is stupidity rather than courage to refuse to recognize danger when it is close upon you."[6]

[6]Sir Arthur Conan Doyle, "The Adventures of the Final Problem," *Strand Magazine* (1893).

CHAPTER 8

Trading in Trendless Markets

Invincibility lies in the defense; the possibility of victory in the attack.

—Sun Tzu

Many investors use momentum indicators to make their trading decisions. Despite the confidence they place in these indicators, most refuse to make a rigorous assessment of their reliability. Unfortunately, without back testing, they have no knowledge of an indicator's measurement error, and without knowing its flaws, making the necessary improvements becomes pure guesswork.

This chapter examines the reliability of a moving average indicator by using a quantitative approach to assess its accuracy as a predictor of future price movements.

Applying a quantitative approach does not prevent you from being a technician. They are not mutually exclusive. Each brings something different to your analysis; collectively, they can significantly enhance your performance.

The discussion on moving averages tackles these meaningful themes:

1. It explains how to construct a moving average. Since these indicators are not perfect, you are always looking to make adjustments to improve their accuracy. If these modifications to your parameters shrink the error score, you increase the precision of your analysis; consequently, there is

a discussion on how to assess the measurement error contained in your forecast.[1]

2. Unlike traditional methods, which use an instrument's price to assess direction, my methods take a multiplicative approach. Throughout the book, I am introducing contributory variables, which increase the predictability of the response variable under investigation.
3. Although most books would have you believe these indicators are flawless, they often are ineffective at predicting price movements. Tracking the performance of a moving average is necessary since this allows you to make adjustments; when it is no longer working effectively, you can react accordingly.

Without making any adjustment to the price of an instrument, its ongoing pattern is difficult to unscramble. A smoothing of scores slows down the action by flattening its connecting lines; this allows us to spot patterns more readily.

Smoothing Scores to Spot Patterns

In trading, a moving average score is the most common procedure for smoothing or flattening the trendline. Although they have their shortcomings, these rolling averages are consistently good at smoothing the past performance of the indicator under investigation; this procedure slows down the movement, thereby eliminating some of its choppiness.

Examples of this are shown using 300 trading days (April 6, 2010, to June 10, 2011). Each of these four figures (Figures 8.1 to 8.4) follows the daily price change of Apple Inc. (ticker: AAPL). In Figure 8.1, it is not easy to spot a pattern, but a 10-day moving average makes it more readable (Figure 8.2).

As you increase the days (=AVERAGE (range of 20 previous trading days)), smoothing the line reduces volatility (Figure 8.3).

Finally, a 50-day moving average (=AVERAGE (range of previous 50 trading days)) makes the trending pattern clearer, but our mission is not clarity, our mission is to strengthen our forecasting ability (Figure 8.4).

[1] A discussion on measuring the predictive error of your study using moving averages is in the appendix.

FIGURE 8.1 Apple's daily price change in the 300 trading days from April 6, 2010, to July 10, 2011. Without smoothing its scores, price patterns are not easy to discern. Converting these price movements into a moving average reduces white noise by flattening the scores of the trend line.

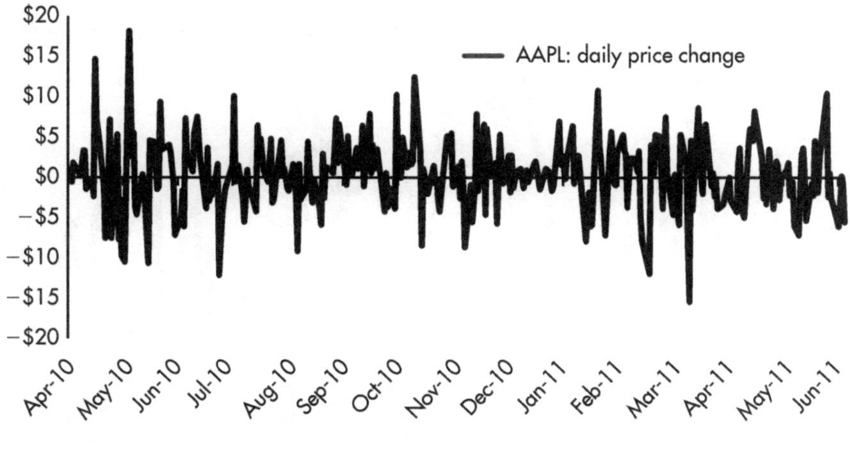

FIGURE 8.2 Apple, using a 10-day simple moving average, begins to flatten the drawn line by creating a 10-day rolling average of its price change.

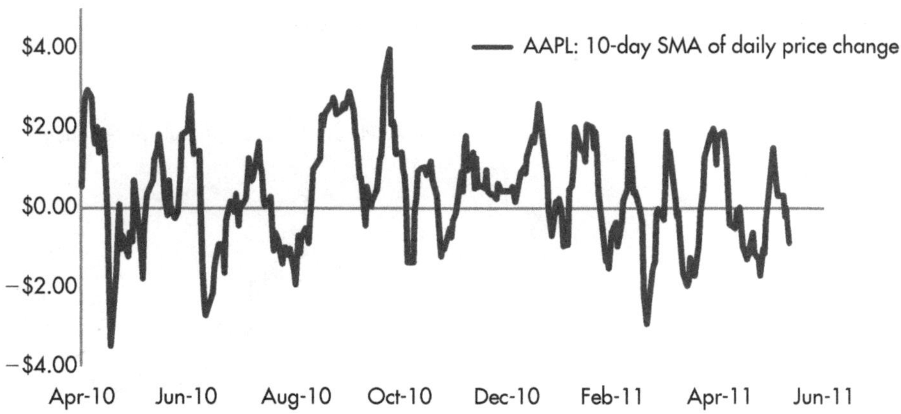

Moving averages use previous scores to make predictions on the basis of a trending pattern. These three line charts depict different scores (using a 10-, 20-, and 50-day parameter); each changes your perspective regarding price direction. As you increase the days, there is less white noise, resulting in a flatter line; however, there is also less opportunity to use these lines as boundaries.

FIGURE 8.3 The black line of AAPL, with a 20-day simple moving average, shows less volatility, but it is still difficult to discern a trading pattern.

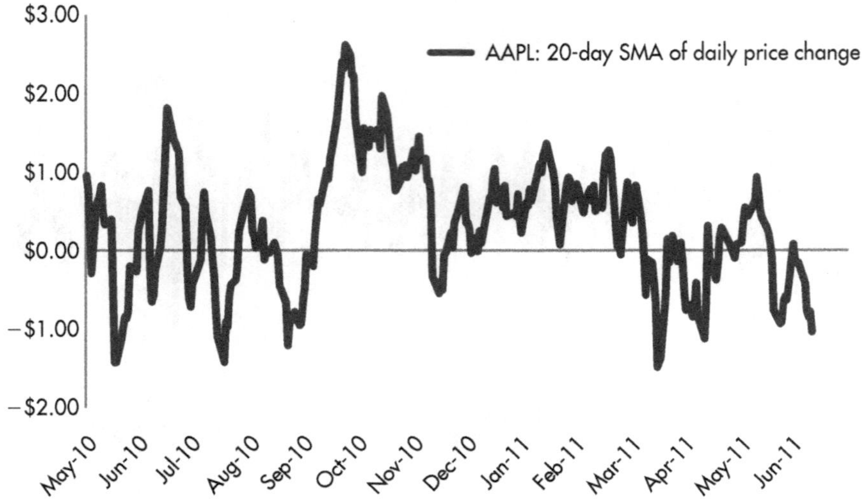

FIGURE 8.4 A 50-day simple moving average flattens the line; this narrows the range of scores across our timeline.

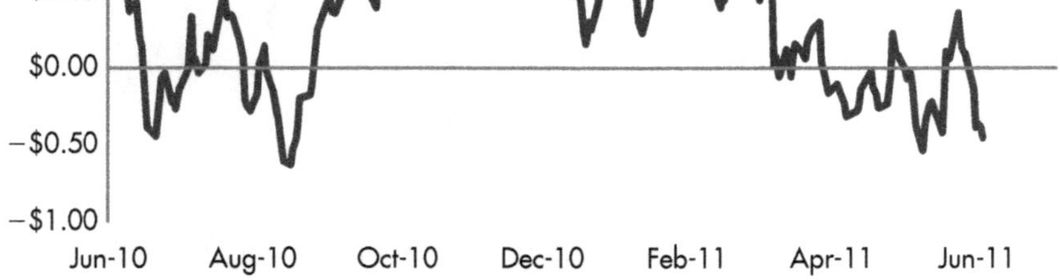

This reductionism decreases the trading opportunities. Support and resistance (SAR)[2] provides market strategists with valuable insight into the process of making prospective trading decisions.

Constructing Simple Moving Averages

When tuning into business stations, the broadcasters often refer to the results of an economic indicator by announcing its four-week simple moving average. The process of creating a simple moving average (SMA) is as follows:

You compute a 4-day SMA by taking the average score of those days under investigation. With these scores: 2, 3, 4, 3, the moving average is (12/4) = 3. If, on the following day, the score is 6, the SMA is 2, 3, 4, 3, 6; remove the earliest day by replacing it with the latest one. After completing this process, the remaining four scores gives us a SMA of 16/4 = 4.

A SMA provides you with plenty of flexibility; you can follow the trending patterns of different intervals (e.g., a time span focusing on a price change of minutes, hours, days, or longer timeframes). When using this indicator, most market participants use trading days by simply taking the average of an instrument's closing price. This is the easy part; the difficulty is determining how many days would give us the greatest degree of accuracy.

This is an important aspect because as you increase the length of your parameter (such as the number of days), the less responsive your indicator is to current prices; however, using more days decreases your trading activity.

In selecting your parameter, the answer is not the same because predictive success varies according to the stock, sector, or commodity you are investigating. When selecting your time frame for constructing a moving average, remember the color of the cat is not important, what matters is if the cat is good at catching mice.

Table 8.1 demonstrates the process of constructing a 3-day SMA for taking a long or short position.

---

[2] Technicians refer to resistance as an advance or series of price advances, which arrive at a previous price, but are unable to break above this imaginary upper line connecting two or more scores. Whereas support is seen as a decline or a series of price declines, which drift down to their previous price, but are unable to break below this imaginary lower line connecting two or more scores.

TABLE 8.1 The calculations begin with a 3-day SMA. When the closing price is above this trading signal, a long position (1) is taken; when the closing price is below the trading signal, a short position (–1) is taken.

Date	Closing Price	3-Day SMA	Trading Position	Price Change	Long	Short
11/01/11	122.00	125.367	short	–3.50		
10/31/11	125.50	127.577	short	–3.10		–3.50
10/28/11	128.60	127.177	long	–0.03	–3.10	
10/27/11	128.63	125.327	long	4.33	–0.03	
10/26/11	124.30	124.280	long	1.25	4.33	
10/25/11	123.05					
10/24/11	125.49					

These are the calculations for a 3-day SMA:

$$\left((\text{time}_1 + \text{time}_2 + \text{time}_3)/\text{n}\right) = \text{predictive score}$$
$$11/01/11(122.00 + 125.50 + 128.60)/3 = 125.367$$
$$10/31/11(125.50 + 128.60 + 128.63)/3 = 127.577$$
$$10/28/11(128.60 + 128.63 + 124.30)/3 = 127.177$$
$$10/27/11(128.63 + 124.30 + 123.05)/3 = 125.327$$
$$10/26/11(124.30 + 123.05 + 125.49)/3 = 124.280$$

This shows the price change difference between trading days:

$$11/01/11 = (122.00 - 125.50) = -3.50$$
$$10/31/11 = (125.50 - 128.60) = -3.10$$
$$10/28/11 = (128.60 - 128.63) = -0.03$$

The results of our calculations are shown in Table 8.2.

Although we can assess profitability, diminishing measurement error is more demanding. Before you can reduce it, you have to quantify it. The following discussion focuses on how to assess measurement error and, more importantly, how to increase your predictive accuracy.

TABLE 8.2 When the closing price is > the trading signal (3-day SMA), a long position is taken; when the closing price is < the trading signal, a short position is taken. We are waiting for the results of executing a short position (–1) on 11/01/11 before entering its price change in the short column.

Date	Closing Price	Direction	3-Day SMA	Trading Position	Price Change	Long	Short
11/01/11	122.00	<	125.367	–1	–3.50		11/02/11
10/31/11	125.50	<	127.577	–1	–3.10		–3.50
10/28/11	128.60	>	127.177	1	–0.03	–3.10	
10/27/11	128.63	>	125.327	1	4.33	–0.03	
10/26/11	124.30	>	124.280	1	1.25	4.33	
10/25/11	123.05						
10/24/11	125.49						

TABLE 8.3 Calculation of a 3-month simple moving average.

Month	Actual Score	Predicted Score	Error Term	Absolute Error	Percentage Error
Jan	11				
Feb	13				
Mar	12				
Apr	15	12.000	3.000	3.000	.200
Average			3.000	3.000	.200

The actual score is your measurement variable. Table 8.3 refers to the closing price for the month (e.g., 11 for January, 13 for February, and 12 for March).[3] In a 3-month moving average, the three earlier months ((Jan + Feb + Mar)/3) produce the forecast for the next month (April = 12).

$$\text{Predicted score} = \left((\text{time}_1 + \text{time}_2 + \text{time}_3)/\text{n}\right)$$
$$(\text{Jan} + \text{Feb} + \text{Mar})/\text{n}) = 36/3$$

An easier way to construct a SMA is to use the statistical function =AVERAGE(range of scores).

[3] Although we are producing a monthly forecast, the statistical application uses the same procedure for any chosen interval.

Although we are forecasting a price of 12, the actual score (April = 15) is above this prediction. The difference between these two scores becomes the error term.

Error Term

What is the difference between the actual score (i.e., monthly price change) and the score we are using to predict a price change for the month in question? This difference becomes our error term. A positive score demonstrates we are below; whereas a negative score demonstrates a predictive score above the actual score. (See Table 8.4.)

The following equation expresses the error in our forecasting:

$$\text{Error} = \text{actual score} - \text{predictive score}$$

Absolute Error

In using the =ABS() function, a positive score remains positive, whereas it converts a negative score into a positive one.

The reason for using this = ABS(cell value) function can be seen in these two hypothetical results (Tables 8.5 and 8.6).

TABLE 8.4 With a prediction of 12, our forecast was $3 below the exact score; consequently, we were underpredicting the closing price.[4]

	Actual Score	Predictive Score	Error	
Apr	15	12	3.000	=15 – 12

TABLE 8.5 By converting a negative into a positive score, we can statistically measure the accuracy of our predictions. Without the conversion, the average of the error term = 0, this makes it difficult for us to perform statistical calculations. Conversely, by using the =ABS function, it turns the negative error score into a positive, this produces an absolute error score of (6/2) = 3.

	Actual	Predicted	Error
	3	0	3
	0	3	–3
Sum			0

[4] In regression analysis (actual score − predicted score) = residual error term.

TABLE 8.6 Since the sum of the error score = 0, it gives us a false impression because it appears as if there is no forecasting error. In order to correct this problem, we create another field. The absolute function transforms a negative to a positive number.

	Actual	Predicted	Error Term	Absolute Error	
	3	0	–3	3	=ABS(−3)
	0	3	+3	3	=ABS(3)
Average			0	3	

TABLE 8.7 By taking the absolute value of the monthly error term, we can report the average percentage error. This term conveys a measurable assessment of our predictive ability. In this case, the average percentage error is 0.238. In attempting to improve our forecasting ability, our objective is to shrink this number.[5]

Month	Actual Score	Prediction	Error	Abs Error	Percentage Error
Jan	11.000	8.000	3.000	3.000	0.273
Feb	13.000	9.000	4.000	4.000	0.308
Mar	10.000	11.333	–1.333	1.333	0.133
Average	11.333	9.444	1.889	2.778	0.238

Percentage Error

A percentage error gives us information about the absolute error term in relation to our measurement (in this case, we are attempting to forecast the closing price for the month).

$$\text{Percentage error} = (\text{absolute error term}/\text{actual score})$$

Using different scores, Table 8.7 shows the calculations for the percentage error term.

How do we know if this error is above or below our forecast? When looking at a positive average error, it indicates the predictive score is below; however, when it is negative, it signifies a predictive score above the actual price of the instrument under investigation.

[5] Anthony Trongone, *Quantitative Methods for Finance and Investing* (Singapore: Cengage Learning, 2008).

Above or Below Expectations

Since many traders have an understanding of moving averages, the appendix contains a more in-depth discussion of these momentum indicators. Table 8.8 is an illustration of a 12-month SMA. There is a description of each measurement term, along with additional examples in the appendix.

This differs from earlier calculations because they are in ascending order. And the predictive score is in the same row as the actual score; this makes it easier to assess the other terms.

This study calculates the 3-day SMA from the earlier 3 months, the average monthly error is positive (2.593). Since these predictive scores are under-predicting, an upward adjustment is necessary. With an increase in our monthly forecast, we are seeking to reduce our average monthly percentage error (0.216).

Figure 8.5 is a line chart showing the predictive price (—) in response to the closing price (—). It is extremely important to ascertain if the predictive score is above or below the closing price.

TABLE 8.8 The calculations show the differences between the monthly price change in comparison to our monthly prediction (3-month SMA). The majority of the predictive scores fall short of the actual monthly sales.

Month	Actual Score	Predicted Score	Error	Absolute Error	Percentage Error
Jan	5				
Feb	8				
Mar	6				
Apr	10	6.33	3.67	3.67	0.367
May	11	8.00	3.00	3.00	0.273
Jun	13	9.00	4.00	4.00	0.308
Jul	10	11.33	−1.33	1.33	0.133
Aug	13	11.33	1.67	1.67	0.128
Sep	15	12.00	3.00	3.00	0.200
Oct	16	12.67	3.33	3.33	0.208
Nov	18	14.67	3.33	3.33	0.185
Dec	19	16.33	2.67	2.67	0.140
Average	13.889	11.296	2.593	2.889	0.216

FIGURE 8.5 With the exception of one month, the predictive scores are below the actual score; therefore, an upward adjustment is necessary.

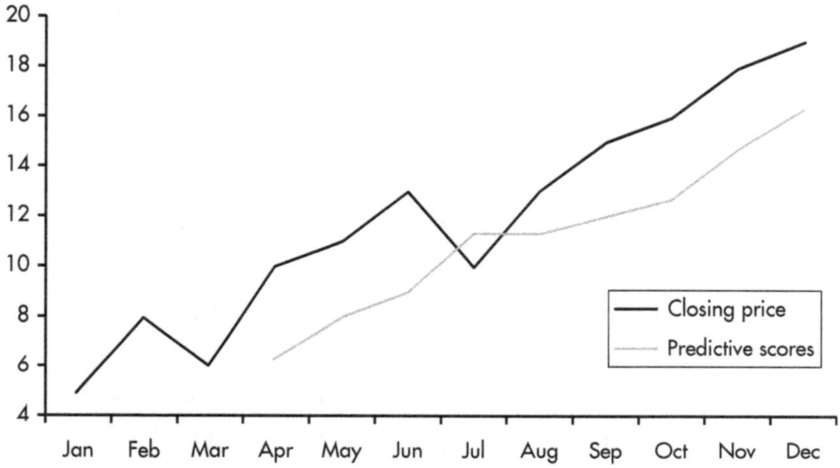

With the exception of July, this 3-day SMA is underpredicting. The actual scores (—) are above our forecast (—); therefore, in order to improve our forecasting an upward adjustment is necessary.

Daily Calculations

Table 8.9 is a 3-day SMA of the spiders. The rightmost columns show the performance outcome by lagging the results of the daily price change. In each case, a long or short position produces inferior results.

A long position with a negative (–$5.27) summary result or a short position with a positive ($1.76) summary result is unprofitable. A moving average is often ineffective when we are trading in a trendless environment.

This daily comparison of the closing price of the spiders with the price predictions (3-day trading signal) illustrates how difficult it is for the gray line to follow along in the direction of the black line.

The predictive score (SMA signal) always follows the closing price of the spiders. Consequently, we refer to it as a lagging indicator because it is trailing the current price of an instrument. This places us at a disadvantage because when rising prices begin falling, or falling prices begin rising, this rolling average signal responds slowly. Fortunately, there are ways to partially compensate for this "lagging" deficiency.

The equations for constructing this worksheet can be seen in Table 8.10.

TABLE 8.9 Either way, a position using a 3-day simple moving average was unproductive.

Date	Closing Price	3-Day SMA	Trading Position	Price Change	Long	Short
11/18/2011	121.98	122.72	–1	–0.13		
11/17/2011	122.11	124.09	–1	–1.97		–0.13
11/16/2011	124.08	125.21	–1	–2.00		–1.97
11/15/2011	126.08	126.07	1	0.62	–2.00	
11/14/2011	125.46	125.48	–1	–1.20		0.62
11/11/2011	126.66	124.71	1	2.34	–1.20	
11/10/2011	124.32	125.12	–1	1.16		2.34
11/09/2011	123.16	125.77	–1	–4.72		1.16
11/08/2011	127.88	126.54	1	1.62	–4.72	
11/07/2011	126.26	126.00	1	0.78	1.62	
11/04/2011	125.48	125.24	1	–0.77	0.78	
11/03/2011	126.25	124.08	1	2.26	–0.77	
11/02/2011	123.99	123.83	1	1.99	2.26	
11/01/2011	122.00	125.37	–1	–3.50		1.99
10/31/2011	125.50	127.58	–1	–3.10		–3.50
10/28/2011	128.60	127.18	1	–0.03	–3.10	
10/27/2011	128.63	125.33	1	4.33	–0.03	
10/26/2011	124.30	124.28	1	1.25	4.33	
10/25/2011	123.05	124.17	–1	–2.44		1.25
10/24/2011	125.49	123.71	1	1.52	–2.44	
10/21/2011	123.97					
10/20/2011	121.66					
				SUM	–5.27	1.76

TABLE 8.10 The formulas for constructing a 3-day simple moving average with the corresponding outcomes.

	A	B	C	D	E	F	G
1	Date	Closing Price	3-Day SMA	Trading Position	Price Change	Long Position	Short Position
2	11/18						
3	11/17	122.11	=AVERAGE (B3:B5)	=IF (B3>C3,1,-1)	=B3-B4	=IF(D3=1, E2,"")	=IF(D3=-1, E2,"")
4	11/16	124.08	=AVERAGE (B4:B6)	=IF (B4>C4,1,-1)	=B4-B5	=IF(D4=1, E3,"")	=IF(D4=-1, E3,"")
5	11/15	126.08	=AVERAGE (B5:B7)	=IF (B5>C5,1,-1)	=B5-B6	=IF(D5=1, E4,"")	=IF(D5=-1, E4,"")

Weighting Moving Averages

When constructing simple moving averages, as you increase the number of days, the SMA places less emphasis on recent performance, because it distributes the same weighting for each day. The reason for using a moving average design is to follow emerging patterns of success or failure. Since each score gets the same weighting, when the price of a stock or commodity has an excessive price move, the distance between the two variables widens. In other words, they are never the front runner; they are always chasing price. How far is the predictive score from the leader? It depends; it is either in the money, or places somewhere with the also-rans, following the frontrunner down the stretch.

One way that you can address this limitation is by weighting the scores. By placing more emphasis on the more recent scores, if the instrument makes an aggressive move, its pace is more responsive. In the following example, we are attempting to predict the closing price of the spiders by using this arbitrary 3-month (WMA) weighting sequence.

In this example (Table 8.11), we are multiplying the closing price by a $(3 \times 2 \times 1)$ weighting sequence. The denominator is the sum $(3 + 2 + 1 = 6)$ of the weightings.

$$= ((123.97 \times 3) + (121.66 \times 2) + (120.33 \times 1)) / 6$$

Denominator = the sum of the weighting $(3 \times 2 \times 1)$ sequence

Sum of weightings / sum of weighting sequence = the predicted score

The calculations for computing the $3 \times 2 \times 1$ weighting signal can be seen in Table 8.12.

10/21/11	123.97	3	371.91
10/20/11	121.66	2	243.32
10/17/11	120.23	1	120.23
		6	735.46

FIGURE 8.6 The choppiness of this sideways market is partially responsible for these dim results.

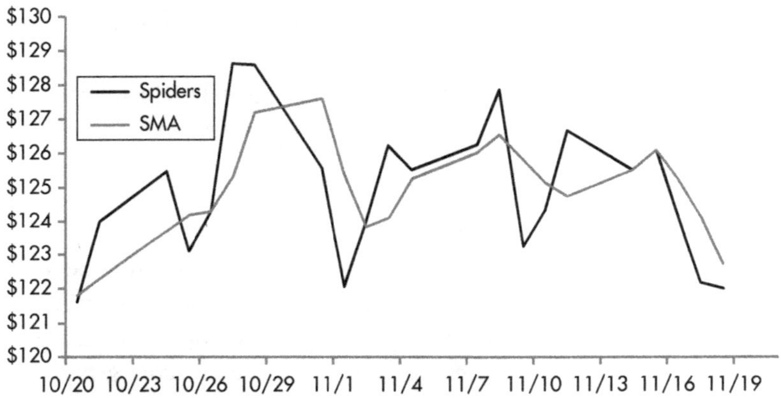

TABLE 8.11 The latest price is given the highest weighting, the earliest the lowest one.

Date	Closing Price	Weighting Sequence	Formula	WMA Signal
10/21/11	123.97	3	123.97 × 3	122.58
10/20/11	121.66	2	121.66 × 2	
10/17/11	120.23	1	120.23 × 1	
Denominator		6		

TABLE 8.12 The formulas for using a 3-day WMA with a 3 × 2 × 1 weighting sequence.

	A	B	C
1	Date	Closing Price	WMA 3-2-1 Weighting
2	11/18	121.98	=((B2*3)+(B3*2)+(B4*1))/6
3	11/17	122.11	=((B3*3)+(B4*2)+(B5*1))/6
4	11/16	124.08	=((B4*3)+(B5*2)+(b6*1))/6
5	11/15	126.08	=((B5*3)+(B6*2)+(B7*1))/6
6	11/14	125.46	
7	11/11	126.66	

TABLE 8.13 With a 3 × 2 × 1 weighting sequence the statistics remain disappointing. With both positions sporting losses, this indicator, by itself, is insufficient.

Date	Closing Price	3-Day WMA	Trading Position	Price Change	Long	Short
11/18/11	121.98	122.37	–1	–0.13		
11/17/11	122.11	123.43	–1	–1.97		–0.13
11/16/11	124.08	124.98	–1	–2.00		–1.97
11/15/11	126.08	125.97	1	0.62	–2.00	
11/14/11	125.46	125.67	–1	–1.20		0.62
11/11/11	126.66	125.30	1	2.34	–1.20	
11/10/11	124.32	124.53	–1	1.16		2.34
11/09/11	123.16	125.25	–1	–4.72		1.16
11/08/11	127.88	126.94	1	1.62	–4.72	
11/07/11	126.26	126.00	1	0.78	1.62	
11/04/11	125.48	125.49	–1	–0.77		0.78
11/03/11	126.25	124.79	1	2.26	–0.77	
11/02/11	123.99	123.58	1	1.99	2.26	
11/01/11	122.00	124.27	–1	–3.50		1.99
10/31/11	125.50	127.06	–1	–3.10		–3.50
10/28/11	128.60	127.89	1	–0.03	–3.10	
10/27/11	128.63	126.26	1	4.33	–0.03	
10/26/11	124.30	124.08	1	1.25	4.33	
10/25/11	123.05	124.02	–1	–2.44		1.25
10/24/11	125.49	124.35	1	1.52	–2.44	
10/21/11	123.97	122.73	1	2.31	1.52	
10/20/11	121.66					
10/19/11	121.13					
				SUM	–4.53	2.54

$$735.46/6 = 122.5767 \text{ (3-day WMA trading signal)}$$

Figure 8.6 charts the performance of this 3 × 2 × 1 weighting along with the price of the spiders.

The formula for predicting the scores is written in the C column. Once you write the formula into the cell, simply highlight it and drag the formula down.

FIGURE 8.7 The 3 × 2 × 1 WMA sequence hangs closely with the daily price of the spiders.

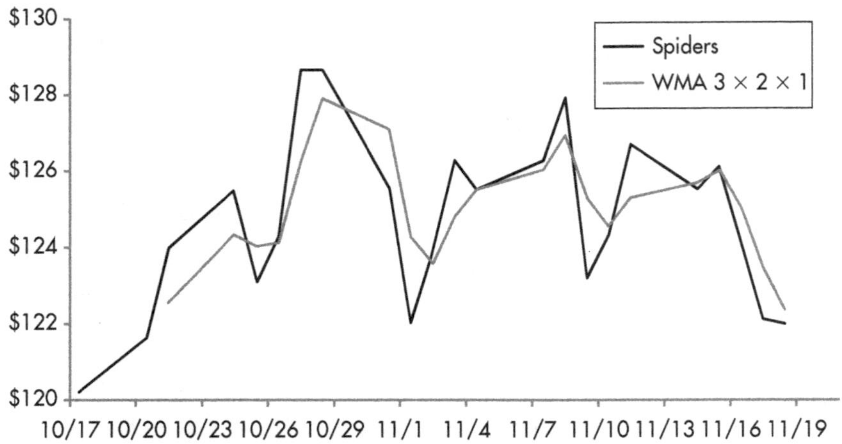

TABLE 8.14 Although this small sample is for illustration purposes, always run a comparison among moving averages.

Spiders	3-Day SMA		3-Day WMA	
	Long	Short	Long	Short
Adv	4	5	4	6
Dec	7	3	7	3
Sum	–$5.27	$1.76	–$4.53	$2.54

This action will automatically enter the remaining formulas for you. Table 8.13 displays the 3-day WMA with its final numbers.

A graphic line comparison of these results can be seen in Figure 8.7.

When running these two different moving averages do some comparison shopping. Table 8.14 displays the results of running a side-by-side comparison of these different methods. Although it uses few cases, its application as well as its interpretation is the same for a full-scale model.

Next, it is important to compare the two rolling averages to assess the difference between their percentage error scores. When comparing these two procedures, you want the one with less measurement error. A closer look at the spacing between the two lines (i.e., the closing price in relation to the predictive score) gives us another comparison measure. Naturally, with

FIGURE 8.8 Always compare the two predictive charts against one another. Examine to see if the SMA or WMA predictive score is a tighter fit.

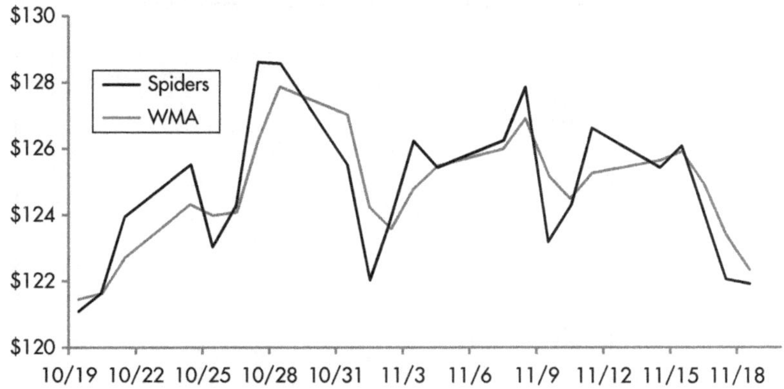

the lower predictive error score, the best-fitting procedure produces less separation; therefore, it affords us more predictive ability (Figure 8.8).

Simulation Analysis

Although the 3 × 2 × 1 weighting seems reasonable, how can we make adjustments without producing a new worksheet? Suppose, we want to change the weighting, how can we get Excel to automatically do the necessary calculations? (See Figure 8.9.)

In the formula bar the equation for "C2" is ((B4*$I$2) + (B3*$I$3) + (B2*$I$4))/$I$5; this computes to a 3 × 1 × −1 weighting sequence, which gives us a profitable solution for both positions.

And, for "C6" it is ((B2*$I$2) + (B3*$I$3) + (B4*$I$4))/$I$5, this computes to ((121.98 × 3) + (122.11 × 2) + (124.08 × −1))/3. If done correctly, with these formulas in place, we can modify the weightings to reflect automatic changes in our calculations as well as in the moving average chart.

In Table 8.15, the weightings are 3 × 1 × −1.

When in a sideways trading market, we sometimes get excessive price changes with advancing days alternating with declining days. When this occurs, a strong weighting on the previous day is a liability.

The t_{-3} weighting uses a negative score; this responds nicely to the price swings as seen in Figure 8.10.

FIGURE 8.9 The advantage of writing the formulas using absolute weightings is that this procedure automatically changes the WMA as you change the weightings in the "I" column.

C2 fx =((B2*$J$2)+(B3*$J$3)+(B4*$J$4))/$J$5

	A	B	C	D	E	F	G	H	I	J
1	date	close	wma	pos	pc	long	short		time	weighting
2	11/18/11	121.98	121.32	1	-0.13				t-1	3
3	11/17/11	122.11	121.44	1	-1.97	-0.13			t-2	1
4	11/16/11	124.08	124.29	-1	-2.00		-1.97		t-3	-1
5	11/15/11	126.08	125.68	1	0.62	-2.00			sum	3
6	11/14/11	125.46	126.24	-1	-1.20		0.62			
7	11/11/11	126.66	127.05	-1	2.34		-1.20			
8	11/10/11	124.32	122.75	1	1.16	2.34				
9	11/09/11	123.16	123.70	-1	-4.72		1.16			
10	11/08/11	127.88	128.14	-1	1.62		-4.72			
11	11/07/11	126.26	126.00	1	0.78	1.62				
12	11/04/11	125.48	126.23	-1	-0.77		0.78			
13	11/03/11	126.25	126.91	-1	2.26		-0.77			
14	11/02/11	123.99	122.82	1	1.99	2.26				
15	11/01/11	122.00	120.97	1	-3.50	1.99				
16	10/31/11	125.50	125.49	1	-3.10	-3.50				
17	10/28/11	128.60	130.04	-1	-0.03		-3.10			
18	10/27/11	128.63	129.05	-1	4.33		-0.03			
19	10/26/11	124.30	123.49	1	1.25	4.33				
20	10/25/11	123.05	123.56	-1	-2.44		1.25			
21	10/24/11	125.49	126.26	-1	1.52		-2.44			
22	10/21/11	123.97	124.45	-1	2.31		1.52			
23	10/20/11	121.66								
24	10/17/11	120.23								
25						6.91	-8.90			
26										

TABLE 8.15 This combination gives more weight to the latest scores, this in turn, reduces the percentage error score.

Time	Weighting
t_{-1}	+3
t_{-2}	+1
t_{-3}	−1
Sum	3

FIGURE 8.10 The predictive line from the new weighting sequence rides tightly on the back of the black line. There are a few exceptions in which it runs below its closing price.

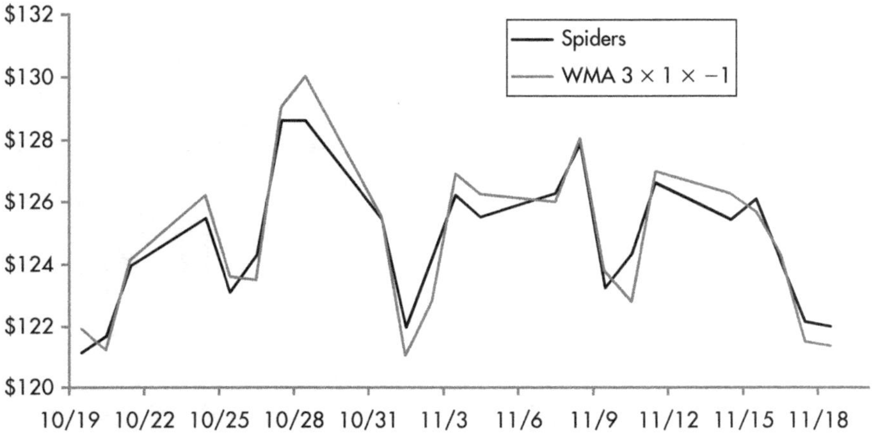

TABLE 8.16 Summary results of the three different analyses.

Spiders 300 Days	Summary	3-Day SMA		3 × 2 × 1 WMA		3 × 1 × −1 WMA	
		Long	Short	Long	Short	Long	Short
Advance	166	96	70	94	72	74	92
Decline	134	78	56	77	57	59	75
Win %	0.553	0.552	0.556	0.550	0.558	0.556	0.551
Summary	$9.33	$5.31	$4.02	$5.40	$3.93	$8.59	$0.74
Average	0.031	0.031	0.032	0.032	0.030	0.065	0.004

In creating this paradigm, you can continue to experiment until you achieve the lowest possible percentage error weighting combination.

After running the statistics, we can assess the performance of the following three moving averages (Table 8.16).

The findings for this study run from September 13, 2009 until November 18, 2011 (300 trading days).

3-day SMA
3-day WMA with a 3 × 2 × 1 weighting sequence
3-day WMA with a 3 × 1 × −1 weighting sequence

These results were not convincing. The 300-day winning percentage was comparable to the other moving average combinations: the long positions

FIGURE 8.11 Not exactly a screaming bull market. In these 300 trading days, the spiders, after three rallies, failed to break past $140, and they take a disastrous slide after penetrating below support in August 2011.

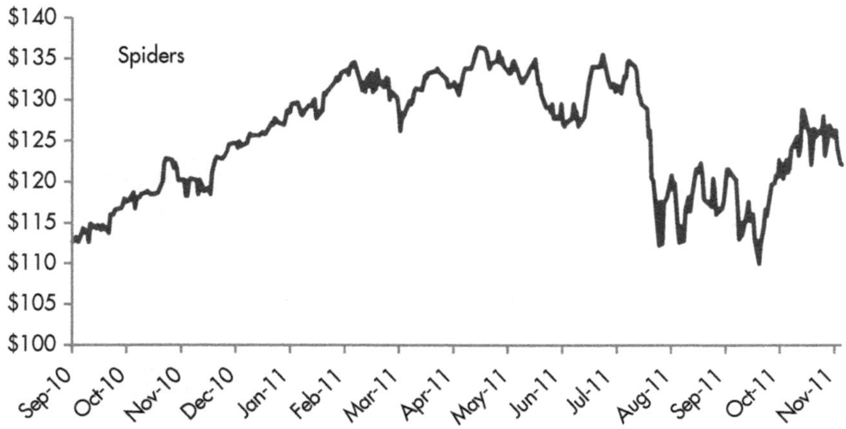

could not significantly improve upon the $0.032 APT, and the short positions were a terrible letdown at picking daily declines. Nevertheless, the best-performing sequence was the ($3 \times 1 \times -1$) unconventional weighting. (See Figure 8.11.)

Surely this run, using a 3-day moving average, would profit from the early stepladder pace of $112 to $133, but falter during the long sideways market. As for taking a short position, the 3 days should produce an inactive trading setting during its early vertical climb, but easily profit from the $22 decline lasting 21 days. This, however, was not the case. Despite the planning, our efforts were unsuccessful; consequently, the next chapter provides some modifications to this approach.

CHAPTER 9

Integrating Variables into a Moving Average

There are no facts, only interpretations.

—Friedrich Nietzsche

This chapter continues with a discussion of using moving averages when trading the spiders. Given its flaws, a simple moving average is too crude an indicator. Standing by itself, it frequently produces inferior results. Correcting this often requires a combination of integrating variables into your analysis, and adopting a different theoretical perspective together with a more adaptable trading model.

Developing a profitable trading system is not always easy. It is an incremental process in which you continuously break things apart and examine the pieces—discarding those ineffective strategies, but retaining those with promise, repeatedly experimenting with them until they are ready for application.

When implementing moving averages part of the problem is the trading environment. That is, when taking a long position, does success require a bull market?

SMAs in a Bullish Setting

Most, if not all, indicators have no immunity from sudden swings in market direction; rolling averages are not the exception, as there are many flaws built into them. We can best illustrate this concept by comparing three moving averages using different time frames.

The analysis for these designs begins by using the September 30, 2003, closing price ($99.95) of the spiders and concludes with the $131.42 closing price on September 1, 2006.[1] Since we are working in an upward trending environment, it favors a long position because of its $31.47 advance in these 737 trading days.

When using the traditional moving average approach found in books on technical analysis, you take a long position when price (black line) rises above the trading signal (100-day SMA; gray line); but offset your position when the price falls below the signal. The biggest drawback for this specific setting is that it restricts you from buying the spiders until its price crosses over the smoothing line; this causes you to miss a large portion of the upswing; therefore, you are never buying at the bottom. This is challenging because after offsetting your long position, this instrument often touches its bottom far below the gray line before making a rapid comeback; however, when playing this system, we cannot take action until the black line crosses above the gray line.[2]

Looking at Figure 9.1, you can see two performance drawbacks: (1) it does not release you from a long position until the spiders are about halfway down each peak, and (2) after rebounding from a bottom this indicator is tardy putting you back into another long position.

Since the 100-day SMA signal is a lagging indicator, when in a long position it does not give us a sell signal until the spiders take a considerable fall. And, when in a short position, it does not give us a buy signal until after the recovery is in force.

Considering these shortcomings, was this 100-day moving average indicator capable of capturing a good part of this $31.47 advance? Not really, a long position gave us $14.02 in profits (287-233-5).[3] When triggering a short position, it was totally incapable of yielding any rewards, losing $17.45 with a 118-93-1 record.[4]

There are different ways to compensate for a moving average score chasing after its actual price.

---

[1]This gives us 367 trading days using the trading days from October 1, 2003, until August 31, 2006.

[2]In the appendix, there is a discussion—along with an illustration—demonstrating the structural flaws of simple moving averages.

[3]In reporting my findings, I am counting each new day as a new trade; therefore, if you are holding a long position, regardless of whether it requires you to retain this direction or take a short position, it is counted as a new trade.

[4]Remember, with a short position, a positive result is reflective of a losing trade. A daily price advance is a losing day, whereas a daily decline is a winning day.

FIGURE 9.1 This is a perfect landscape for a moving average play. In spite of upward trending prices, the 100-day moving average is a lagging indicator; therefore, it is slow to respond.

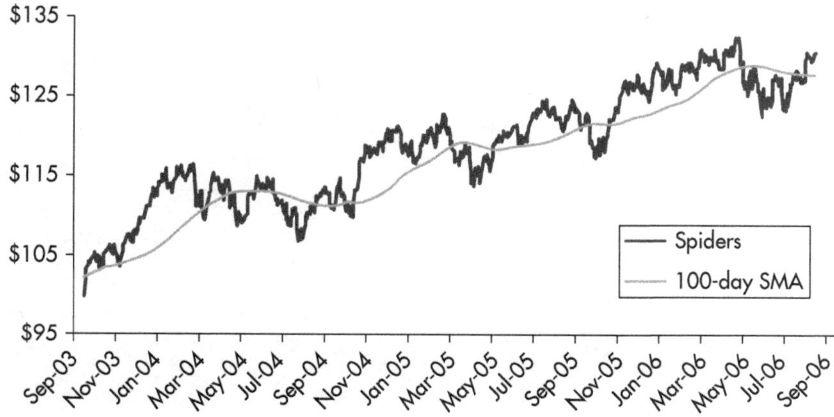

Being more of a trailing indicator, the 100-day SMA reacts more slowly; whereas, those with fewer days are going to be more responsive to changes in price. After all, in looking at the line chart of the spiders, the 10-day SMA hangs closely around its closing price (Figure 9.2); therefore, it appears as if it is a more promising play.

Although a shorter time frame should be more responsive for capturing recent price moves, the results are surprisingly disappointing on both sides of the aisle. A long position generates a paltry sum ($3.86); whereas, the result of a short position is dreadfully disappointing.

How effective was the 3-day SMA in this bullish setting?

Table 9.1 is a side-by-side comparison of three simple moving averages. By far, the 3-day produced the worst performance for either a long (–$12.88) or short ($42.25) position.

The analysis of these three SMAs runs from October 1, 2003, until August 31, 2006 (737 trading days).

Apparently, in a bullish setting, a SMA with more days is the better play. For instance, when looking in either direction, the 100-day was the best performer. Responsible for its success were 529 long positions (the 10-day with 429, the 3-day with 416). With 71.78 percent of its trades being buys, it is the closest to simply sitting on a long position. And, with the spiders pocketing $31.47 in 737 days, any study featuring more long positions with fewer shorts is going to have a huge advantage.

FIGURE 9.2 The 10-day SMA signal hangs closer to the closing price of the spiders, but its performance results are disappointing.

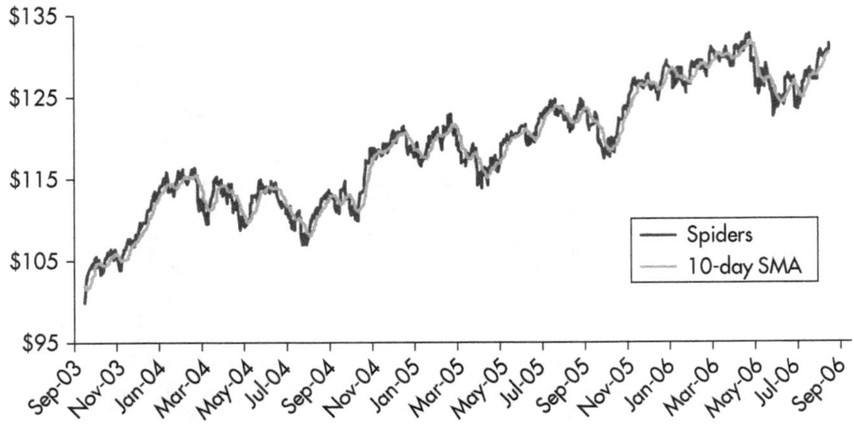

TABLE 9.1 The results show three simple moving averages. Despite the trading parameter, the performances are ugly; however, the best metrics come from the 100-day SMA.

Spiders	3-Day		10-Day		100-Day	
737 days	Long	Short	Long	Short	Long	Short
Trades	416	321	429	308	529	208
Advance	216	189	235	170	291	114
Decline	195	131	192	134	233	93
Ties	5	1	2	4	5	1
Win %	0.519	0.589	0.548	0.552	0.550	0.548
Summary	–$12.78	$44.25	$3.86	$27.61	$17.83	$13.64
Average (APT)	–0.0307	0.1379	0.0090	0.0896	0.0337	0.0656

Categorizing Variables

In the previous investigation on moving averages, the findings were disheartening. As you recall, this strategy gave us a buy signal when the closing price of the spiders was above its 10-day moving average. When we do not put restrictions on our predictor variable, it can compromise our results. For instance, one pressing question to answer is whether its performance is better at predicting future price movements when the signal is far away from the closing price of the spiders or slightly below it?

Again, we are evaluating the results of holding a long position from today's closing price to the closing price of the following trading day.

In these three separate cases the trading signal differs in strength. When taking a long position in the spiders, do these three situations perform differently?

1. The closing price of the spiders is $123, the 10-day moving average is $120; therefore, the signal is $3.00 below the closing price.
2. The closing price of the spiders is $123, the 10-day moving average is $121.50; therefore, the signal is $1.50 below the closing price.
3. The closing price of the spiders is $123, the 10-day moving average is $122.70; therefore, the signal is $0.30 below the closing price.

Can we improve on the disappointing performance of the spiders when using a10-day SMA (Oct 1, 2003 to Aug 31, 2006)? In running this analysis in the previous chapter, we had 429 days calling for a long position, resulting in $3.86 in profits. Considering that the spiders had a run of $31.47 in 737 trading days, this performance was grossly inferior.

A column chart displaying the excessive volatility of a 10-day SMA signal is shown in Figure 9.3. This indicates an environment of excessive buying and selling; such overtrading (churning) is costly, because of commission fees.

FIGURE 9.3 This shows the whipsaw action of the 10-day SMA trading signal. This is informative because it measures the range of its trading signal. With this information, we can measure performance when its score is above +2 or below −2.

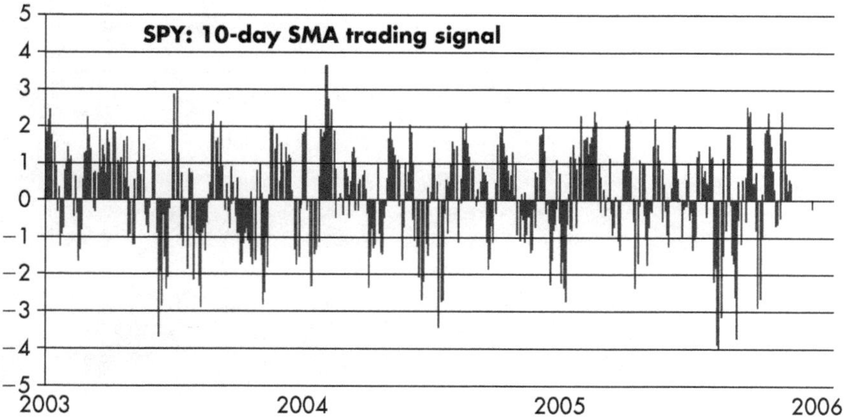

By investigating the trading signal on the basis of the distance from the closing price, we want to improve performance. When calculating a moving average, the "trading signal" acts as the difference between the closing price of an instrument and its moving average score. In this case, the calculation is as follows:

Trading signal = the closing price of the spiders − its 10-day simple moving average

Clearly, once we construct a breakdown of the various categories of this trading signal, it may augment our predictive powers. By turning the results of this signal into a categorical variable, we can assess its performance in arbitrary settings.

This study runs 737 trading days, starting with a position at the closing bell on September 30, 2003, until the closing bell on August 31, 2006. The investor takes a long position when the trading signal > 0.

Table 9.2 shows the results of taking a long position in each of these seven categories, with a spacing of $0.50, between these two variables.

These seven categories show the complexity of using statistics as a basis for your trading decisions. Since the earlier study was not broken down by brackets, a long position was taken despite the distance between the two variables (closing price > 10-day simple moving average).

With a $3.86 profit in 429 trading days, there were some categories (gray shading) capable of passing this benchmark. When the trading signal was barely positive, it gave us $5.88 in revenue; but the best bang for the buck

TABLE 9.2 A slight increase or an excessive signal (gray shade) was capable of outperforming this 10-day SMA of the spiders.

10-Day Trading Signal	n	Mean	Sum
> 0.00 to ≤ 0.499	98	0.0600	5.88
≥ 0.50 to ≤ 0.999	130	–0.0003	–0.04
≥ 1.00 to ≤ 1.499	89	–0.0796	–7.08
≥ 1.50 to ≤ 1.999	72	0.0625	4.50
≥ 2.00 to ≤ 2.499	33	–0.0476	–1.57
≥ 2.50 to ≤ 2.999	5	0.3220	1.61
≥ 3.00	2	0.2800	0.56
Summary (> 0.00)	429	0.0090	3.86

TABLE 9.3 With one profitable category (83 of the 308 trades), when in a bullish setting, the spacing between the closing price and the 10-day SMA was not a meaningful factor.

10-Day Trading Signal	n	Mean	Sum
< 0.00 to > −0.499	96	0.0845	8.11
≤ −0.50 to ≥ −0.999	83	−0.0655	−5.44
≤ −1.00 to ≥ −1.499	53	0.2906	15.40
≤ −1.50 to ≥ −1.999	35	0.0577	2.02
≤ −2.00 to ≥ −2.499	20	0.1090	2.18
≤ −2.50 to ≥ −2.999	15	0.0887	1.33
≤ −3.00	6	0.6683	4.01
Summary (< 0.00)	308	0.0896	27.61

came after a 2.50 trading signal. In between, the results were a crapshoot with three of the four delivering losing outcomes.

Markets often reach unsustainable performance heights. In this case, after the signal reaches 1.00, it sets the stage for the worst-performing categories; nevertheless, a signal in excess, that is, over 2.50 became too powerful an upswing for contrarians not to counterattack. When such an imbalance occurs, it often captures buyers' attention, as contrarians go against price momentum.

When applying this strategy, an investor takes a short position when the signal < 0.

Table 9.3 shows the results of taking a short position in each of these seven categories, with a spacing of $0.50 between these two variables.

With such a narrow margin, this strategy does not appear profitable, but set against an unrelenting bullish landscape ($27.61 advance in 308 trading days), a short position is always at a serious disadvantage.

Still, after the fact, it appears absurdly simple to believe we can rectify this problem by simply not taking a short position in an upward trending market. This backward thinking corresponds to the race handicapper who can always pick the winner after the race, but unfortunately, we cannot trade the past.

Contributory Variable

A contributory or independent variable is the indirect cause behind your results. They often supplement your findings, as these predictor variables serve to strengthen the accuracy of your analysis.

Given the strong performance of the spiders, these results remain disappointing. A 10-day moving average—above or below its closing price—is still not providing us with a workable approach. Whenever my results are inadequate, a good fix is to throw another predictive variable into the mix.

When including another variable, it has to function by supplementing the results of the already existing moving average indicator. Each variable, by itself, influences our response variable, but when acting together, they often produce a piggyback effect. That is, when working together these two variables lift results, not additively, but, on occasion, they produce a multiplicative effect.

It is best to start with another momentum variable, one that complements our 10-day moving average by demonstrating the trending direction of this indicator. One way to accomplish this is to compare the closing prices of the spiders, one on the previous trading day from another one taken a few days back.

Rate-of-change (ROC) is an indicator that subtracts the existing closing price from a previous closing price. In this case, we are evaluating an 11-day ROC to show the direction of the 10-day SMA.

Basically, we are looking to ascertain if the 10-day SMA is assuming an upward or downward trend. In Table 9.4 the closing price is \$126.08; however, going back 11 days it was at \$127.88; therefore, its trendline is pointing down. The statistical computation for an 11-day ROC is as follows:

$$\text{ROC11} = (\text{closing price } t_{-0} - \text{closing price } t_{-11})$$

In this case, the ROC11 score of –\$1.80, on November 15, 2011, subtracts its closing price (\$126.08) from October 31, 2011(\$127.88). Given this score, we can infer a downward trending ROC score, despite its positive trading signal.

When accounting for an interaction of these two momentum variables, there are four trading possibilities:

1. A long position with the closing price > 10-day SMA AND the ROC11 > 0 (closing price t_0 > closing price t_{-11}).
2. A long position with the closing price > 10-day SMA AND the ROC11 < 0 (closing price t_0 < closing price t_{-11}).
3. A short position when the closing price < 10-day SMA AND ROC11 > 0 (closing price t_0 > closing price t_{-11}).
4. A short position when the closing price < 10-day SMA AND ROC11 < 0 (closing price t_0 < closing price t_{-11}).

TABLE 9.4 In this more recent worksheet of the spiders, the ROC11 indicator (11/15/11 to 10/31/11) is negative ($126.08 – $127.88 = –$1.800), but its 10-day simple moving average is calling for a long position (its close of $126.08 is > 10-day SMA $125.144).

Spiders	Close	10-Day	ROC	SMA Signal
11/15/11	126.08	125.144	–1.800	1
11/14/11	125.46	125.386	–0.800	1
11/11/11	126.66	125.346	–1.970	1
11/10/11	124.32	125.777	0.020	–1
11/09/11	123.35	125.872	0.300	–1
11/08/11	127.88	125.389	2.390	1
11/07/11	126.28	125.310	2.310	1
11/04/11	125.25	125.182	3.590	1
11/03/11	126.25	124.723	5.120	1
11/02/11	123.99	124.437	1.410	–1
11/01/11	122.00	124.495	1.770	–1
10/31/11	127.88	123.730	5.310	1
10/28/11	126.26	123.361	5.750	1
10/27/11	128.63	122.549	7.880	1

The next question is what happens when we combine these interacting effects? Seen from the perspective of a long position, will the spiders perform better when the ROC11 is positive or negative?

When taking a long position, a supplementary research question asks how the spiders perform on the following day when you apply this directional (ROC11) indicator?

Table 9.5 reports the findings of this analysis, which begins on October 1, 2003; it runs until August 31, 2006.

The inclusion of this variable supplements this analysis because a negative ROC11 (i.e., its t_{-0} price falls below its t_{-11} closing price), was able to sharpen performance by registering a gain of $1.51 in 56 trades.

How do the spiders trade on the following day when you apply this directional (ROC11) indicator? (See Table 9.6.)

Although the moving average summary score of $27.61 remains the same after we incorporate this 11-day ROC variable, its inclusion creates a trading opportunity using a short position.

TABLE 9.5 There is some disparity between the two ROC categories. Clearly, when the price of the spiders weakens (ROC11 < 0), it strengthens the return on each trade ($0.0270 APT).

Long Position	ROC11 > 0	ROC11 < 0	Trading Signal > 0
Trades	373	56	429
Advances	202	33	235
Declines	169	23	192
Ties	2	0	2
Win %	.542	.589	.548
Average	$0.0063	$0.0270	$0.0090
Summary	$2.35	$1.51	$3.86

TABLE 9.6 Despite the daily advance of the spiders, a short position was profitable when this momentum ROC11 indicator was on the upswing, but when the ROC11 was on the downswing, a short position was a fatal mistake.

Short Position	ROC11 > 0	ROC11 < 0	Trading Signal < 0
Trades	64	244	308
Advances	31	139	170
Declines	32	102	134
Ties	1	3	4
Win %	.484	.570	.552
Average	–$0.0445	$0.1248	$0.0896
Summary	–$2.85	$30.46	$27.61

When the closing price was above its previous close, it resulted in a profitable return. On the contrary, when the closing price was below its previous close, it resulted in a $0.1248 APT loss. Remember that a positive score when taking a short position is unprofitable.

The investigation found an inverse relationship between the two momentum indicators:

1. When the 10-day SMA is positive (long position), the spiders perform best when its price is turning down (ROC11 is negative).
2. When the 10-day SMA is negative (short position), the spiders perform best when its price is pointing up (ROC11 is positive).

TABLE 9.7 This analysis reports the results of a long position, given the SMA $> 0 +$ ROC11 < 0 (this indicator's closing price (t_{-0}) is below its previous close (t_{-11})).

Long Position with ROC11 < 0		
10-Day SMA Trading Signal	**n**	**Sum**
> 0.00 to < 0.499	27	2.84
≥ 0.50 to < 0.999	18	0.44
≥ 1.00 to < 1.499	8	–2.09
≥ 1.50 to < 1.999	2	0.64
≥ 2.00 to < 2.499	1	–0.32
≥ 2.50	0	0.00
Summary (> 0.00)	56	1.51

It is not uncommon to increase performance by incorporating another variable into your analysis. In this case, the ROC11 produces favorable results, but selecting one does not come easy; it takes some imagination. In this case, we are trying to determine the direction of the simple moving average signal when its trending pattern is rising or falling. When the ROC11 is positive (negative) there is the expectation of an upward (downward) trending simple moving average signal. This is another distinction between the closing price being above or below its SMA signal.

Finally, we want to return to the more profitable categorical variables. A factorial design gives us the opportunity to run these categorical variables together with ROC ($t_0 - t_{-11}$) to determine how they function with one another.

The category barely creeping into positive territory with a 17-10 record ($2.84 APT) took advantage of this inverse combination (SMA > 0 + ROC11 < 0).

These findings consist of the two recommendations from the earlier study. Their findings show us the results of the 56 long positions with a declining momentum indicator (Table 9.7) and the results of the 64 short positions with an advancing momentum indicator (Table 9.8).

Finally, a glimpse of paradise occurs for short sellers as they collect $3.18 when the SMA signal is below a loss of one dollar (Figure 9.4).

Most books stop here, giving you a false impression of a profitable trading system. But, this is just the beginning, not the end. Why, because *we don't trade the past, we trade the future!*

TABLE 9.8 This analysis reports the results of a short position, given the SMA < 0 + ROC11 > 0 (this indicator's closing price (t_{-0}) is above its previous close (t_{-11})).

10-Day SMA Trading Signal	n	Sum
< 0.00 to > −0.499	44	−1.50
≤ −0.50 to > −0.999	17	−1.68
≤ −1.00 to > −1.499	3	0.33
≤ −1.50	0	0.00
Summary (< 0.00)	64	−2.85

FIGURE 9.4 The spiders present a good shorting opportunity when the trading signal is < −.90 and the ROC11 > 0.

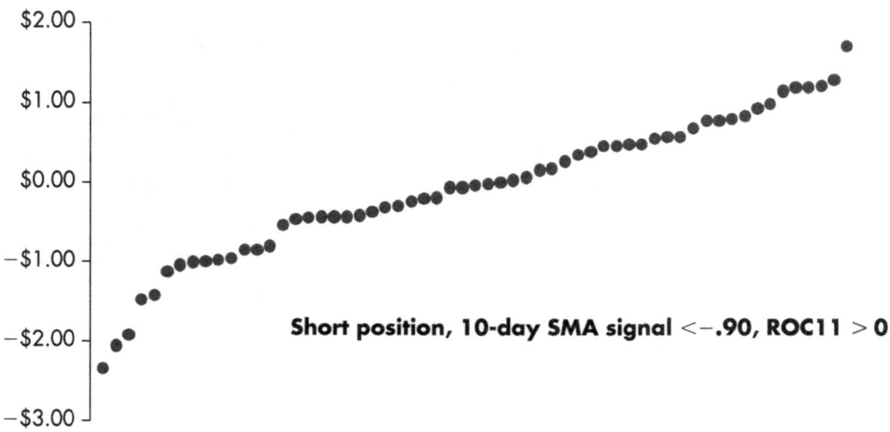

Cross-Validation

Another way of tracking the performance of a study is to run a cross-validation analysis. This procedure verifies the reliability of your previous results. It is always important to reassess your findings before putting your money to work. One practical solution is to run the design using the past as a screening study; once you produce your findings, run the analysis again using the current days as a benchmark. If the performance numbers for the two separate studies are similar, the study validates your results.

TABLE 9.9 Despite a $4.07 profit in 300 trading days of the spiders, the 10-day SMA results run contrary to conventional wisdom.

SPY	10-Day Simple Moving Average Long	Short
Trades	185	115
Advance	101	65
Declines	84	50
Average	−0.0401	0.0998
Summary	–$7.41	$11.48

Since we already have the results of the earlier analysis, all that is left is to run another one using the same two variables. Once we confirm these results, they increase our confidence in the reliability of our earlier findings.[5]

In this investigation, we are re-creating the same analysis within a more current setting. In these previous 300 trading days, the spiders, closing at $112.49, on September 17, 2010, ran up to a closing price of $116.56 on November 23, 2011. Although shorter in design, this price run replicates the positive performance of the earlier study. Given a $4.07 run, this does not alter our hypothesis. We expect a long position to be profitable, but a short position to be unprofitable.

Table 9.9 contains 300 trading days; it runs from September 17, 2010, until November 23, 2011.

Again, the results of running a SMA were counterproductive. Of course, we would simply go against traditional theory because the results are pointing us in a different direction; that is, a long position has a $7.41 negative outcome; whereas, a short position has an $11.48 positive outcome.

In looking at these two outcomes, will the ROC11 indicator have a positive or negative impact on our response variable? (See Table 9.10.)

After running a cross-validation study we expect the two studies to show similar results (Table 9.11).[6]

There were large performance discrepancies between the two studies. Since the more recent study fails to support the earlier results, it is not a tradable system!

---

[5]In writing this book, I am never "fishing" for results that would corroborate my earlier findings. For example, I am simply downloading the previous 300 days ending on Thanksgiving 2011.
[6]The earlier study had three days with a $0.00 price change.

TABLE 9.10 Clearly, there is a performance distinction between the two momentum directional indicators.

10-Day Simple Moving Average with ROC				
300 Days	**Long Position**		**Short Position**	
SPY	**ROC > 0**	**ROC < 0**	**ROC > 0**	**ROC < 0**
Trades	147	38	36	79
Advance	83	18	19	46
Declines	64	20	17	33
Win %	.565	.474	.528	.582
APT	–.0184	–.1239	.0467	.1241
Summary	–2.70	–4.71	1.68	9.80

TABLE 9.11 A comparison of the two studies demonstrates inconsistencies between them.

10-Day Simple Moving Average with ROC11				
	Long Position		**Short Position**	
SPY	**ROC > 0**	**ROC < 0**	**ROC > 0**	**ROC < 0**
September 30, 2003, to August 31, 2006 (737 trading days)				
Trades	373	56	64	244
Summary	$2.35	$1.51	–$2.85	$30.46
September 17, 2010, to November 23, 2011 (300 trading days)				
Trades	147	38	36	79
Summary	$–2.70	–$4.71	$1.68	$9.80

Long-Term Analysis

What if we take a more extensive examination of a simple moving average when trading the spiders by expanding the number of days in our study?

This study runs from October 1, 2003, to November 23, 2011.

Again, we are expecting the following outcomes:

- A long position to produce a positive outcome
- A short position to produce a negative outcome

Table 9.12 reports contrasting results for these two trading positions.

TABLE 9.12 This table takes us back some 2,000-plus trading days; it clearly shows a simple 10-day moving average (without the ROC indicator) is not working. Unlike the earlier two studies, this includes the bear market. Of course, such long-term negativity significantly weakens the results of taking a long position.

	10-Day SMA	
SPY	**Long**	**Short**
Trades	1,204	849
Advance	656	463
Declines	546	380
APT	–0.0338	0.0656
Summary	–40.70	55.73

After all, with these inferior results, why stubbornly try to fit a round peg into a square hole? When the workings of a money-making system are staring you in the face, do you go with conventional wisdom, or do you go with what is working?

What is amazing here is that we have our results, but before applying them to our trading day, remember the previous statement by Jean-Jacques Rousseau (1762), "man is born free but lives everywhere in chains."[7]

Since the results of this indicator are counterproductive, the question is why are we enslaving ourselves to a dysfunctional theory? When we get stuck in this predicament it is best to move on by constructing an integrative tradable system that relies on the ongoing movements of each charting combination.

So far, the summary scores of the four-pattern sequence are not going to increase our investment accounts, but once you study the charting patterns, it opens the door for some interesting plays. (See Table 9.13.)

Generating Interactive Profits

By transforming results into a running summary, we can discover emerging patterns of success or failure. This turns into a proactive trading system, I refer to it as GIA, which stands for generating interactive profits.

This study runs from October 1, 2003, to November 23, 2011.

[7]Jean-Jacques Rousseau, *The Social Contract* (1762).

TABLE 9.13 With 2,000-plus trading days, this is a good indication of how the 10-day SMA responds to price movements in the spiders. There is a meaningful separation between the two ROC11 directional outcomes.

10-Day Simple Moving Average with ROC11				
2,053 Days	**Long Position**		**Short Position**	
Sum	**ROC > 0**	**ROC < 0**	**ROC > 0**	**ROC < 0**
Trades	1,046	158	165	684
Advance	562	94	85	378
Declines	482	64	79	301
Win %	.537	.595	.515	.553
Average	–.0264	–.0825	.0072	.0797
Summary	–27.66	–13.04	1.19	54.54

FIGURE 9.5 Technicians can pick their spots immediately when trading this combination.

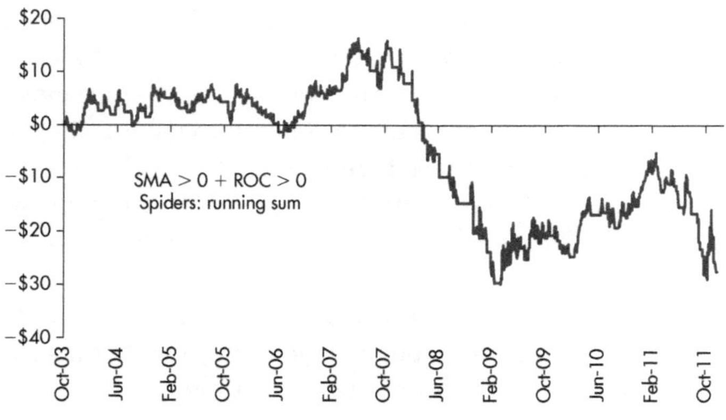

The contributory variables are the following:

10-day SMA
11-day ROC

The response variable is the daily trading activity for the spiders (closing price t_{-0} – closing price t_{-1}).

With two variables, we can extract more information about trading the spiders. Along with the two simple moving average possibilities, there are two ROC directional patterns. This provides investors with four trading charts, in which they can easily apply their technical analysis skills (Figure 9.5).

FIGURE 9.6 Slow starting, this combination consists of small steady price movements. It closely hugs the breakeven line before dropping $27.92 in seven straight losses. In February 2009, it does begin to recoup a portion of its earlier declines.

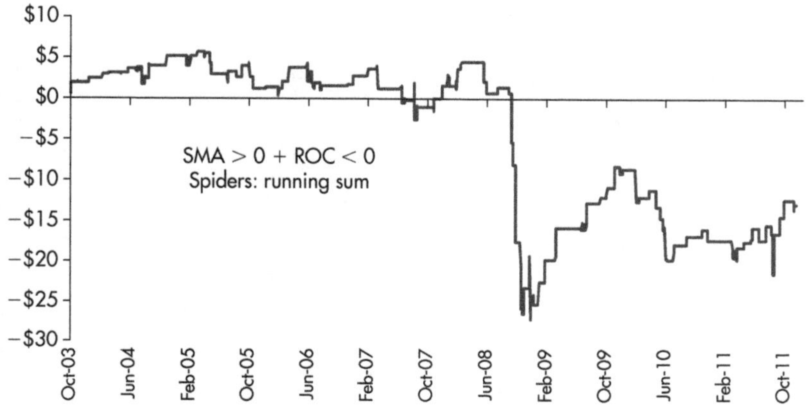

The SMA > 0 + ROC > 0 combination is seen in Figure 9.5. It begins with a sideways market, showing multiple bottoms with varying peaks; a long position at breakeven appears to be profitable. Once reaching its summit, the combination takes a precipitous fall, finally penetrating below support, which happens to be at this breakeven line. Thereafter, it is nothing but a downhill journey, finally showing some consolidation at –$30. After touching support, it undergoes two years of improvement. In February 2011, it falters, falling back down to a running summary loss of –$27.66.

Figure 9.6 shows the running summary for the SMA > 0 + ROC < 0. It holds steady for six years, however, a seven-day losing streak takes it down hard.

Early on, by sitting on the breakeven point, this SMA > 0 + ROC < 0 combination creates an opening for those seeking to sell as rising prices make their way to resistance or to buy as falling prices come down to support.[8]

---

[8]You can take a long position when prices are at support. Providing prices advance, you close your long position prior to reaching resistance, but if prices fall below support you unload your position to prevent further damage. Conversely, you have the opportunity to take a short position as the price comes into the vicinity of resistance with the intention of offsetting it slightly before support. On those days when the market goes against your order, you have to quickly offset your position.

This form of channel trading is designed to maximize return but minimize risk. Unfortunately, once prices break past support or resistance (SAR) investors often react impulsively; consequently, it takes discipline to successfully incorporate this strategy because when prices break above resistance or below support, the loss can be devastating; therefore, you have to scramble with everyone else playing this strategy to reverse your position.

FIGURE 9.7 Another slow start, but this combination has increasingly lower summary lows, accompanied by successive rebounds to an upper boundary. A short position works well, until the beginning of the bull market, where it makes its way back to earlier resistance.

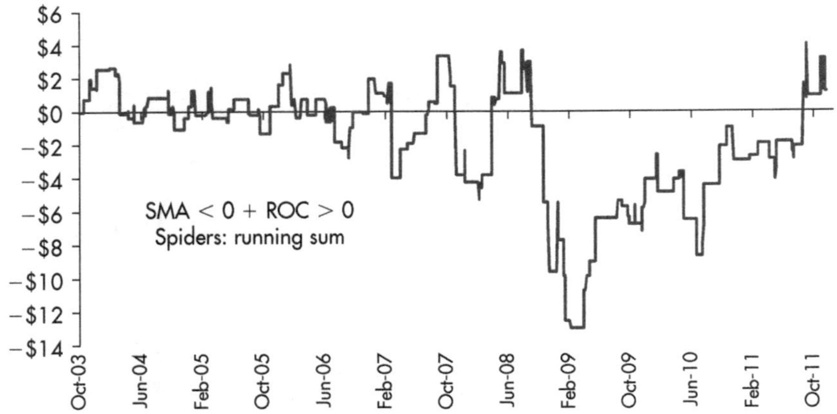

The best trading opportunity came after it fell below breakeven to a summary loss of –$27. With the emergence of the bull market, this combination advances $20 before taking another fall.

Given 158 trades, this system's price moves are unsteady. With the exception of taking a short position, at the start of its $25-plus fall or in taking a long position after the indecisiveness in February 2009, there are few tradable plays. Meanwhile, these seven straight losses demonstrate how a performance streak can overpower our summary statistics.

Figure 9.7 tracks the SMA < 0 + ROC > 0, this maintains a similar pattern as the earlier two combinations, but its recovery rises past breakeven.

This SMA < 0 + ROC > 0 sequence does put together a string of profitable short bets. The bull market, however, is instrumental in creating a strong recovery above the breakeven line. With few trading opportunities, 165 trades in 2,000-plus days, the lines of this summary chart are choppy; nevertheless, with agility a chartist can produce a good percentage of profitable trades.

It is interesting to see how this combination is unable to pierce resistance. More fascinating is its ability to produce a series of breakdowns from this upper boundary, particularly since these breakdowns continuously make new bottoms until this sequence confronts the bull.

Figure 9.8 reports the results when both indicators are negative (SMA < 0 + ROC < 0); this combination produced a steady stream of profits.

Although this SMA < 0 + ROC < 0 generates a long stream of advancing trades, it requires a contrarian's determination to play this

FIGURE 9.8 The arrangement does not follow the earlier combinations. Its steady rise to $60 makes it worth shadowing.

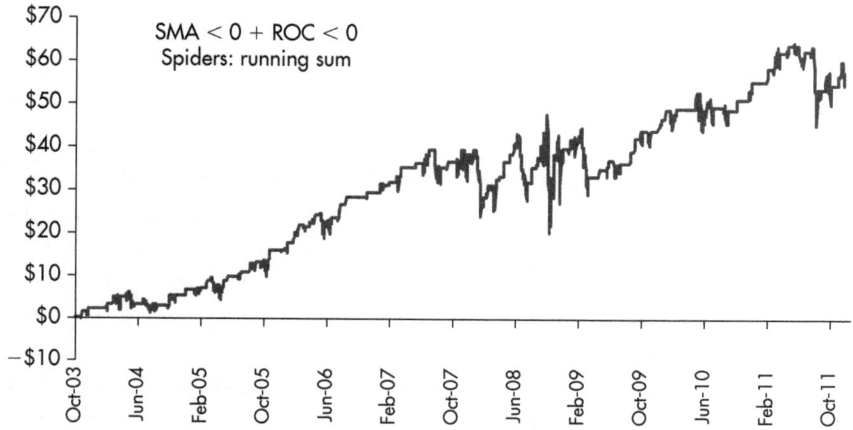

sequence successfully because it goes against the book. When in a bearish market, this combination gives up some ground, but quickly recovers in a bullish market environment, as it amasses a powerful rally. Part of its success comes from investor's willingness to consent to a buy-on-the-dips trading mentality.

Unlike the other strategies experiencing a slow start, this one has early success. And, in contrast to the three earlier charts, this one does not appear to have two incongruous halftimes.

As I stated in a June 2006 feature article, trade the chart, not the system.[9] We can greatly improve our chances for success "by trading the results of each sequence separately; you can come away with a more profitable trading decision. This GIA system is proactive as it gives you the opportunity to put your technical skills into play."[10]

Despite positing the effectiveness of moving averages, after running an analysis, the descriptive statistics found no meaningful performance advantage. Even with the inclusion of another variable (ROC) or the integration of these variables, we were unable to produce results outperforming this 2,000-day trading environment. Consequently, in our discussion on momentum indicators we were unable to support the recommendation for their use in a long bullish setting. Seen from this perspective, without validating your

[9]Anthony Trongone, "Trade the Chart, Not the System," *Technical Analysis of Stocks & Commodities* (June 2006).
[10]Trongone, "Trade the Chart, Not the System," 44–47.

results, do not put confidence in these long-held "facts." After interpreting the results of your analysis, if your findings run contrary to conventional wisdom it is best to go against the grain.

Summary

In summary, there are plenty of favorable opportunities for those active traders willing do the necessary work. Some aspects of uncovering new systems, such as breaking an instrument apart into smaller settings and integrating more indicators into your analysis, as well as drawing a running summary of the performance results of your findings, are a necessary requirement for success when developing momentum indicators.

Since the market is constantly moving, the effectiveness of these indicators is sometimes questionable. When taking a long-term trading approach, they may disappoint; however, they do have spurts of remarkable success. Seen from this perspective, it is important for us to monitor their progress. When they are performing effectively they are good at predicting price direction. Paradoxically, there are many occasions when their signals do offer us a profitable way to bet against them. In any case, knowledge of the existing patterns is a rewarding enterprise because their direction gives you some insight into the collective thinking of market participants.

CHAPTER 10

Going against the Grain

A person who is too nice an observer of the business of the crowd, like one who is too curious in observing the labor of bees, will often be stung for his curiosity.

—Alexander Pope

After making an extensive study of moving averages, we would be remiss not to adopt a different strategy. A crossover moving average (CMA) captures the difference between two moving averages with differing durations. This popular indicator has us subtracting two simple moving averages. Although there are numerous variants, we will begin with a simple 3-8 day combination.[1]

Crossover Moving Averages

The calculation for a 3-8 crossover is

Score = 3-day simple moving average – 8-day simple moving average

The 3-day SMA provides a faster response; the 8-day SMA a slower response. When the price of the 3-day (shorter period) is above the 8-day (longer period), it is seen as a bullish crossover indicator; when below it is seen as a bearish crossover indicator.

[1] Of course, any combination of moving averages can be studied. I prefer to use a sequence formulated by Leonardo Fibonacci, a thirteenth-century mathematician from Pisa, Italy. The Fibonacci numbers are as follows: 0, 1, 1, 2, 3, 5, 8, 13, 21, 34, 55, ... His book *Liber Abaci* (1202) had a profound impact on European commerce.

TABLE 10.1 A 3-8 crossover score subtracts the 3-day SMA from the 8-day SMA. A positive score occurs when the shorter day outpaces the longer day's moving average; this is indicative of a bullish setting.

	Daily Price $ Change	3-day SMA	8-day SMA
Jan 12	1.20	1.00	0.30
Jan 11	0.60		
Jan 10	1.20		
Jan 9	0.40		
Jan 8	0.20		
Jan 5	–1.00		
Jan 4	–0.40		
Jan 3	0.20		

Naturally, in the construction of these crossover averages, there are many possible derivations. Often, one may hold for weeks, but without running an analysis, producing the most profitable weighting combination usually gives us spotty results.

Table 10.1 demonstrates a calculation of a 3-8 crossover score at the closing price on January 12. The lighter shade represents the 3-day score.

The 3-8 crossover score is positive ((1.0 – 0.3) = 0.70); consequently, it is a bullish indicator, predicting an increase in price on the next day.

Notice how the 3-day performance surpasses its counterpart; this produces a positive score. A negative tally is seen as a precursor of downward trending prices. As we have seen from the earlier two chapters, under no circumstance accept this unequivocally without running an analysis to ascertain the veracity of this supposition.[2]

Table 10.2 shows the results of a 3-8 crossover simple moving average combination, with the following assumptions.[3]

$$\text{3-day SMA} > \text{8-day SMA} = \text{bullish crossover setting}$$
$$\text{3-day SMA} < \text{8-day SMA} = \text{bearish crossover setting}$$

[2] Anthony Trongone, "Momentum Indicators in a Free-Falling Market," Interactive Data Corporation www.esignal.com (February 6, 2009).

[3] You can experiment with a WMA by assigning different weightings to the two moving averages.

TABLE 10.2 Without any statistical manipulation, the average daily price increase for these 635 days was $0.0530. In comparison, when the crossover setting was positive it was unable to perform satisfactorily (a $2.29 profit in 390 trading days). Completely missing the mark was the bearish crossover setting. This strategy forces us to take a short position, but its $0.1280 APT was grossly counterproductive; which implies that we would have done better taking a long position in this bearish setting.[4]

Spy	Bullish Crossover Setting	Bearish Crossover Setting	Summary
Trades	390	245	635
Adv	219	133	352
Dec	171	111	282
APT	$0.0059	$0.1280	$0.0530
Sum	$2.29	$31.37	$33.66

TABLE 10.3 This shows a 10-day daily price change for the spiders. The 3-8 crossover price runs above 2.000 on October 28, 2011. Thereafter, we are assessing the performance over the next few trading days.

Date	Closing Price	PC	3-Day SMA	8-Day SMA	3-8 Crossover
10/28/2011	128.60	–0.03	127.177	124.604	2.573
10/27/2011	128.63	4.33	125.327	123.851	1.475
10/26/2011	124.30	1.25	124.280	122.801	1.479
10/25/2011	123.05	–2.44	124.170	122.585	1.585
10/24/2011	125.49	1.52	123.707	122.268	1.439
10/21/2011	123.97	2.31	122.253	121.675	0.578
10/20/2011	121.66	0.53	121.790	121.141	0.649
10/19/2011	121.13	–1.45	121.313	120.881	0.432
10/18/2011	122.58	2.35	121.793	120.204	1.590
10/17/2011	120.23	–2.34	121.103	119.443	1.661

The dates of this study are from June 25, 2009, until December 30, 2011 (635 trading days).

The closing price of the spiders on June 26, 2009, was $91.84. Its closing price on December 30, 2011, was $125.50; this represents a $33.66 increase in price.

[4] When using a 3-8 day crossover moving average, a $0.00 result accounts for any discrepancy in these numbers.

After confirming these results, it becomes obvious that this crossover strategy was ineffective when going long in a bullish setting or going short in bearish setting. Once again, when the numbers are disappointing, a more restrictive trading environment often points us in the right direction.

We can begin by evaluating the results of a 3-8 crossover price when this score is excessively positive. Table 10.3 shows the daily price changes for the spiders. The crossover score ran to 2.573, which signifies a strong 3-day rally. Given this condition, we want to know how the spiders perform after an explosive run. On October 27, 2011, the \$4.33 daily price change was responsible for pushing the 3-8 crossover above 2.000.

After the 3-8 crossover score rises above 2.000 (see Figure 10.1), should an investor take a short position in the spiders over the next few days? In this study, we are investigating the performance of the spiders one, three, and eight days after reaching this 2.000 target price.

Besides displaying the days over 2.000, this boundary chart is a good representation of price volatility when trading the spiders. More recently, the frequency of this 3-8 crossover price, stepping outside these ± 2.000 boundaries should be seen as an early warning sign of troubling times ahead.

Before providing the results of taking a long position, when the 3-8 crossover score is above 2.000, it is instructive to show how the spiders perform during those days in which the 3-8 crossover price resides within this ± boundary.

FIGURE 10.1 After computing a 3-8 crossover score, the line chart delineates those days above 2.000 (upper boundary) and below −2.000 (lower boundary). In this study, however, we are looking for a snapback in the price of the spiders once it breaks over the upper line of the 2.000 crossover score.

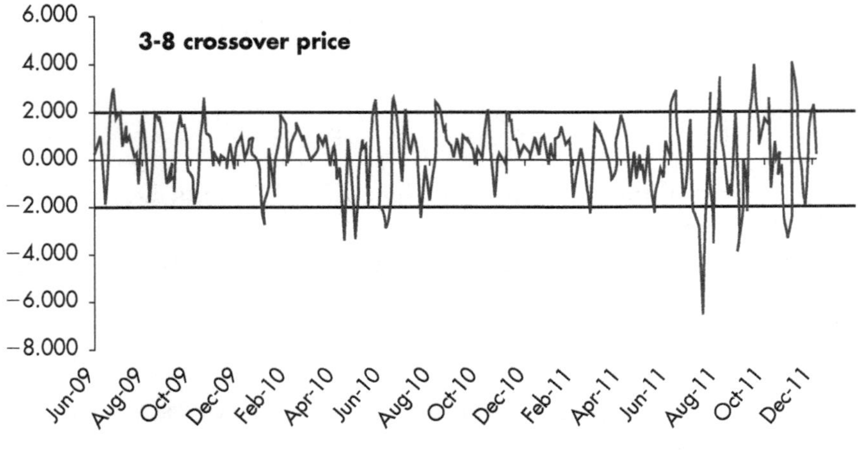

FIGURE 10.2 A dual axis chart showing the spiders' performance together with a 3-8 crossover price. The biggest price spurts occur when this crossover price resides within a narrow boundary.

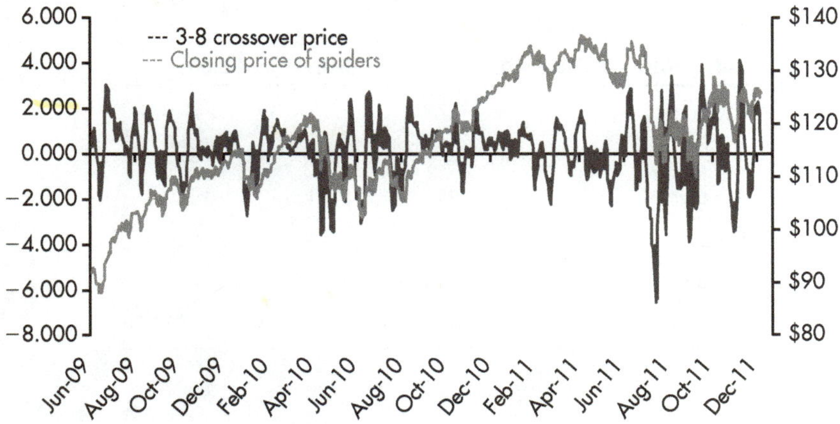

This study, however, focuses on the results of the spiders when they sit above the upper (2.000) boundary. Although it does not offer many plays, when they do break above this watermark, does this cultivate investor indecisiveness, and when uncertainty reigns, is it likely to take these 500 companies down because traders are betting against existing momentum?

Figure 10.2 clearly shows resistance at the upper boundary, making it tempting to take a short position at a price slightly above 2.000; therefore, we want to put this assumption to the test by running the analysis.

This analysis differs from earlier studies because it evaluates three response variables. We normally make the next trading day our performance measure, but this study examines the summary price of the spiders one, three, and eight trading days after the 3-8 daily SMA finishes the trading day above 2.000.

In this study, we are investigating the spiders from June 26, 2009, to December 30, 2011; findings appear in Table 10.4.

When comparing a 3-day against an 8-day moving average, a positive crossover score indicates recent buying pressure.[5]

[5] This is another study in which we begin our analysis early, but collect our numbers at a later date. In other words, we officially report our results from June 26, 2009; however, in order to run an 8-day SMA, it requires us to use June 16, 2009, as the unofficial starting date. And, since a score above the upper boundary comes four days before the final trading day of 2011, the final n × 8 summary does not contain the five daily change scores arriving in 2012.

TABLE 10.4 This study examines three different daily pricing outcomes, the next day (n × 1), the sum of the next three days (n × 3) and the sum of the next eight days (n × 8), after the crossover difference between a 3-day SMA minus an 8-day SMA penetrates above the +2.000 boundary.

3-day SMA – 8-day SMA	**Crossover > +2.00**		
Crossover	n × 1	n × 3	n × 8
Trades	47	47	47
Advance	25	21	21
Decline	22	26	26
Average	–$0.3879	–$0.7343	–$0.6145
Summary	–$18.23	–$34.51	–$28.90

After skyrocketing to above 2.000, the spiders trading in this bullish crossover setting were incapable of sustaining a strong price run. On the ensuing day, this frothy run was starting to overflow; this can be seen by its average loss of $0.3879. However, the biggest drop came from summing the scores of the subsequent three days (a loss of $0.7343 APT).

After generating such an excessive crossover score, this negative reaction was felt for eight days (Table 10.5). It is not uncommon for a crossover score to produce consecutive days over the upper boundary; therefore, the summary for three (n × 3) and eight (n × 8) days contain duplicate summary scores. As a result of this, you are increasing your bet each day the spiders reside over +2.00.

This study continues with an evaluation of the same response variables; however, it evaluates the summary performance of the spiders, one, three, and eight trading days after the 3-8 daily SMA penetrates below the −2.000 mark.

The chartist can see many developing patterns across these 635 trading days, but what is appealing to contrarians is when the spiders break down below a supporting price of −2.000. In making this the basis of our next study (see Table 10.6), we are questioning the performance of the spiders after finishing the day below this lower boundary.

This excessively bearish run below the lower boundary offers the contrarian some rewarding possibilities. Since the three daily settings exhibit an

TABLE 10.5 The gray shade consists of those days in the upper (2.000) boundary. The summary calculation for these days often contains duplicate dates.

Date	Close	Price Change	3-day SMA	8-day SMA	Crossover	n × 1	n × 3	n × 8
12/19/2011	120.29	–1.30	121.357	122.884	–1.527			
12/16/2011	121.59	–.60	121.840	123.689	–1.849			
12/15/2011	122.19	.45	122.327	124.273	–1.946			
12/14/2011	121.74	–1.31	123.000	124.776	–1.776			
12/13/2011	123.05	–1.16	124.437	125.166	–0.730			
12/12/2011	124.21	–1.84	124.737	125.406	–0.670			
12/09/2011	126.05	2.10	125.577	125.504	0.073			
12/08/2011	123.95	–2.78	125.647	124.754	0.893			
12/07/2011	126.73	.47	126.403	124.224	2.180	–2.78	–2.52	–6.44
12/06/2011	126.26	.04	125.780	122.925	2.855	.47	–.21	–4.67
12/05/2011	126.22	1.36	125.350	121.713	3.637	.04	–2.27	–4.03
12/02/2011	124.86	–.11	124.940	120.834	4.106	1.36	1.87	–3.12
12/01/2011	124.97	–.02	123.337	120.184	3.153	–.11	1.29	–1.92

n × 3 uses a 3-day summary score for the subsequent 3 trading days.
n × 3 for 12/07/2011 = –$2.52 =SUM(12/08 + 12/09 + 12/12)
n × 3 for 12/06/2011 = –$0.21 =SUM(12/07 + 12/08 + 12/09)
n × 3 for 12/05/2011 = –$2.27 =SUM(12/06 + 12/07 + 12/08)

TABLE 10.6 When the spiders sit below the lower boundary (a 3-8 SMA crossover score below −2.000), the daily price change summary for the next day (n × 1), next three days (n × 3) and the next eight days (n × 8) recovers smartly.

3-day SMA – 8-day SMA	Crossover < −2.00		
Crossover	n × 1	n × 3	n × 8
Trades	47	47	47
Advance	24	29	26
Decline	23	18	21
Average	$0.2919	$0.7272	$0.8947
Summary	$13.72	$34.18	$42.05

FIGURE 10.3 The closing price of the cues displays a landscape with a varied terrain.

opposite reaction, this involves taking a position against downward momentum. The comeback progressively gains strength, as this contrarian system produces generous results over the next eight days.

Contrasting Styles

In this study, we bring back the =RANK function. This daily evaluation compares the closing price of the cues over 30 trading days.

This study (Figure 10.3) contains 400 trading days and runs from April 9, 2010, until November 4, 2011.

This 400-day closing price chart of the cues displays increasing volatility. After a rocky start, this index fund runs uphill. Thereafter, it stays in a sideways trading pattern, while holding at a price of $54, before rising again in its third futile attempt to surpass a price of $60. But this time, the cues break down below support. In doing so, it misled everyone who thought a short position was the better play, as it fell to an intraday price of $49.99, but kept vacillating until finally heading back toward resistance.

Positioning Pieces

The =RANK function is very flexible. It does not have to rank every score in your worksheet; it can perform a "rolling" ranking, which confines your analysis to a specific duration. In this investigation, we are running an ascending rank of the cues (ticker: QQQ) on its closing price. Although the study consists of 400 trading days, the rank function includes an evaluation of 30 consecutive trading days.[6]

After assigning an ascending ranking (a rank of 1 is the highest closing price; 30 is the lowest closing price) of the previous 30 trading days, what performs best?

Interestingly, we are evaluating a comparison of those rankings at the highest or lowest extremes. Of course, the best performance could come from those scores stuck in the middle of the pack; therefore, this study consists of three categories of scores with different rankings:

1 to 5 ranking
11 to 20 ranking
26 to 30 ranking

After ranking the closing price of the past 30 trading days of the cues, this study examines the following day's daily performance for each of the three ranking categories.

In addition to rating the three categories by their performance scores, we have to equate them to the advance in the cues over 400 trading days from April 9, 2010, to November 4, 2011. Tables 10.7 and 10.8 demonstrate the mechanics for evaluating these three categories.

The findings for each category for these 400 trading days are in Table 10.9.

A ranking of 11 to 20 was the best category, as evidenced by its 47-37 record and its ability to collect $7.60 of the $9.06 advance in the cues.

Once you rank the scores, you get an understanding of the recent positioning of an instrument's closing price. This is helpful because many indicators produce a trading signal without giving you information on the closing price in comparison to its pricing history.

---

[6] As in other studies, sometimes it is necessary to increase the days in your analysis to run certain indicators (such as a 10-day moving average). In order to rank the days from 371 to 400, we have to use additional days. For instance, April 9, 2010, is the starting day; for you to give it a rank of 30 days, you have to go back to include another 29 trading days.

TABLE 10.7 Those dates not qualifying in this study do not receive a performance score; however, Nov 3, 2011 is within the "1 to 5" category and the two earlier dates are in the "11 to 20" category.

	A	B	C	D	E	F	G
1	**Date**	**Close**	**Price Change**	**30-Day Ranking**	**Rank 1 to 5**	**Rank 11 to 20**	**Rank 26 to 30**
2	11/04/11	57.80	–.30	8			
3	11/03/11	58.10	1.18	5	–0.30		
4	11/02/11	56.92	.48	12		1.18	
5	11/01/11	56.44	–1.51	15		0.48	
6	10/31/11	57.95	–.99	6			

TABLE 10.8 The outside rankings use the =IF statement, whereas, the Rank 11 to 20 category uses a =IF(AND) statement.

Date	Close	PC	Ranking	Rank 1 to 5	Rank 11 to 20	Rank 26 to 30
11/04/11	57.80	=B2-B3	=RANK(B2, B2:B31)			
11/03/11	58.10	=B3-B4	=RANK(B3, B3:B32)	=IF(D3<=5, C2,"")	=IF(AND (D3 > 10, D3<21),C2,"")	=IF (D3>=25, C2,"")
11/02/11	56.92	=B4-B5	=RANK(B4, B4:B33)	=IF(D4<=5, C3,"")	=IF(AND (D4 > 10, D4<21),C3,"")	=IF (D4>=25, C3,"")
11/01/11	56.44	=B5-B6	=RANK(B5, B5:B34)	=IF(D5<=5, C4,"")	=IF(AND (D5 > 10, D5<21),C4,"")	=IF (D5>=25, C4,"")
10/31/11	57.95	=B6-B7	=RANK(B6, B6:B35)	=IF(D6<=5, C5,"")	=IF(AND (D6 > 10, D6<21),C5,"")	=IF (D6>=25, C5,"")
10/30/11	58.94	=B7-B8	=RANK(B7, B7:B36)	=IF(D7<=5, C6,"")	=IF(AND (D7 > 10, D7<21),C6,"")	=IF (D7>=25, C6,"")

TABLE 10.9 The poorest records belong to the two outlying categories. A modest ranking generates the most success.

	30-Day Ranking of the Cues			
	1 to 5	**11 to 20**	**26 to 30**	**Total**
Trades	149	84	74	400
Advance	83	47	35	216
Decline	65	37	38	182
Average	.0058	.0905	.0157	.0227
Summary	\$0.87	\$7.60	\$1.16	\$9.06

Trading Bands

Since we are evaluating an index fund's performance in respect to its recent price, a discussion on support and resistance (SAR) is necessary. Trading bands are lines drawn above as well as below the existing price. Lines drawn above represent price resistance (Figure 10.4); lines drawn below represent price support (Figure 10.5).[7]

The most common trading strategies occur when these bands are in the vicinity of resistance:

1. A breakout from the upper band (resistance)—take a long position as you follow the current direction of rising prices.

FIGURE 10.4 The three combinations of playing the upper band.

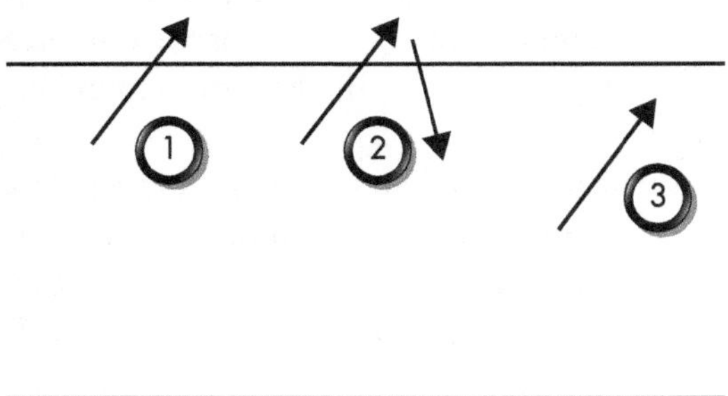

[7] Additional information on resistance can be found in the following articles: Anthony Trongone, "Caution: Resistance Ahead," eSignal.com (May 25, 2012); Anthony Trongone, "Rubbing against Resistance," eSignal.com (June 1, 2012); Anthony Trongone, "Warning: Bear Activity," *Technical Analysis of Stocks & Commodities* (September 2012).

FIGURE 10.5 The three combinations for playing the lower band.

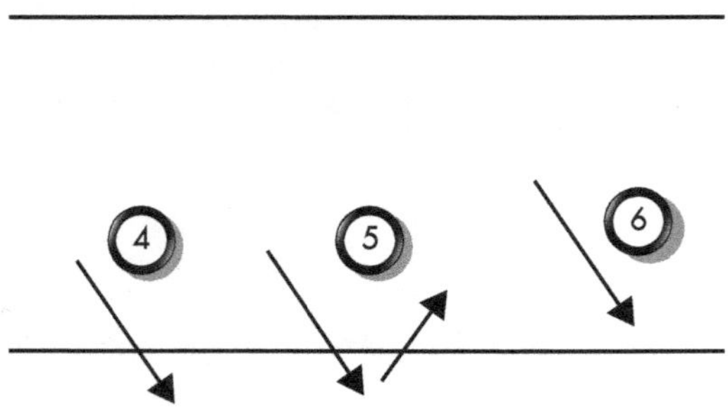

2. A breakout above the upper band, but the instrument is unable to sustain this price momentum, the result is that it breaks back down—take a short position with the expectation that prices will sustain this downward direction.
3. Prices run toward the upper band, but the expectation is for a turnaround before the price of this instrument touches it—take a short position with the expectation of lower prices as this instrument is unable to break past resistance.

The most common trading strategies occur when these bands are in the vicinity of support:

1. Price penetration below the lower band (support)—take a short position with the continued expectation of falling prices.
2. A breakout below the lower band, but the instrument is unable to sustain this price momentum, the result is that it breaks back above support—take a long position with the expectation prices will sustain this upward direction.
3. Prices run toward the lower band, but the expectation is for a turnaround before the price of this instrument touches it—take a long position with the expectation of higher prices, as this instrument is unable to penetrate below support.

Technicians refer to these lines as envelopes because they enclose the current price of an instrument with drawn lines. The one above the existing price acts as resistance; the other, below, functions as support. These envelopes are indicative of a trading strategy in which we take an opposite position as prices approach these drawn boundaries.

Another popular approach is to use them as a breakaway strategy for pricing volatility. For example, some bands work by placing the upper band one standard deviation above price, whereas they anchor the lower line one standard deviation below the existing price.

Although there are many trading strategies, intraday traders encounter the same common weakness when they apply these indicators: They do not draw these lines from market volatility within the same intraday period, but calculate this moving average from earlier intraday periods. Common sense tells us there is less volatility before the opening bell; therefore, the bands are in a narrow trading range. Once the bell rings, pricing volatility automatically increases, which produces explosive price swings in an environment of artificially tight bands; this generates excessive trading action.

After the opening bell these wild price swings eventually widen the bands, but as the morning progresses market activity begins to slow down; this creates mild price swings in a wide trading band, which impedes trading action.

In the afternoon the window of opportunity narrows; that is, until we confront an increase in activity in the final hour of trading when the market experiences more pricing volatility. When we encounter this situation, it expands the width of these bands, but after the closing bell activity comes to a halt, making it difficult to take a position because the bands are wide, but price swings are relatively mild.

Seen from this perspective, it is artificially creating more or fewer trading prospects. Therefore, when using these banding strategies, I suggest taking a more inclusive approach by comparing volatility within the same time frame; that is, if you are trading in the 09:30 to 10:30 hour, use this hour in your analysis to make comparisons. Although most of your focus should be on the recent pricing volatility during the hour under investigation, if you prefer to use an earlier setting, be sure to make the necessary modifications.[8]

Pullbacks in Price

Pullbacks in price are powerful; they often produce an explosive counterreaction. They frequently show us success, but when they fail to work they can quickly take us to our emotional dark side. The basis of playing these systems appears to be conceptually comparable for prices moving in either direction; however, holding on to this perception can be very costly.

[8] Anthony Trongone, "Using Momentum Indicators in a Free-Falling Market," Interactive Data Corp., www.esignal.com (February 6, 2009).

Using a short-term parameter, such as a 3-day SMA, affords more activity, but this action occurs in a frenzied trading environment (Figure 10.6). It can be a workable strategy, but impossible for investors who do not have the discipline to retain their emotional equanimity when confronting a choppy market. When prices are bouncing around, it produces a trading atmosphere that requires a rapid execution of your orders.

The 50-day SMA is more conducive for most investors, as it requires less trading activity (see Figure 10.7).

FIGURE 10.6 A 3-day SMA has plenty of noise. It allows more activity, but in this environment, it elicits more emotionally driven trading.

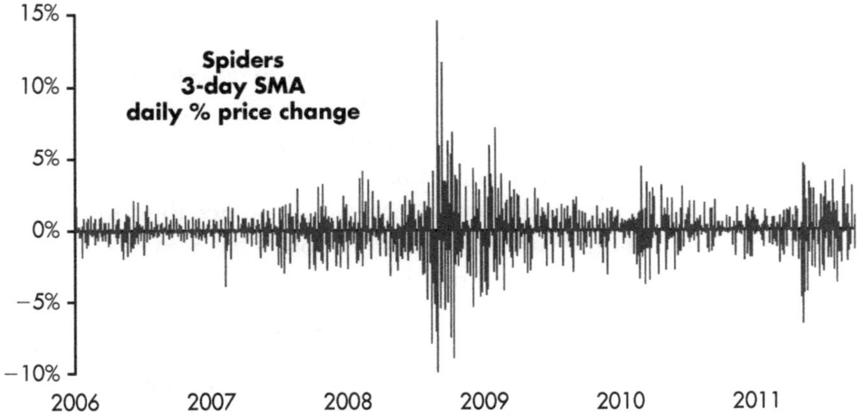

FIGURE 10.7 A 50-day moving average of the spiders' percentage daily price change provides more transparency. An opportunity appears to exist after prices fall below −0.25 percent.

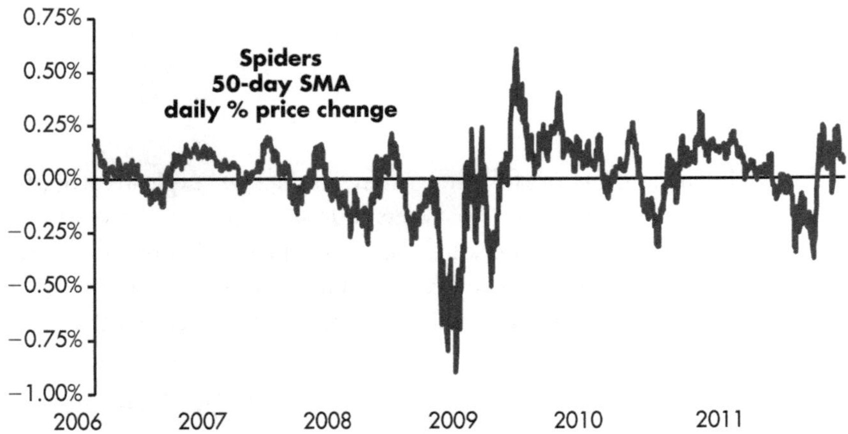

In looking at this line chart of a 50-day SMA, a long position, after residing below −0.25 percent, appears to be a profitable strategy. The question is, when do you take your profits or accept your losses?

An exit strategy, as important as it is, receives less attention in comparison to entering a position. In this study, this process is simplified because it requires you to offset a long position three trading days after buying the spiders.

Naturally, many of these trading plays stack together. For instance, once the spiders achieve this downward distinction, they may suffer a series of declines. When confronting a continuous run of days below −0.25 percent (buy signal), despite the long 2008 downturn, this study encourages you to take another long position.

The question is after the 50-day SMA penetrates below −0.25 percent, how do the spiders perform over the following three trading days?

We begin this study on January 3, 2006; it runs 1,511 trading days, ending on December 30, 2011.

The 50-day simple moving average of the closing price of the spiders becomes our predictor variable; once the trading signal is below −0.25 percent, it becomes our response variable. You take a long position in the spiders at the close of the trading day. You hold this long position for three trading days, promptly selling it at its closing price (see Table 10.10).

Since F4 is blank, traders take no action. F5 has a 1 in its cell value, which means we are taking a long position for the three ensuing days. The sum of these three days is reported in cell G5 ($5.16 = 2.07 + −0.78 + 3.87).

TABLE 10.10 The 50-day SMA of the spiders falls below −0.25 percent, this releases a buy signal. The response variable is the value of holding this long position over the next three trading days.

	A	B	C	D	E	F	G
1	**Date**	**Close**	**$ Change**	**% Change**	**50-Day SMA**	**–0.0025**	**3-Day Sum**
2	10/10/2011	119.58	3.87	0.033	–0.0013		
3	10/07/2011	115.71	–0.78	–0.007	–0.0021		
4	10/06/2011	116.49	2.07	0.018	–0.0020		
5	10/05/2011	114.42	2.08	0.019	–0.0028	1	5.16
6	10/04/2011	112.34	2.41	0.022	–0.0032	1	3.37
7	10/03/2011	109.93	–3.22	–0.028	–0.0038	1	6.56
8	09/30/2011	113.15	–2.90	–0.025	-0.0032	1	1.27

In order to compute this 3-day price change, we apply a formula that combines two functions. You can accomplish this by using the IF statement, which confines your selection to (F5 = 1). Providing this statement is *true*, you want the equation to sum the next three trading days; if it is *false*, leave this cell empty.

=IF(F5 = 1, SUM(C2:C4),"")

$(3.87 + -0.78 + 2.07) = 5.16$

The results of this equation can be seen over this extensive study. Most of the activity occurs in the winter of 2008 (Figure 10.8).

There are long stretches of inactivity, but when the system is active, the plays have a tendency to come fast and furious. Obviously, when there are consistently long downturns there is a disadvantage in trading this system. Putting aside these drawbacks, this system is a good one (the results are in Table 10.11), but be on the lookout for bear traps.

A respectable winning percentage with a remarkable \$0.63 APT is not shabby. Certainly, despite the impact of bear footprints, this system had its profitable moments. More importantly, this statistical design allowed us to introduce a two-function statement.

The downside of using this system occurs when equities enter into negative territory; in this situation you can take a beating. These precipitous drops are unforgiving, as they can descend rapidly into unforeseen territory; making it difficult to escape unscathed, both financially and emotionally.

FIGURE 10.8 Generally a profitable 3-day run, this strategy takes a beating during the bear market.

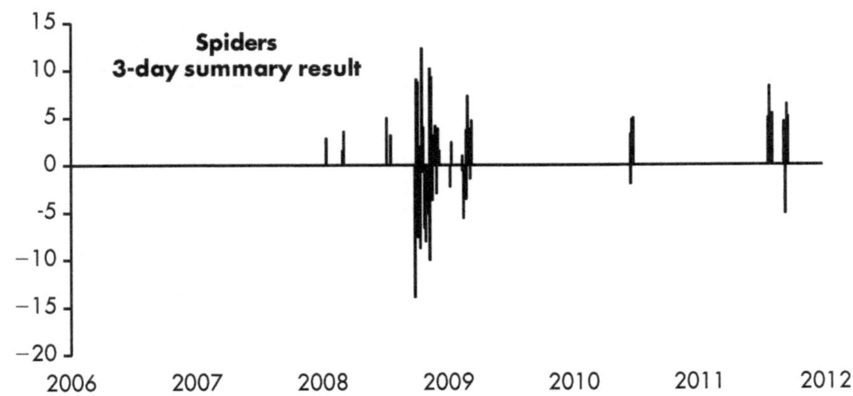

TABLE 10.11 Some notable numbers appear when summing these 94 long positions. With 1 play for every 16 trading days, this is a negative, but an impressive \$0.63 APT profit is worth the wait.

3-Day Summary Score of a Long Position in the Spiders	
Trading Days	1,511
Trades	94
Advance	55
Decline	39
Win %	.585
Average	0.6302
Summary	\$59.24

Intraday Range

This study investigates the regular trading session of the spiders. More specifically, it evaluates the intraday price swings from its closing price.

The definitions for this study pertain to the intraday prices when trading the spiders during the day session.

H	indicates highest intraday price
L	indicates lowest intraday price
PM	represents the afternoon closing price

$$\text{H} - \text{PM} = \text{highest price} - \text{close}$$

After attaining its highest price, a drop in the spiders leaves a wide space between its highest – closing price, this is indicative of a large positive number; whereas, a small positive number indicates less spacing between these two intraday prices.

$$\text{PM} - \text{L} = \text{closing price} - \text{lowest price}$$

When the closing price rises far from its lowest price, it produces a large positive number; conversely, a small positive number occurs when the closing price stays in the vicinity of its lowest price of the trading day.

We want to assess the daily performance of the spiders when the $\text{H} - \text{PM} > (\text{L} - \text{PM} + \$0.50)$.

TABLE 10.12 This worksheet produces vital information. It includes the =IF statement for the response variable.

Date	Op	Hi	Lw	Cl	Pc	H – PM	PM – L	H – PM > (PM – L + $0.50)
11/08/2011	126.92	128.02	125.71	127.88	1.62	.14	2.17	
11/07/2011	125.39	126.39	124.20	126.26	0.78	.13	2.06	
11/04/2011	125.23	125.70	124.01	125.48	–0.77	.22	1.47	
11/03/2011	125.27	126.50	123.60	126.25	2.26	.25	2.65	
11/02/2011	123.83	124.40	122.79	123.99	1.99	.41	1.20	
11/01/2011	122.03	123.51	121.52	122.00	–3.50	1.51	.48	1.99
10/31/2011	127.16	127.26	125.32	125.50	–3.10	1.76	.18	–3.50
10/28/2011	128.00	128.85	127.80	128.60	–0.03	.25	.80	
10/27/2011	127.63	129.42	125.96	128.63	4.33	.79	2.67	

This investigation begins on June 1, 2010, and continues until December 30, 2011. Its contributory variable is H – PM > (PM – L + $0.50).[9] Its response variable is the daily price change difference in the spiders when comparing two consecutive trading days.

The research design for constructing this system can be seen in Table 10.12 (close t_{-0} – close t_{-1}).

When the H – PM is > $0.50 above the PM – L, there was a meaningful performance difference between the two categories (Figure 10.9). Although the winning percentages were similar, the average return was superior. When this occurs, it is instructive to diagram the daily results.

This strategy (H – PM > (PM – L + $0.50)), despite fewer trading opportunities, is worth chasing considering its $29.50 profit in 114 trades (Table 10.13). On the flipside, the earnings resulting from a downward vertical move (H – PM < (PM – L + $0.50)) were only mildly profitable; therefore, it does not make the grade as a restrictive trading system.

The increase in the frequency of trading opportunities found at the conclusion of Figure 10.9 is often a symptom of a changing landscape. Until we receive these numbers, we cannot run an analysis; therefore, the outcome remains speculative.

[9] Experiment with using $0.50 in the equation H – PM < (PM – L + $0.50); its effectiveness will vary according to the price of the spiders and market volatility, as well as many other factors. Furthermore, when you encounter large fluctuations in price, assign a percentage score to replace a fixed $ amount.

TABLE 10.13 This shows the results H – PM > (PM – L + \$0.50), as well as the remaining trading days.

Spiders	H – PM > (PM – L + \$0.50)	H – PM < (PM – L + \$0.50)
Trades	114	288
Advance	62	152
Decline	51	136
Win %	.543	.528
Average	\$0.259	–\$0.040
Summary	\$29.50	–\$11.53

FIGURE 10.9 The black lines represent the H − PM > (PM − L + \$0.50); whereas, the gray lines are indicative of the H − PM < (PM − L + \$0.50).

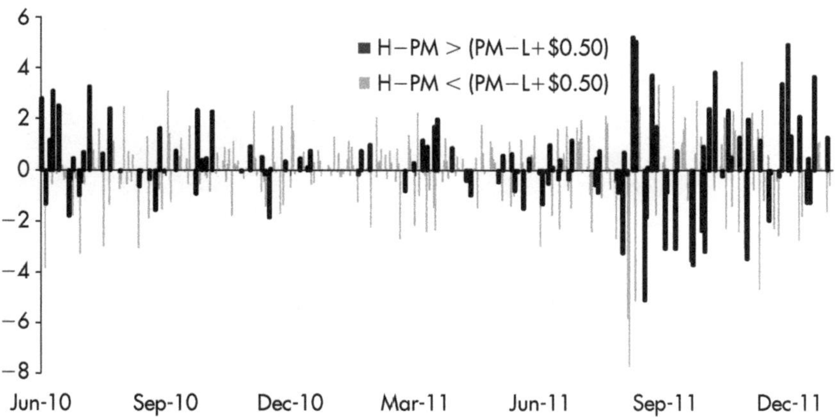

Summary

A comparison of momentum strategies going against the existing pattern does offer some interesting contradictions. Which one is the better strategy? The current trading environment is often the best metric for making this distinction. The natural reaction is to follow pricing momentum, by aggressively attacking excessive strength; however, many of these studies show how you can get stung by observing the activity of crowds without knowing how the market functions when there is excessive volatility.

CHAPTER 11

Restrictive Trading Systems

It is better to create than to learn! Creating is the essence of life.

—Julius Caesar

This chapter offers a more introspective examination of restrictive trading systems. Since they have constrictive trading parameters, they do not produce everyday plays. Despite less frequency, the beauty of playing these systems lies in their impressive winning percentage.

Although remaining inactive when the market is sprouting wings is not easy, the good news is that even with fewer prospects, as your experience grows, you will uncover more of these highly dependable plays to supplement your trading strategy.[1]

While many systems require an analysis of the current environment, these restrictive systems do not have this requirement because their trading parameters are fixed. For example, in taking a long position when the spiders close the regular session finishing within a few pennies from their lowest price of the day, we do not have to concern ourselves with current pricing indicators, spikes in trading volume or other contributory variables. We are simply looking to see if the closing price of the spiders is within $0.08 of its lowest price.

[1] Anthony Trongone, "Trading When Less Is More," *Technical Analysis of Stocks & Commodities* (February 2004).

Going with Momentum

One of the most intrinsically rewarding trading moments comes when you start the day with a relatively light position; as the day continues, the market stumbles badly, but after falling to its lowest point of the day, you begin buying shares. Moments later, the market reverses direction, as we watch the price change column on our trading screen switch from red to green.

After a devastating loss, many day traders can make a persuasive argument for taking a long position. It appears to be an alluring play, but is it worth putting our greenbacks to work? After all, picking bottoms is not easy, but perhaps we can be more successful if we wait until early morning volatility begins to fade.

Not everyone performs best in the morning hours; some investors would be better waiting until later in the day. Analogous to horses bolting from the starting gate, for many it is best to implement your decision after they begin jockeying for position as they go into the first turn; once they are on the backstretch, the dust settles, making it easier to predict the finish of the race.[2] Similarly, this study, which has a strong percentage of success, has you taking a position after early-morning volatility subsides by placing either a buy stop or sell stop order at or slightly after 11:00.

In looking at how the spiders react after this instrument runs above its 11:00 price, is it better to run with or against momentum? In going with momentum, in order to place an order without being at your trading platform, we would have to place a buy stop order; conversely to go against momentum, we would place a limit order to sell (top half of Figure 11.1).

FIGURE 11.1 There are two divergent paths for our investigation from the 11:00 price.

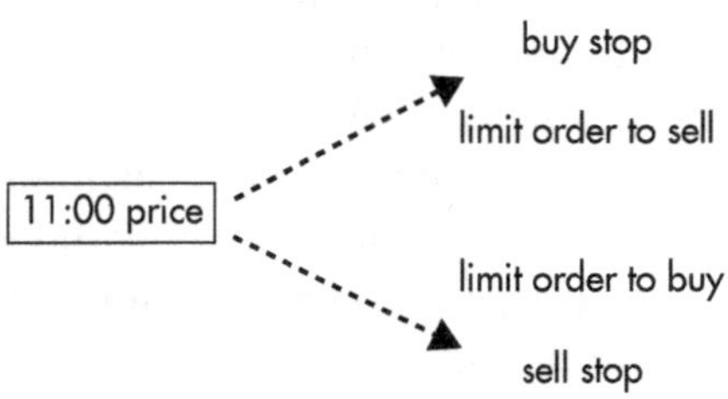

[2] Anthony Trongone, "Take Your Profits or Let It Ride," *Technical Analysis of Stocks & Commodities* (August 2008): 22–28.

The figure introduces a study using the 11:00 price as a springboard to taking a trading position in the equities market. As prices advance, a sell position can be a profitable play, but if they retain their upward path, does it become more difficult for bears to turn against this rising tide of bullish sentiment?

On the other hand, when the spiders make a considerable move below the 11:00 price, is taking a position against downside momentum a good play? That is, as prices slip past a certain point, do bears come to dominate afternoon action? Both these assumptions seem plausible, but until we put them through the paces of an analysis, take them as conjecture—not fact!

I begin this analysis with the buy side of this combination, by taking a long position with a buy-stop order when the price advances three-quarters of a percent above the 11:00 price.

What action would you take if the spiders rise 0.75 percent from the 11:00 price—is it better to take a long or short position? More specifically, we are looking for this advance to occur between 11:00 and 16:00 in the trading day. The entry point of taking either position comes with a buy stop order in place shortly after 11:00.

In this system, without the price rising to your entry position, there is no fill. Providing that the spiders advance to this price, we are questioning the benefit of taking a long or short position. By testing the long position at a price 0.75 percent above the 11:00 hour, the performance results are the opposite of taking a short position.[3]

Besides this system's effectiveness, after producing the results, there is the advantage of not doing any more analysis; simply enter two orders at a price above and below the 11:00 price.[4] Since you are trading on a strong move away from this price, you do not have the pressure of placing your position until after 11:00, but definitely do it before it reaches above or below your target price.

When placing a buy-stop order you are buying shares long as the price rises above its existing price. If the order fills, you want the spiders to keep rising.

With the 11:00 price of the spiders at $100, you would place a buy stop order at $100.75.

---

[3] If the 11:00 price of the spiders is at $100, a buy occurs at $100.75. If the market closes at $101.75, a buy position gives you a $1.00 profit, whereas, taking a short position at $100.75, gives you a $1.00 loss.

[4] As with all systems, once it is in place, you still have to monitor its results, but since it is a restrictive system, the tracking of your systems performance occurs infrequently.

The calculation for taking a long position when a stock is at a price of \$100 at 11:00 hours:

$$= 100 \times 1.0075$$
$$= 100 \times (100 \times 0.75\%) = \$100.75$$

Providing the price reaches your buy-stop order, you would be entering into a long position at \$100.75.[5]

Before starting the process of executing any trades, always seek more information. Would it strengthen your conviction if you knew the performance of the spiders from 11:00 until 16:00 over these 1,379 trading days?

This exchange-traded fund (ETF) began trading on April 20, 2006, at an 11:00 price of \$131.13. On October 7, 2011, its 16:00 price stood at \$115.69. Despite this loss, our objective is to produce profitable results by taking a long position in a losing environment.

Since the focus of this study is on a percentage score away from the 11:00 price, the calculation of outlying scores is a necessary requirement (Table 11.1).

In comparison to the 1,379 trading days, the 11:00 to 16:00 summary price change took a mild spill (–\$7.11). This slight loss becomes our

TABLE 11.1 The results of trading the spiders from 11:00 until 16:00 reveal a \$7.11 decline with a winning percentage at 0.518.[6]

Trading Range: 11:00 to 16:00, 4/20/2006 to 10/07/2011	
10th percentile	–1.086%
15th percentile	–0.788%
85th percentile	0.767%
90th percentile	0.970%
Sum	–\$7.11
Mean score	–0.0052
Stdev	1.130
Record: 715-653-11	

[5] Although these stop orders do not give this exact price, we are making this assumption when doing our calculations.

[6] Setting our stop orders at ± 0.75 percent from the 11:00 price accounts for approximately 15 percent of our negative (15th percentile = −0.788 percent) and positive (85th percentile = 0.767 percent) outlying scores.

benchmark for success, with a long position we want to improve on this average per trade (APT) profit. Figure 11.2 displays the daily price movements of the spiders during these five hours.

We are subjecting our analysis to different price settings, such as the sizeable setback, as well as the long upward run (2009 to 2011) in the spiders. Therefore, once we assess the efficacy of this strategy, it is necessary to draw a line chart demonstrating a running summary of this system's performance.

With such an extensive setting, always run an analysis of the more recent trading activity. In this case, we are comparing the findings of 1,378 days with the final 100 days of this study (Table 11.2).

FIGURE 11.2 The closing price of the spiders displays some diverse trading settings. A sharp downward movement at the conclusion of this study (100 trading days) did not prevent this system from establishing a 21-8 winning record with $6.95 in profits.

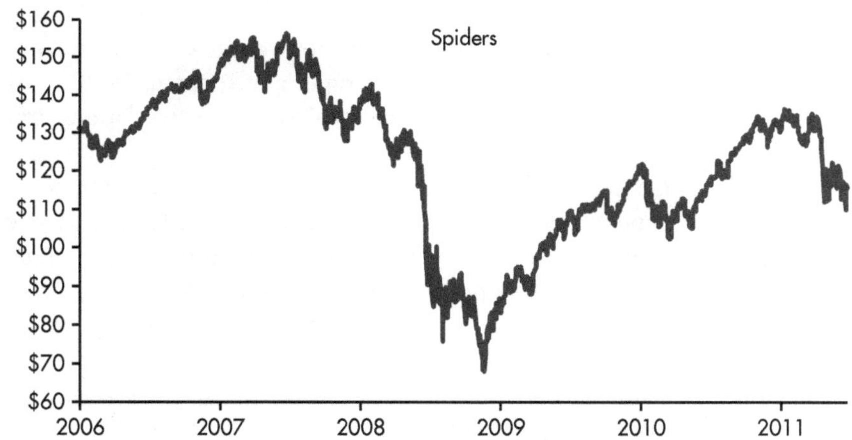

TABLE 11.2 Given this negative trading environment, this was a remarkable run, bagging $44.28 in profits; especially striking was its 21-8 record with a $0.24 APT return at the conclusion of this study.

1,378 Trading Days	> 0.75 Percent 11:00 Price	Previous 100 Trading Days
Advance	198	21
Decline	134	8
Win Percentage	0.596	0.724
Summary	$44.28	$6.95
Average	$0.133	$0.240

Despite qualifying as a restrictive system, we were able to produce 332 trades in 1,379 days (24 percent trading activity).

A $44.28 return was admirable, but how has this system done lately? In the concluding 100 days, a 1,000-share long position gave the momentum investor a return of $6,950. Certainly, when you consider the acute downward descent during these 100 days, these results become even more remarkable.

A line chart (Figure 11.3) of the running performance of this three-quarter system is instructive because it shows the flat line, a long upward trending pattern, and a dampening of this preexisting trendline along with another burst of rising energy in 2011.

This clearly shows how long some systems take before they begin to catch fire. Remarkably, most of its success comes during a devastating 2008 bear market, but when the spiders recover, this system runs along a flat line for two years, finally, showing another upturn after a slight downturn.

There are many surprises here; for instance, depending on when you run your analysis, even a successful system will not always give us a winning performance on a steady basis. Additionally, it shows an inverse performance between these two summary charts; this was especially apparent in 2008. It demonstrates that without performing an analysis these revelations can remain buried beneath the surface.

If the price of the spiders falls 0.75 percent from its 11:00 price, is it better to take a long or short position? More specifically, we are looking for this decline to occur between 11:00 and 16:00 in the trading day. The entry point of taking either position comes with a sell-stop order in place shortly after 11:00.

FIGURE 11.3 A running summary after taking a long position in the spiders demonstrates a very bumpy ride before shifting into overdrive.

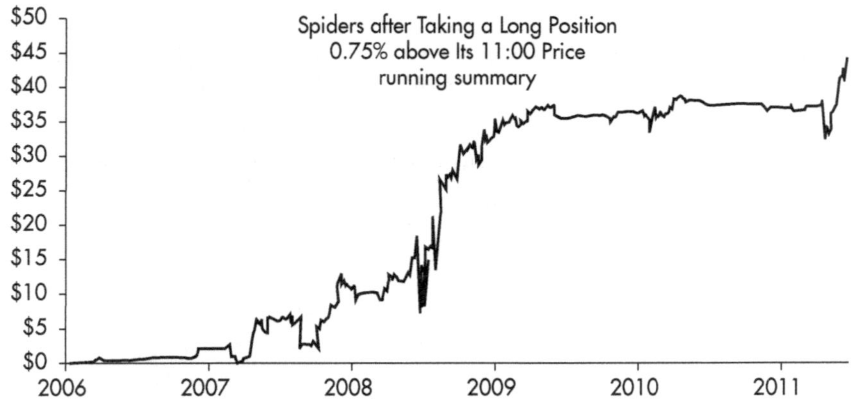

TABLE 11.3 A short position was able to produce favorable, but anemic results.

1,378 Trading Days	< −0.75 Percent 11:00 Price	Previous 100 Trading Days
Advance	195	20
Decline	214	19
Win Percentage	0.477	0.513
Summary	–13.60	–2.22
Average	–$0.033	–$0.057

When placing a sell-stop order you are selling shares short at a price below its existing price. Providing the order fills, you want prices to keep falling below your sell-stop order.

The calculation for taking a short position when a stock is at a price of $100 at 11:00 hours:

=100 × .9925 $99.25
=100 – (100 × 0.75%) $99.25

With the 11:00 price of the spiders at $100, you would place a sell-stop order at $99.25.

With a negative return, we would expect a short position to outperform its counterpart. But again, without running the analysis, it is pure speculation. Table 11.3 provides the results for taking a short position 0.75 percent below the 11:00 price.

Considering the $7.11 loss over 1,379 trading days, a short position at 0.75 percent below the 11:00 price does not appear to be a productive strategy. Of course, a running summary (Figure 11.4) provides a more informative perspective of this system's long-term performance.

Although a short position using this strategy was unimpressive, its best performance came during the 2009 to 2011 bullish backdrop. Apparently, when in a bull market, on a bad day, traders are more likely to take their winnings; this forces the price of the spiders to sustain its southerly direction.[7]

Despite these uninspiring results, we still have to continue testing this afternoon strategy. For instance, what if we wait for a stronger downturn

[7] There were 73 days with both sides (i.e., either above 0.75 percent and below 0.75 percent or below 0.75 percent and above 0.75 percent) producing trades during this 11:00 to 16:00 time frame.

FIGURE 11.4 The uniqueness of this system occurs during the bullish market (2009 to 2011); as the spiders run to a price of $140, this system experiences its best short trades.

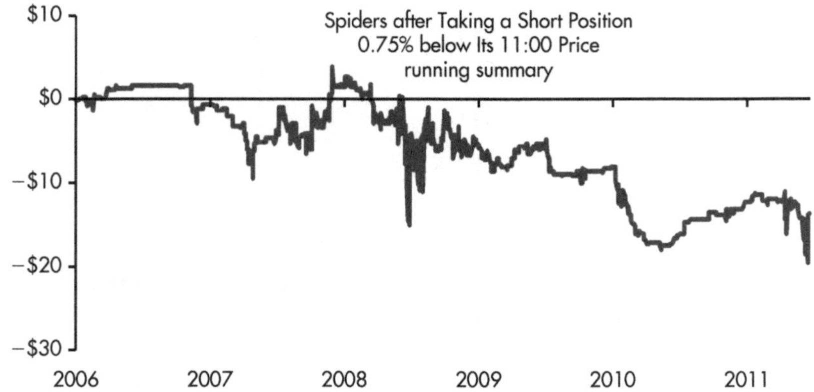

before taking a short position? Actually, too far below the 11:00 price inspired a rally. Suffering a loss of 1.5 percent below the 11:00 price made things worse, resulting in a $21.46 advance in 150 trades ($0.143 APT).[8]

After-Hours Performance

Sometimes, extreme pricing conditions deliver the best prospects; unfortunately, when the basis of a strategy originates from outlying scores, they produce few trading samples. In order to produce enough cases, we have to go back 1,201 days. Unlike other studies, this one focuses on after-hours trading; specifically, between the 16:00 to 18:00 hours from January 3, 2007, until October 7, 2011. During these days the spiders, with a $3.24 advance during these two hours does not appear to merit any action.

After either an advance of 40-plus cents or a decline of 40-plus cents from 16:00 to 18:00, would it be profitable to take a contrarian position at 18:00, offsetting this position at 08:00 hours on the next morning of trading?

[8] Since the percentage move away from the 11:00 price will not happen immediately, it is not necessary for you to be at your trading desk. Although you do want to place these orders before they move either above or below their target price, it still remains a workable system for those who cannot access their trading screens until midday.

FIGURE 11.5 On the basis of a strong advance (left y-axis begins with an advance of > \$0.40) from 16:00 to 18:00 hours, this scattergram displays the results of taking a short position at 18:00 until offsetting it at 08:00.

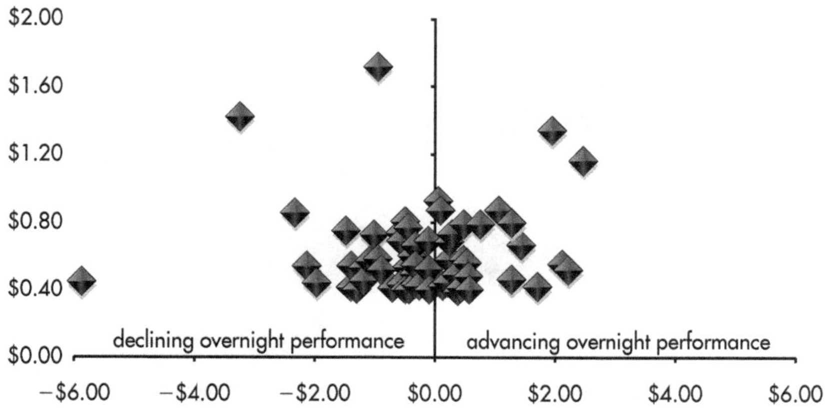

Failure is often a far better teacher; in this case, success (a > \$0.40 gain) and failure (a < \$0.40 loss) are equally persuasive at producing a memorable lesson. After an advance of 40-plus cents in these two hours, the spiders fell \$16.10 in 63 trades, with an APT loss of \$0.256; a short position is a consideration. Meanwhile, after a decline of 40-plus cents, holding a long position in the spiders overnight from 18:00 to 08:00 put \$22.75 in your pocket (an APT gain of \$0.250 in 91 trades).

Within these two hours, there is considerably less trading activity. When the equity markets experience these excessive price swings, it often elicits a strong emotional reaction from traders; therefore, when price swings in this afterhours setting become too aggressive, will they produce different results in the 12-hour overnight session?

We can answer this question by drawing a scattergram displaying two variables. The y-axis (dependent variable) is on the left and the x-axis (independent variable) is on the bottom of this scatter chart.

After an explosive move in the spiders, the scattergram (Figure 11.5) shows the results of taking a short position at 18:00 until 08:00. The left side, which delineates the 35 declining scores, has one outlier responsible for \$5.95 of the \$16.10 in losses. Although the majority of scores cluster together, the bias is toward the negative side.

In looking at the scattergram (Figure 11.6) showing the results of a \$0.40 decline within these two hours, the statistics favor another contrarian position, but it is never easy to take a position that runs against current market momentum, especially when sentiment is so strong.

FIGURE 11.6 The upper axis of this scattergram shows the results of the overnight when taking a long position after a debilitating decline of 40-plus cents. The left axis begins with a loss of $0.40 to its largest setback at –$1.97. This strategy has 57 advancing against 34 declining overnight sessions, a $22.75 profit.

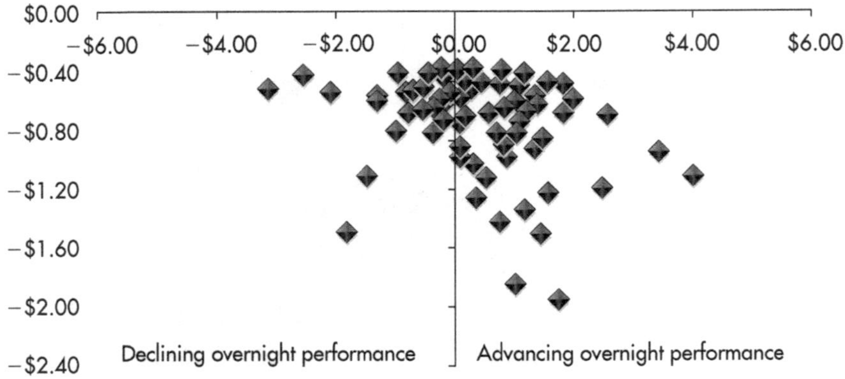

Clearly, the right side of the scattergram dominates the landscape; therefore, the opportunities for profits are available to those day traders willing to take a long position after an extensive loss of 40-plus cents in these two hours. The scattergram displays the winning positions on the right side of breakeven; furthermore, it shows five outlying scores over $2.00 against three under –$2.00.

A loss over $1.00 in these two hours is uncommon. Apparently, after prices came crashing down, investors saw this correction as if it were a one-day fire sale. By the opening bell, the average return was $0.93 with an 11-2 record. Think about this: although the news is negative, surely for the spiders to take such a fall, past news had to be grim; most likely, however, the story creating a doomsday scenario was different from today's. In essence, in these situations, we are always betting against bad news; nevertheless, we are not in the business of making predictions about how egregiously bad the story is in comparison to past downturns. We are simply contrasting the performance of the spiders after a comparable loss. In tracing the history of this condition, considering the 12-5 record, the market was sufficiently resourceful. (Table 11.4 reports the summary findings for this study.)

Table 11.5 sets aside the largest losses in this two-hour evening session.

Given a loss of < $1.20 in the earlier time frame, there was a single setback against nine tries. Together, the $8.79 return was two pennies shy of a $1.00 APT profit. These riveting comebacks appear to be a repetitive investing theme.

TABLE 11.4 The performance statistics of a large price swing in the 16:00 to 18:00 after hour's session. Clearly, a contrarian position was the better play.

1,201 Trading Days Jan 3, 2007 to Oct 7, 2011	18:00 to 08:00 > +$0.40	 < –$0.40
Advance	28	57
Decline	35	34
Win Percentage	.444	.626
Summary	–$16.10	$22.75
Average	–$0.256	$0.250

TABLE 11.5 These were the worst performing scores in the after hours session (16:00 to 18:00). The overnight reaction (18:00 to 08:00) of these dreadful two-hour results can be seen in the right column.

16:00 to 18:00 After Hours	18:00 to 08:00 Overnight Session
–$1.97	$1.74
–$1.87	$1.03
–$1.52	–$1.80
–$1.51	$1.45
–$1.44	$0.77
–$1.37	$1.17
–$1.27	$0.37
–$1.24	$1.57
–$1.22	$2.49

Preventing Disaster

Restrictive trading systems do not always present a trading opportunity; very often they are there to prevent you from taking a position in an unproductive setting. This upcoming study proves how these systems do not always have to focus on success, as your findings can sometimes prevent you from entering a position in a hostile trading environment.

TABLE 11.6 A 5-day SMA using the past five days of the 09:30 to 10:30 hourly setting.

Date	z930	z103	z113	k93_103	k103_113	5-Day SMA
11/29/2011	120.05	120.66	120.51	.61	–.15	.30
11/28/2011	119.54	119.96	119.99	.42	.03	.05
11/25/2011	116.38	117.37	117.27	.99	–.10	–.15
11/23/2011	118.06	117.18	116.88	–.88	–.30	–.34
11/22/2011	119.39	119.77	118.83	.38	–.94	–.14
11/21/2011	120.20	119.54	119.12	–.66	–.42	–.18

z930 opening 09:30 price
z103 opening 10:30 price
z113 opening 11:30 price
k93_103 hourly price change from 09:30 to 10:30
k103_113 hourly price change from 10:30 to 11:30
5-day SMA 5-day simple moving average of the 09:30 to 10:30 hourly price change
=AVERAGE(5 day price change of the k93_103)
11/29/11 = (.61 +.42 +.99 + −.88 +.38) =.30
11/28/11 = (.42 +.99 + −.88 +.38 + −66) =.05

The dates in the study begin on July 24, 2009; it runs until November 29, 2011.

In these 594 trading days, the spiders took a $9.00 spill; consequently, a long position was at a disadvantage. Nevertheless, were there some price components of the earlier hour responsible for the bulk of this loss?

Providing the equities market has a strong 5-day performance in the opening hour of trading (09:30 to 10:30), will this have a positive or negative effect on the next trading hour?

More precisely, the independent variable occurs when the 5-day moving average in the opening hour of trading (09:30 to 10:30) is > $0.30. The dependent variable is the performance in the spiders between the 10:30 to 11:30 trading hour (see Table 11.6).

Within the 10:30 to 11:30 hourly setting (k103_113) the spiders fell $9.00 in 594 days; however, when the 5-day SMA of the 09:30 to 10:30 price was positive. That is, when this momentum indicator was > 0, the 10:30 to 11:30 hour fell $9.89 on 332 occasions.

Most of the damage occurred when this hourly rise was > $0.30. In the 65 days in which the spiders were above this $0.30 mark, the next hourly summary loss was $6.63. Most day traders fixate on the opening hour; if it runs up, they are more likely to jump in, but an early upswing in price can often produce a bear trap.

In the 15 days when this momentum indicator saw a decline of < –.50, the spiders slid \$2.08 (a −\$0.139 APT decline). Considering the small sample, this system probably deserves a pass; nevertheless, knowledge of these results can save you from making a costly mistake.

Why does a 5-day SMA of the earlier hour impact the 10:30 to 11:30 hour? When there is causation without causality, any explanation without a supporting theory will fabricate a specious argument. Sometimes the results of your analysis will produce reliability but it comes without a theoretical basis, that is, prediction can come without explanation, but trading on theory without a proven track record is not going to manifest success. In other words, prediction without understanding trumps a system having the underpinnings of sound academic reasoning but no predictive ability.

Playing a Widening Range

This system is seeking a profitable return by playing the opening hour range (highest – lowest hourly price) of the spiders. The study runs 602 days from July 14, 2009, until November 29, 2011. We begin by evaluating those scores with the widest range price difference between the highest – lowest price in the spiders in the opening hour of the regular trading session.

Release of economic indicators at 10:00 can produce artificially wide price spikes. And with the explosion of trading volume, price movements are often very aggressive.

The =PERCENTILE function can calculate these extremes in trading volume and accomplish the task of profiling a difference in this hourly trading range. Certainly, with this function we can assess the performance among different ranges; however, this study takes aim at those 60 trading days with the widest range.

The =PERCENTILE(range of hourly scores, 0.90) function creates the percentiles with \$0.10 increments when trading the spiders from 09:30 to 10:30. Table 11.7 reports these scores for these 602 trading days.

The 90th percentile = \$1.34.

With 602 trading days (July 14, 2009, to November 29, 2011), we are confining this study to the 60 days generating a range (highest to lowest price) above \$1.34.

On the basis of these (09:30 to 10:30) percentiles, does a profitable opportunity exist in the following hour? More specifically, when the hourly range reaches above \$1.34, does it warrant a long position?

TABLE 11.7 The range of scores for the spiders between 09:30 to 10:30 showcases their percentiles for these 602 trading days.

Spiders: 602 Trading Days	
09:30 to 10:30 Percentile	**Range, Highest to Lowest**
0.10	\$0.45
0.20	\$0.54
0.30	\$0.62
0.40	\$0.70
0.50	\$0.77
0.60	\$0.85
0.70	\$0.96
0.80	\$1.10
0.90	\$1.34

In taking the difference of the highest price from the lowest price, this study investigates those trading days with an hourly range above \$1.34 (90th percentile). This study examines the hourly price change in the spiders from 10:30 to 11:30.

In the 60 days when these conditions were present, the ensuing hour was unable to produce an admirable W-L record (30-29-1), but against a –\$7.84 backdrop (602 trading days) in the 10:30 to 11:30 hour, the \$4.76 return is an impressive turnaround.

This raises another meaningful question. When the 09:30 to 10:30 session trading range is > \$1.34, was there a performance difference in the 10:30 to 11:30 session when there was an opening hour price advance or decline?

The following study examines two conditions. What is the result of trading in the 09:30 to 10:30 hour with a (highest to lowest) range > \$1.34, when the price change for the spiders is either positive or negative?

The 90th percentile = highest – lowest price for the spiders during these 602 trading days was \$1.34; therefore, we are running the analysis on the basis of the following conditions:

09:30 to 10:30 range > \$1.34 AND 09:30 price > 10:30 price
09:30 to 10:30 range > \$1.34 AND 09:30 price < 10:30 price

TABLE 11.8 These are the results of using a restrictive system with two trading parameters when assessing the performance of the spiders in the three-hour afternoon session (13:00 to 16:00). The findings demonstrate how both conditions were able to outperform the $1.92 advance in 374 days in which this system was not in play.

Results of Trading the Spiders from 13:00 to 16:00

Trading Conditions	n	APT	Sum
> .004% + restrictive range	13	.1423	$1.85
< –.004% + restrictive range	11	.2227	$2.45
Neither condition applies	374	.0051	$1.92

The response variable focuses on taking a long position in the spiders at 10:30, but offsetting this position at 11:30.

Given the 60 qualifying days with a $4.76 summary return, was there a performance difference when contrasting the price change in the preceding hour? No, there was no appreciable difference between these hourly (09:30 to 10:30) conditions, an advance had a 14-12-1 record with $2.43 in profits; whereas a decline had a 16-17 record with $2.33 in profits.

Certainly, when the range in the opening hour of trading is at its widest (> $1.34), those 60 trading days easily outperform the 542 trading days (602 – 60); nevertheless, when placing our attention on the outlying scores does this give us a trading opportunity?

In restricting our analysis to those 60 days with an opening hour range of $1.34, does a strong loss in the opening hour (< –$1.00) outperform a strong gain (> $1.00)?

No, the 10:30 to 11:30 price change for the 17 plays with an opening hourly decline < –$1.00 came to a sum of $0.22; whereas for those 12 days with an opening hourly advance > $1.00 came to a sum of $0.21.

A Study Using Two Different Time Frames

After a strong overnight gain extending into the 11:00 hour, if the price of the spiders is relatively flat over the following two hours (11:00 to 13:00), does this offer us a trading advantage in the final three hours (13:00 to 16:00) of the regular trading day?

Alternatively, if the cues rise or fall significantly from the closing price to the 11:00 price, but, in either case, they spend the next two hours trading with modest gains, does this give us a percentage play for the remaining three hours of the regular trading day?

This is unlike the earlier studies because the trading conditions occur over two different settings; that is, the price of the spiders from the closing bell until the 11:00 hour, along with the two-hour midday setting (11:00 to 13:00), set the parameters for this analysis.

This study covers some 398 days; it runs from June 7, 2010 until December 30, 2011. It consists of two pricing conditions (either a 0.4 percent advance or a 0.4 percent decline), along with another pricing condition within the 11:00 to 13:00 time frame, before it can qualify as a restrictive trading system. Consequently, after satisfying the earlier condition, we make an evaluation of the later condition.

The advancing price condition begins with a positive price move in excess of 0.4 percent from the aftermarket session (16:00) until 11:00 hours of the next trading morning. With this requirement satisfied, we turn to the 11:00 to 13:00 setting. Providing the price stays within a range of 0.4 percent, we place a long position at 13:00 before selling it at 16:00.

The declining price condition begins with a negative price move in excess of 0.4 percent, from the aftermarket session (16:00) until 11:00 hours of the next trading morning. With this requirement satisfied, we turn to the 11:00 to 13:00 setting. Providing the price stays within a range of 0.4 percent, we place a long position at 13:00, before selling it at 16:00.

Although these are encouraging numbers (see Table 11.8) they left us with only 24 plays in 398 days. In spite of this limitation, the system does supplement our existing plays.

Trading Patterns

One systematic approach does not cover every pricing formation. Although the many restrictive systems require continuous trading days to assess performance, some work by using those days within a specific pricing pattern. In a feature article, "Situational Trading," I wrote how an analysis containing a long series of trading days will water down your results.[9] This statement takes on more significance when you are making an assessment of a trading formation which takes a few days to unwind.

[9] Anthony Trongone, "Situational Trading," *Technical Analysis of Stocks & Commodities* (October, 2009).

FIGURE 11.7 Unlike a continuous study of an instrument, certain configurations, such as this "V" formation require those days specific to the pattern under investigation. The circle inscribing this pattern illustrates the conclusion of a sharp downturn, as well as the onset of a strong recovery, as the price of this instrument abruptly changes course.

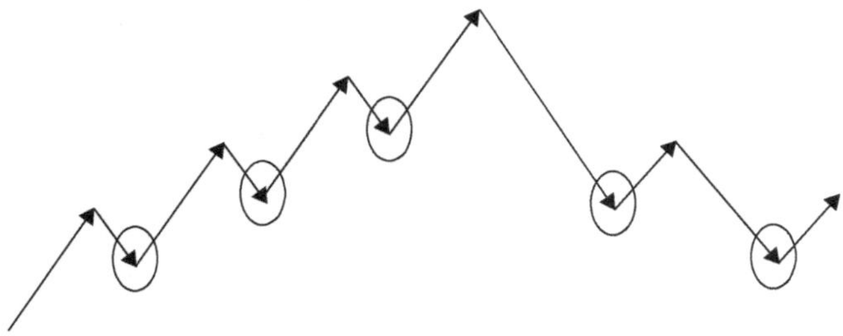

Figure 11.7 demonstrates how prices correct, but immediately turn around—this produces a short-term pattern; technicians refer to this as a V-shaped trading pattern.

Any book on undertaking the study of charting patterns will offer the reader a considerable assortment of configurations, each mandating its own distinctive analysis in the study of those days leading into as well as completing this pricing pattern.

Summary

Although these systems do not present many trading opportunities, they offer us favorable percentage plays. Seen from this perspective, the experience of creating these restrictive systems will bolster your confidence. This upbeat optimism will inspire you to construct an abundance of these high-percentage plays. Although you have these systems on call, you have to be willing to temper your enthusiasm, waiting for the moment to play your hand when the market is ripe for the pickings. As in poker, when you are dealt a poor hand, it is best to fold early. Similarly, in investing, if the probability for taking a position is unattractive, it is best to observe the action without contributing to the pot.

CHAPTER 12

Identifying the Shifting Characteristics of Volume

Avoid strength, attack weakness.

—Sun Tzu

Most market strategists perceive trading volume to be a leading indicator of future price movement. So far, despite its importance, our concentration has been on price, not volume. They believe in making a collective assessment of both these variables before rendering any trading decision.

Although few day traders would refute this statement, most consider volume to be a less meaningful indicator of future price movements. This partially explains why some market participants do not adequately study the impact volume has on the instruments they are trading.

Since trading activity has dynamic properties, it cannot be studied in isolation. This is analogous to submerging a bucket below the surface of a rapidly flowing river: once you carry it to shore, the water in the bucket no longer retains the river's turbulence. Seen from this Eastern perspective, the visual signposts in a day of strong market activity become less effective because blending all the different components of the trading day into a daily score often dilutes our results.

Along with the hourly changes in trading volume, there are discernible differences in the comparison among trading days. Take, for instance, this 50-day moving average of trading activity for the spiders in Figure 12.1.

The rolling traces of this 50-day simple moving average (SMA) of trading volume draw upon some of the problems of using such a simplistic premise.

FIGURE 12.1 Since the 50-day SMA of trading volume for the spiders wavers over these five years, an adjustment reflective of these widespread variations is advisable.

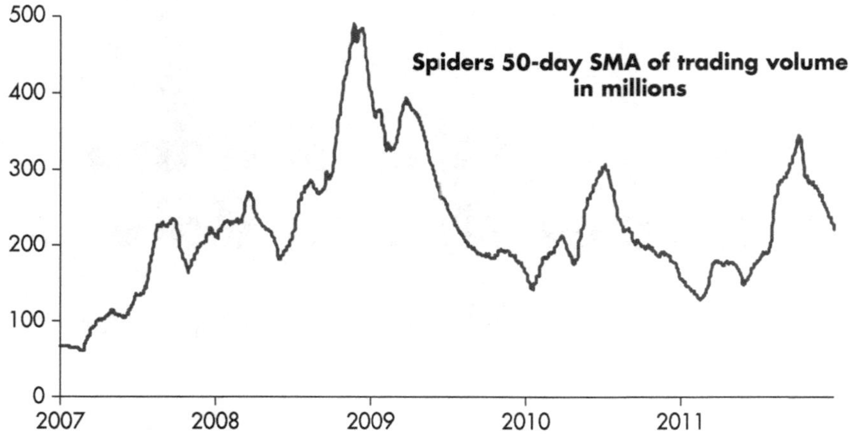

While it is easy to perceive the wide dispersion in trading activity, do we make the necessary adjustments?

Volume Distortion

In my 2011 article on trading volume, I discuss how traders do themselves a disservice by pitting current trading activity against a moving average because "they aggregate all these trading days without making allowances for the strength or weakness of price movements."[1]

Table 12.1 is an account of trading volume by different daily price movements. The average 1,260-day trading volume at 226.40 million shares is far below a day in which the spiders had an excessive daily price change.

The findings cover the dates from January 3, 2007, to December 30, 2011. These five years display a comparison of the four pricing categories when there was a percentage increase or decrease in the daily price of the spiders. I include the trading days along with the average trading volume (ATV) of the spiders, as Table 12.1 demonstrates the discrepancy of activity by price.

Take for example the bottom category (showing a loss of < -2.00 percent); its average volume is 378.64 million shares in 106 trading days. My

[1]Anthony Trongone, "Comparative Trading Volume," *Technical Analysis of Stocks & Commodities* (February 2011), 28–32.

TABLE 12.1 Given a comparison of the average trading volume of the spiders, with those excessive price swings, all four categories were above the 1,260-day average; this substantiates the case for making modifications.

1,260 Trading Days Spiders	Comparison of Average Trading Volume 226.40 Million Shares	
	Trading Days	**Average Volume**
+1.00 to +2.00	152	228.78
> +2.00%	84	347.95
−1.00 to −2.00	142	267.12
< −2.00%	106	378.64

TABLE 12.2 This shows the numerical discrepancy between those trading days with a percentage either above or below the 1,260-day average volume of 226.40 million shares. When the losses were excessive, few days were below this daily average.

Daily % Change Spiders	Number of Trading Days below/above 1,260-Day Average Volume of 226.40 Million Shares	
	Below Average	**Above Average**
+1.00 to +2.00	95	57
> +2.00%	15	69
–1.00 to –2.00	47	95
< –2.00%	6	100

point is that, for such an extensive loss, this is our comparison, not the 1,260-day average of 226.40 million shares.

Table 12.2 presents the trading days above versus below the average trading volume within each of the four pricing categories.

A modest percentage gain was indicative of trading volume below (n = 95) outpacing the days above average (n = 57); however, given a 2-plus percentage gain, buyers became more willing to participate in the strong rally producing 15 days below to 69 days with above-average volume.

The question remains, when redistributing the categories to reflect the average trading volume specific to each category, can this improve our predictive ability?

The spiders, when falling by a percentage plus decline, the above-average category had 95 of the 142 days, but an extensive loss was clearly no contest,

TABLE 12.3 Next-day performance of the spiders. After a daily price change, the statistics favor a short position after an excessive rise, but a long position after an excessive fall in the spiders.

Daily % Change	Performance Summary by Category		
Spiders	Days	$ Next-Day Performance	APT
+1.00 to +2.00	152	–39.64	–0.261
> +2.00%	84	–17.94	–0.214
–1.00 to –2.00	142	23.45	+0.165
< –2.00%	106	30.62	+0.289

TABLE 12.4 In the presence of a strong daily price move, the expectation for future price direction corresponds to expanding or contracting volume.

Daily % Decline	Below Average	Above Average
	Trading Environment	
> +1%	bearish	bullish
> +2%	bearish	bullish
< –1%	bullish	bearish
< –2%	bullish	bearish

giving a 100 to 6 advantage to those days above the average of these 1,260 days. These dominating statistics imply the obvious: Without incorporating price into your assessment of trading volume, it is likely to undermine your results.

What was the next-day performance of the spiders following an excessive percentage price change? Table 12.3 answers this question by reporting the performance of the four pricing categories.

If you do not separate average volume by categorizing changes in price, you are subscribing to the bullish/bearish traditional standard (see Table 12.4).

A rise in price accompanied by strong volume produces a bullish market, but bearish when trading activity is weak. On the downside, traders become optimistic when prices fall in an environment of weak volume, but pessimistic about future price if activity is strong.

TABLE 12.5 After a percentage advance, the below-average category is by far the worst performer. A percentage price decline brought success despite either volume condition; however, the clear winner came on the trading day after an excessive loss volume above its average.

Spiders: n = 1,260	**$ Summary of Next Trading Day**			
	Average Volume = 226.40 Million			
01/03/07 to 12/30/11 Daily % Change	**n**	**Below Average**	**n**	**Above Average**
+1.00 to +2.00	95	−39.90	57	0.26
> +2.00%	15	−0.14	69	−17.80
−1.00 to −2.00	47	9.54	95	13.91
< −2.00%	6	3.32	100	27.30

Consequently, we would expect the following results within each category:

- A positive day with above-average volume will outshine a positive day with below-average volume.
- A negative day with below-average volume will outshine a negative day with above-average volume.

Seen from this theoretical perspective our research questions are as follows:

- After a day following an increase in the price of the spiders, will above-average volume produce an advance in price (bullish); conversely, will below-average volume produce a decline in price (bearish)?
- After a day following a decrease in the price of the spiders, will below-average volume produce an advance in price (bullish); conversely, will above-average volume produce a decrease in price (bearish)?

In this investigation we are examining the change in the daily closing price ($t\text{-}_0 - t\text{-}_1$) of the spiders (see Table 12.5).

With the below outpacing the above average in the mild positive category by a 95 to 57 margin, this brought some disappointing results; nevertheless, a sustainable loss of $39.90 in 95 trading days supports our contention of a bearish environment. Conversely, the $17.80 loss in 69 plays was not supportive of a bullish setting after a day with above-average trading volume and a return in excess of 2 percent.

TABLE 12.6 After a 2 percent advance the ATV was 347 million, the above/below-average differences were similarly negative; however, on those days with a 2 percent decline the ATV was 378 million, the results of this condition were similar to the performance of the spiders, with the above-average category once again putting together a very impressive performance (+$25.69).

Spiders: n = 1,260	$ Summary of Next Trading Day			
	Average Volume = 347.95 Million			
> +2.00%	n	Below Average	n	Above Average
	49	−$9.89	35	−$8.05
	Average Volume = 378.64 Million			
< −2.00%	n	Below Average	n	Above Average
	64	$4.93	42	$25.69

Two of the categories had weak results; therefore, they were unable to produce decisive findings. And with one category having only six cases, it is hard for us to make a directional statement.

Turning to a slightly negative category, the two volume alternatives had equally positive results. And, after a strong loss with above-average volume, the 100 trades sporting a $27.30 advance certainly were not bearish; consequently, this goes against conventional wisdom.

After making the necessary modifications, by incorporating the average daily volume of these excessive single-day price swings, what were the performance results of the spiders on the following day? (See Table 12.6.)

This $25.69 profit in the spiders ran contrary to conventional wisdom, as a bearish day with excessive trading volume brought positive results on the following trading day.

Volume Adjustment When Encountering an Excessive Loss

Can we shed more light on this topic, by switching to another equities index fund with a shorter duration (June 30, 2010, to November 11, 2011)? Although these statistics can change drastically by replacing the spiders with the cues, the column chart (Figure 12.2) supports my thinking on this sensitive topic, because it demonstrates the variability in trading volume over

FIGURE 12.2 Trading volume in millions demonstrates long-term variations. The peaks in daily activity produce an upward bias in the average score.

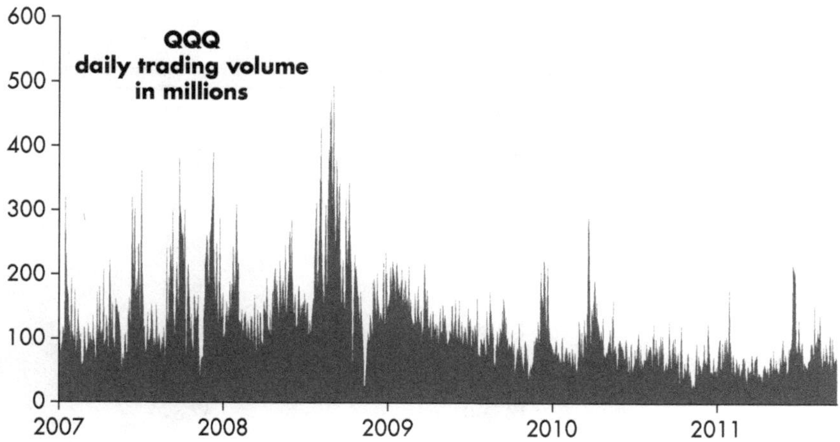

TABLE 12.7 These results corroborate the earlier study. As with the spiders, a modestly strong turnaround came on the trading day following an excessive loss with above-average trading activity.

Daily % Decline 06/30/10 To 11/11/11 QQQ	Number of Trading Days Below/Above 600-Day Average Volume of 82 Million Shares			
	Below Average		Above Average	
	Trading Days	$ Sum	Trading Days	$ Sum
−1.00% to −2.00%	20	−$3.02	34	$3.41
< −2.00%	4	$0.78	31	$6.16

an extensive trading range. And it gives further evidence on how trading activity vacillates depending on the comparison among time frames.

In the 600 trading days under investigation, the average trading volume for the cues was 82.11 million shares. Traditionally, as this is our watermark, a positive trading day with activity above this daily average is seen as bullish; below it, bearish. When the cues had a mild percentage decline, there were 24 days with below-average trading volume in comparison to 65 days with above-average trading volume (Table 12.7).

An outlying score can either inflate or deflate moving averages (particularly when trading around the holidays); this can be rectified by ranking trading activity.

TABLE 12.8 Excess trading volume can inflate or deflate the mean score; a ranking of the scores, however, produces less statistical distortion.

QQQ Ranking	Jan 3, 2011 to Nov 15, 2011 (in millions)	
	10 Largest Volume Days	10 Smallest Volume Days
1	214.10	25.34
2	205.88	30.13
3	204.72	35.02
4	193.65	36.21
5	176.29	36.82
6	151.84	37.35
7	143.78	37.74
8	137.00	37.82
9	132.78	38.05
10	129.96	38.06

Ranking Scores

By ranking the trading volume, we would expect less skewness among outlying scores. The next illustration (Table 12.8) accounts for the highest trading days by daily volume.

After subtracting the ranking score between two consecutive days ($t_{-1} - t_{-0}$), will a large change in volume strengthen or weaken the performance of the cues on the following trading day?

In order to answer this question, this study uses the dates from January 3, 2011, to November 16, 2011 (221 trading days).

December 31, 2010: closing price of the cues $54.46
November 16, 2011: closing price of the cues $57.17

A ranking of 1 has the highest trading volume; consequently, a ranking of 221 represents a trading day with the least activity (see Table 12.9).

Since the highest volume days receive the lowest ranking, when comparing two successive trading days, an increase in trading volume produces a positive score. Conversely, a decrease in trading activity produces a negative score.[2]

[2]Of course, the sequence of subtracting a ranking score between days is an individual preference.

TABLE 12.9 With 221 days in this study, 60.50 million shares (10/31/2011) were given a ranking of 121. On the following trading day, there was a strong increase in activity (99.90 million shares), which represents the 19th-busiest trading day. The question is, will this 102 ranking difference between two consecutive trading days have an impact on the price of the cues?

Date	Closing Price	Volume/ Million	Ranking Volume	Difference in Ranking
11/15/2011	58.13	52.18	150	39
11/14/2011	57.49	44.62	189	−48
11/11/2011	57.85	54.47	141	−49
11/10/2011	56.78	65.97	92	−13
11/09/2011	56.81	69.52	79	28
11/08/2011	58.88	62.88	107	−11
11/07/2011	58.21	65.51	96	17
11/04/2011	57.80	61.51	113	−55
11/03/2011	58.10	78.99	58	42
11/02/2011	56.92	65.12	100	−81
11/01/2011	56.44	99.90	19	102
10/31/2011	57.95	60.50	121	77

FIGURE 12.3 Select the "is greater than" option within the AutoFilter command.

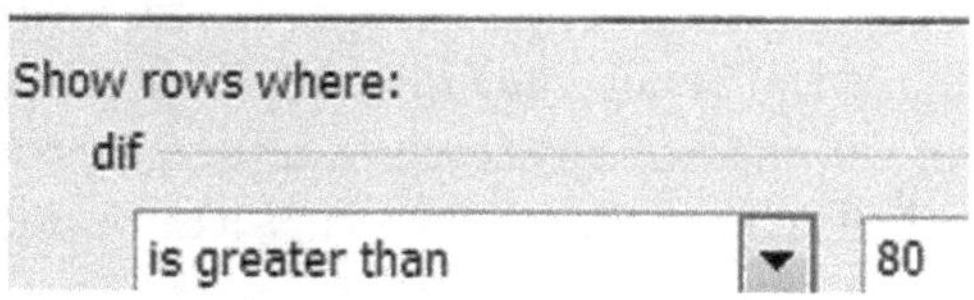

The difference in ranking the volume of two consecutive days results in some fractious scores. Do wider differences have an impact on performance?

Figure 12.3 shows how to produce the results when a ranking "is greater than" 80 when using the AutoFilter command.

Table 12.10 presents a negative ranking (decrease in trading volume), while Table 12.11 shows a positive ranking (increase in trading volume) between two trading days.[3]

[3]Since this study has 221 trading days, the results will be profoundly different once you either increase or decrease the number of trading days.

TABLE 12.10 A wide negative change in the daily ranking of trading volume was responsible for producing profits when trading the cues.

Rank Scores Volume Decreases	n	\$ Sum	\$ APT
−1 to −30	54	−8.30	−0.154
−31 to −80	32	8.88	0.278
≤−81	23	8.40	0.365

TABLE 12.11 When trading volume increases between days, the ranking difference is positive.

Rank Scores Volume Increases	n	\$ Sum	\$ APT
1 to 30	56	0.13	0.002
31 to 80	39	−10.74	−0.275
≥ 81	17	3.49	0.205

A wider ranking difference between trading days was accompanied by more meaningful price swings on the following trading day.

With these results, it is feasible to consider using comparative rankings for trading volume. This procedure, however, does not take into account the widespread differences in trading volume over many days. This is a concern, because as we increase the trading days in our study to make our findings more robust, the guiding principles of a normal bell curve become apparent. Consequently, when a small advance or decline in the outside edges occurs, it causes more of a reaction in contrast to the majority of scores assembling around the center of activity.

Fortunately, we can mitigate some of this concern by using the =RANK function differently. Before we design a new study using this "rolling rank" function, a discussion on the comparative analysis of the trading activity of exchange-traded funds (ETF) index funds in the current market place is helpful.

Disharmonious Narratives

After a significant downturn, there is a tendency for the market to overshoot its target; when investors realize this phenomenon, they begin prowling for bargains by taking an opposite position causing the market to abruptly change its directional course. In most cases, when evaluating a pattern with an abrupt downturn accompanied by a sudden recovery, "changes in trading volume were a meaningful harbinger of the beginning of the downturn as well as a turnaround in the price of the stock or commodity."[4]

Unfortunately, trying to get a historical read on trading volume for the overall market has become more difficult. With all the new ETFs hitting the marketplace, it has eaten into the daily trading activity of the traditional standard bearers. For instance, how many byproducts are there of the spiders, the cues, or even the gold (GC) contract? With all these copycat offerings, they disperse the volume among them. This dissemination of trading activity makes historical comparisons a less precise indicator.

Seen from this perspective, a comparison process between two instruments is a good way to circumvent this thorny issue. Below is a discussion of a proportional assessment between the daily trading volume of the spiders in comparison to the E-mini S&P 500 (ES) contract.

A ratio is a mathematical relationship between two numbers. In this case, we are comparing differences in the 50-day SMA between the two trading instruments.

Here, we are studying the trading activity between two instruments representing the same index, the S&P 500. We will look at the 50-day moving average of the spiders in relationship to the 50-day moving average of the ES commodity contract.

When using ratios, customarily, the larger number is the numerator and the smaller one is the denominator.

For instance, the 50-day average trading activity (Figure 12.4) for these two instruments over the previous 1,342 trading days (from October 10, 2006 to Thanksgiving 2011) are as follows:

Spiders	= 214.3 million
ES contract	= 1.993 million
Ratio	= 214.3/1.993 = 108

For every contract, it takes 108 shares of the spiders; this ratio becomes our tipping point. As a consequence, this is our fulcrum: below 108, the

[4]Anthony Trongone, "Situational Trading," *Technical Analysis of Stocks & Commodities* (October 2009), 12–16.

FIGURE 12.4 Comparison of daily trading activity between the spiders against the ES continuous contract. After constructing a 50-day SMA of trading activity, it divides the 50-day spiders by the 50-day ES contract.

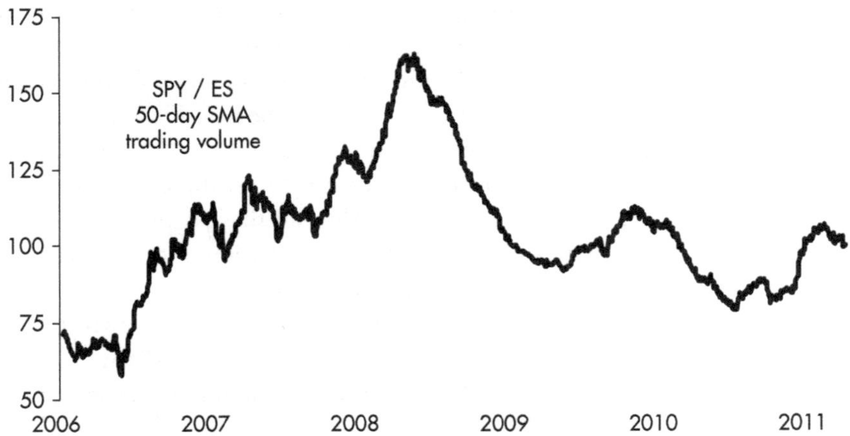

spiders draw less trading activity; above 108 the spiders draw more activity in comparison to the ES contract.

When holding the futures contract at 2 million shares, we can discern changes in this ratio by adjusting the volume in the spiders.

160 million/2 million = 80
200 million/2 million = 100
240 million/2 million = 120

A score below 108 implies less comparative activity for the spiders. The line chart clearly demonstrates a difference in trading activity between these two instruments, but the spiders having been unable to hold firmly over this benchmark since 2008, the question is: Are they losing their appeal, or is the commodities contract commanding more attention?

One way to answer this question is to compare similar instruments.

Cues	= 119.2 million
NQ contract	= 328,000
Ratio	= 119.2 million/328,327 = 363

A score at 363 implies comparative trading activity. Unlike the SPY/ES combination, this tandem's early going (2006 to 2008) holds across a steady flat line, before rising strongly (Figure 12.5). When it begins to drop, its descent falls below 350.

FIGURE 12.5 Comparison of daily trading activity between the cues against the NQ continuous contract. After constructing a 50-day SMA of trading activity, the comparison divides the 50-day of the cues by the 50-day NQ contract.

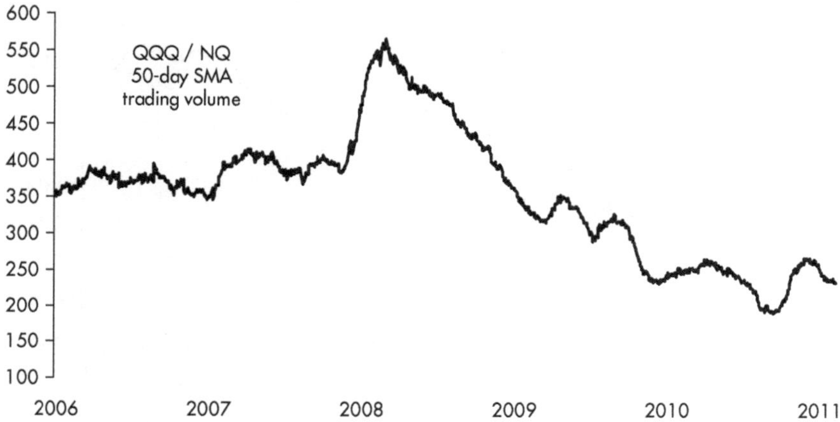

Clearly, there is either less demand for these index funds, or their weakness is the result of competition among ETFs. Going forward, what is the reliability of using past activity of these ETFs to reflect the present? And with the continuous growth of these new ETFs, is it contaminating the daily trading volume of companies?

Trade Your Findings, Not the Axiom

In order to reduce the variability between weeks, these three popular ETFs are using a four-week simple moving average for volume (left axis) and price (right axis). These three dual axis charts report the weekly closing price along with weekly trading volume (in millions). They can be seen in Figures 12.5 (SPY), 12.6 (QQQ), and 12.7 (GLD).

One aspect apparent in both charts is the existence of a fear factor that surfaces whenever these two index funds have the slightest drop in price. The volume spikes occur when traders forcefully react by expanding volume, which is likely due to the emotional scars they still have from the previous bear market (October 2007 to March 2009).

The SPDR GOLD shares (GLD) have a similar response, an unrelenting bull market, but no appreciable increase in trading activity.

The differences among these three funds partly pertain to the instrument, more specifically; this reflects investors' attitudes about future pricing.

FIGURE 12.6 The spiders' weekly averages show rising prices but stagnant trading volume.

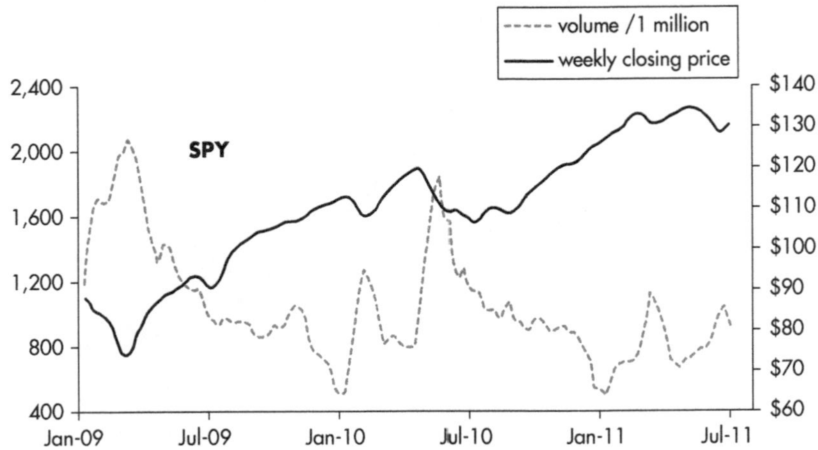

FIGURE 12.7 Practically the same trading landscape, but there is an inverse correlation between the rising price of the cues in relation to its falling trading volume.

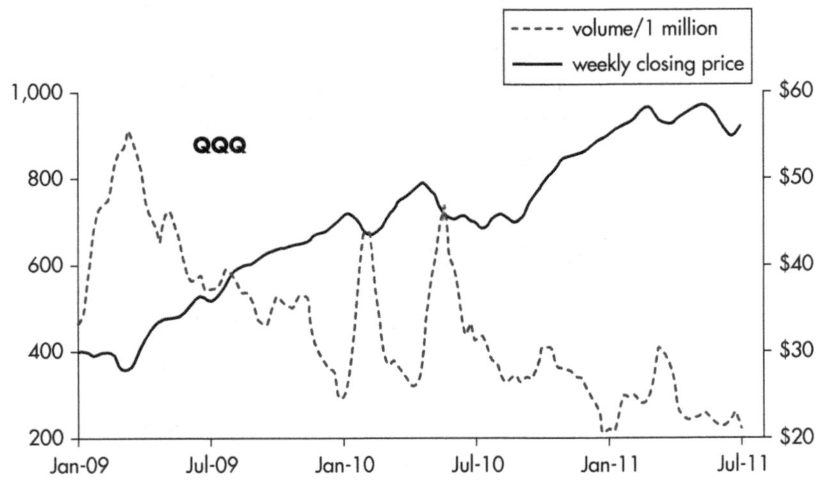

With the fiscal crisis, market specialists were very bullish on gold, believing it would offset exposure to any economic negativity; therefore, investors missing earlier runs saw any drawdown in price as a buying opportunity. These perceptions of invincibility support this buying pattern, but they do not exist forever. Nevertheless, for our purposes, be mindful of these pockets of opportunity when a decrease in price increases speculation, which expands trading activity.

FIGURE 12.8 Again we are showing a four-week moving average of both variables to reduce the choppiness. The early vertical spikes occur before a drop in the price of gold (SPDR GOLD); however, as the price of this precious metal becomes brighter, these spikes occur after a slight drop in price as investors begin buying on the dips.

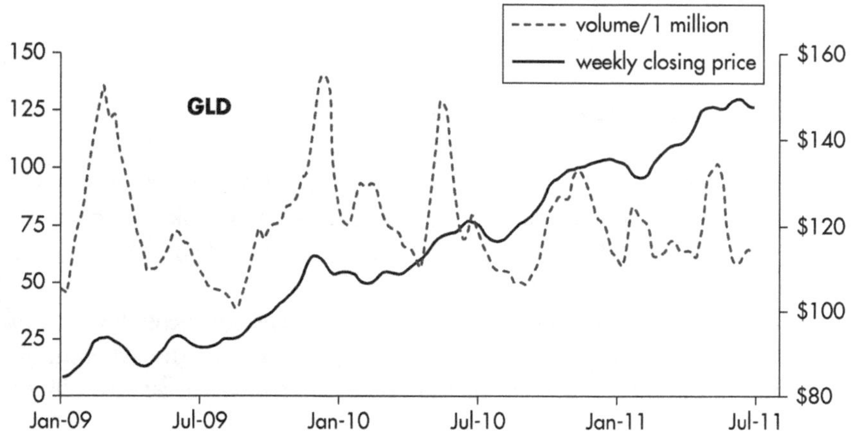

No Substitute for Thinking

Although the markets have been on the rise, trading volume has not kept pace, but has continued its downward descent. This has mystified many market strategists because a situation of rising prices with contracting volume flies in the face of technical analysis.

This grounding principle is definitely not apparent in these three charts (Figures 12.6 to 12.8). Most, if not all, academic books describe a bull market as a rising market accompanied by acceleration in trading volume; however, in these examples, weekly activity decelerates.

My explanation for this can be found in a weekly article for Interactive Data Corporation (www.esignal.com). An examination of these three charts demonstrates how past turbulence influences the minds of investors. Apparently, the aftermath of an extensive equities collapse often exerts a psychological aspect playing on the ability of investors to correctly act in response to the ongoing directional pattern of the market.[5]

The meltdown in the fall of 2008 left investors with a strong aversion to risk. Beaten and battered over 340 days, they swore off trading. As the rally began on March 10, they stayed away from their computer screens. Lightly

[6]Anthony Trongone, "Trade the Chart, Not the Investment Principle," Interactive Data Corporation, February 9, 2010, www.esignal.com.

positioned, they were more inclined to root against a market comeback than for it. Despite the recovery, they refused to participate. Instead of following the momentum, they let their feelings take precedence over logical thinking. Since these investors took some excruciating losses, there were not willing to experience more pain.

Early-Morning Trading Volume

One critical piece of information that most market strategists overlook is early morning trading volume. A majority of daytraders look to the futures market for forecasting direction, but when the focus is solely on price, there is less conviction in the strength of their findings.

Before taking a position become knowledgeable about the earlier trading setting. This study examines excessive trading volume in the ES contract between 06:00 to 09:00 to assess its impact on price movements from 09:00 to 11:00.[6]

This study runs from June 2, 2010, to November 25, 2011 (386 trading days).

Outlying scores can be found by using the following function:

=PERCENTILE (range of trading volume,.90)
90th percentile = 232,529

Once you obtain this score, run an =IF statement, for trading volume above 232,529. With this information we want to acquire an understanding of the sequence of the outlying scores prior to taking a trading position.

This onslaught of trading volume is often very informative; it customarily warns us of changes in market behavior. In this case (Figure 12.9), the ES contract takes a strong thrashing, recovers some, but confronts another round of excessive trading activity before crashing down.

A comparison of early morning volume among days is informative; however, performing a "rolling" rank analysis of early morning volume is often a better precursor of future price direction.

---

[6]You can easily replace the ES contract with the spiders. In the hour from 07:00 to 08:00, the average trading volume for the spiders was 930,631, but with the median at 686,037, it tells us that some days had excessively high volume within this hour (January 30, 2007, to January 6, 2012).

FIGURE 12.9 The days with excessive volume (above the 90th percentile > 232,529) in the ES contract within this three-hour range (06:00 to 09:00) are increasing in frequency, which causes a sharp decrease in price.

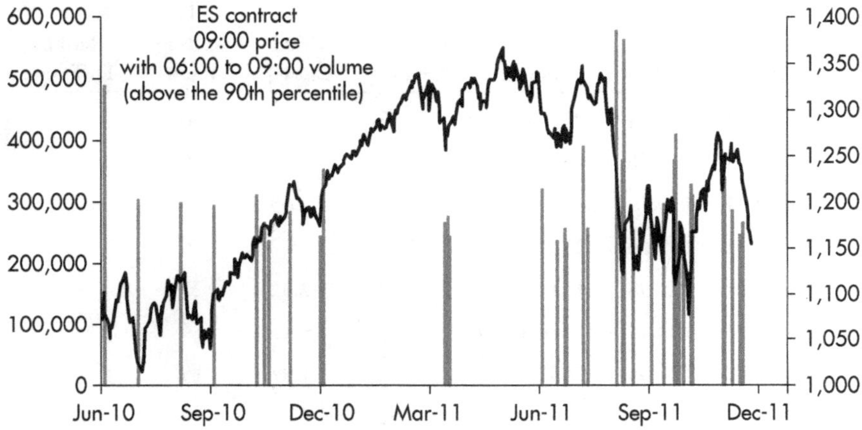

Thirty-Day Rolling Ranking

Earlier we ran a ranking study (using the =RANK function) on trading volume for the 221 days under investigation. After assigning a ranking score from 1 to 221, we took the ranking score difference between two consecutive days.

In this study, we are investigating the spiders over 570 days; we are not using the =RANK function over the 570 trading days, but a "rolling" rank of the closing price of the spiders over the previous 30 days. In order to produce a ranking difference, subtract the 30-day ranking between consecutive days ($t\text{-}_1 - t\text{-}_0$), as in Table 12.12.

This rectifies the earlier problem of an ETF losing trading volume because of competing byproducts.

The rank formulas for the three dates are given below:

11/25/11 =RANK(c2,c2:c31)
11/23/11 =RANK(c3,c3:c32)
11/22/11 =RANK(c4,c4:c33)

Unlike the earlier study, we are evaluating volume in a short-term framework. For instance, 414 million shares (11/01/11); it gets a 3 for its ranking, because it is the third-highest trading day in past 30 days. This rolling rank model addresses the shortcoming of uneven patterns

TABLE 12.12 The 30-day ranking scores of the closing price of the spiders demonstrate how the rolling ranking model functions in this short trading environment.

	A	B	C	D	E	F	G
1	Date	Close	Volume	Price Change	Price Lag t_{-1}	30-Day Rolling Rank	Ranking Difference
2	11/25/11	116.34	99,556,980	−.22		30	−10
3	11/23/11	116.56	223,964,569	−2.63	−.22	20	1
4	11/22/11	119.19	215,986,143	−.47	−2.63	21	−5
5	11/21/11	119.66	228,508,379	−2.32	−.47	16	5
6	11/18/11	121.98	215,062,788	−.13	−2.32	21	−17
7	11/17/11	122.11	330,064,090	−1.97	−.13	4	11
8	11/16/11	124.08	234,785,173	−2.00	−1.97	15	14
9	11/15/11	126.08	184,192,038	.62	−2.00	29	1
10	11/14/11	125.46	158,973,173	−1.20	.62	30	−0
11	11/11/11	126.66	189,674,278	2.34	−1.20	30	−11
12	11/10/11	124.32	231,347,018	1.16	2.34	19	−14
13	11/09/11	123.16	336,971,570	−4.72	1.16	5	19
14	11/08/11	127.88	224,088,063	1.62	−4.72	24	6
15	11/07/11	126.26	196,184,911	.78	1.62	30	−10
16	11/04/11	125.48	248,867,478	−.77	.78	20	−7
17	11/03/11	126.25	286,067,470	2.26	−.77	13	8
18	11/02/11	123.99	244,533,308	1.99	2.26	21	−18
19	11/01/11	122.00	414,961,250	−3.50	1.99	3	19
20	10/31/11	125.50	227,500,425	−3.10	−3.50	22	2

of trading volume over many days. This occurs when using a short-term moving average, which may be an unfair representation of activity because of outlying scores or around holidays (such as the light activity on November 25, 2011, known as Black Friday), which produces a moving average showing less activity.

This form of ranking better retains the integrity of the scores; however, a 30-day rolling average may not be the most precise yardstick for every instrument. The best approach for predicting scores with less measurement error is to experiment by running the numbers.

TABLE 12.13 This shows the performance results of the spiders using a 30-day rolling rank of trading volume. Most of the negative returns occurred when there was no ranking difference between days; nevertheless, there were setbacks for those two categories with a rolling rank score between ± 21 to 30.

30-Day Rolling Ranking	Trades	$ Sum	APT
−21 to − 30	11	−5.80	−.527
−11 to − 20	65	12.23	.188
−1 to − 10	195	17.71	.091
= 0	48	−21.95	−.457
1 to 10	170	9.98	.059
11 to 20	67	4.80	.072
21 to 30	14	−3.59	−.256
Sum	570	13.38	.024

The study consists of 570 trading days (August 24, 2009, until November 25, 2011). With an increase of $13.38 in the spiders, the expectation is for positive results. Nevertheless, without including price as a variable, will a 30-day rolling ranking of trading volume reflect a price improvement in the spiders on the following trading day (Table 12.13).

These findings afford us some insight into trading volume. A positive or negative ranking from 1 to 20 was profitable; however, when the ranking had no change or was above ± 20 the results were negative. Of course, we can increase our knowledge by incorporating the daily price change of the spiders into this preliminary investigation.

Ranking Intraday Sessions

When trading intraday, a ranking of volume for two consecutive trading sessions is a powerful predictor of price direction.

Take for example, trading the ES contract from midnight to 06:00; knowledge of trading activity during these six hours is instructive; however, by including activity from 06:00 to 08:00, does it strengthen our forecasting ability?

The contributory variable takes on two successive timeframes:
ES contract trading volume: 00:00 to 06:00
ES contract trading volume: 06:00 to 08:00

TABLE 12.14 This row of statistics shows the ranking differences for February 3, 2012. When equating a ranking of 491 in the earlier setting (v0006) to the 309 ranking in the 06:00 to 08:00 setting (v0608), the rank difference was positive (182); therefore, it signifies a strengthening of activity in comparison to the earlier setting.

Date	vm 00_06	vm 06_08	z8 Price	z11 Price	Rank v0006	Rank v0608	Rank Difference	08:00 to 11:00 Price Change
2/3/2012	65,595	49,429	1,323.00	1,338.25	491	309	182	15.25

Once you have these scores, subtract the ranking differences between them. For instance,

$$\text{intraday ranking volume} = (06{:}00 \text{ to } 08{:}00) - (00{:}00 \text{ to } 06{:}00)$$

A ranking of 1 represents the busiest trading day; 599 characterizes a setting with the lowest trading activity.

When comparing the two ranking scores, a negative score indicates less trading activity in the earlier setting, while a positive score indicates more trading activity in the earlier setting (Table 12.14).[7]

The dependent variable in this investigation is the ES contract when trading from 08:00 to 11:00. The dates of the study run from October 21, 2009 to February 17, 2012.[8]

Given a comparative weakness in volume there were differences in the categories, the 115 days with the smallest ranking difference gave back −121.75 points (Table 12.15). The 59 widest scores gave those investors looking to go long the best opportunity for success by generating 77.75 points.

Although small differences brought 75 points in profits (Table 12.16), an analysis of the 24 days with a widest positive ranking sank some 76 points (a −3.18 APT loss).

Inclusion of these two predictor variables provides more information regarding investors' beliefs about the market opening. When we want to acquire an understanding of morning movements, some insightful information pertains to whether volume is contracting or expanding.

[7]Since the six-hour setting averages 108k while the two-hour setting averages 58k, the earlier setting trades more contracts, but we are subtracting the difference between ranking scores, which implies a comparative volume difference between these two settings.

[8]Traditionally, on days surrounding holidays, there is no trading from midnight to 06:00.

TABLE 12.15 A negative score is indicative of weakening volume in the 06:00 to 08:00 setting. That is, in comparison to the six-hour setting (00:00 to 06:00), the two-hour setting had a comparative decrease in trading activity. In these 307 trading days, there was a −24.50 point loss when trading from 08:00 to 11:00 in this equity contract.

Ranking Category	Trades	$ Sum	$ APT
from −1 to −50	115	−121.75	−1.059
from −51 to −150	133	19.50	0.147
from −151 to −250	48	68.25	1.422
LT − 250	11	9.5	0.864
ES: SUMMARY POINTS	307	−24.50	−0.080

TABLE 12.16 A positive score is indicative of strengthening volume in the 06:00 to 08:00 setting. That is, in comparison to the six-hour setting (00:00 to 06:00), the two-hour setting had a comparison increase in trading activity. In these 287 trading days, there was a 61.25-point loss when trading from 08:00 to 11:00 in this equity contract.

Ranking Category	Trades	$ Sum	$ APT
from 1 to 50	114	75.00	0.658
from 51 to 150	110	–99.25	−0.902
from 151 to 250	39	39.25	1.01
GT 250	24	–76.25	−3.18
ES: SUMMARY POINTS	287	−61.25	−0.213

Summary

Surges in trading volume are the collective expression of fear. Although the fear of losing money elicits more of a reaction, day traders dread the possibility of missing a profitable opportunity. As we have seen, when early-morning trading volume strays from its normal activity, it deserves more attention. Since this is a reflection of group emotion, it often acts as a predictor of future volatility.

Although a comparative assessment of trading activity often is a good indicator, by itself it can be a temperamental yardstick. Since holidays, shortened trading days, or summer doldrums act as sources of reduced activity, they are not a symptom of market sentiment; therefore, they require a revision in our analysis.

Including trading volume in your studies often enhances your predictive ability, but there are times when it is fraught with measurement error. Nevertheless, carefully observe excessive amounts of trading activity; they are often a flashing red light for aberrant price swings.

Our inclination is to tag along with the reaction of the crowd, but by avoiding strength, we can frequently reduce our exposure to loss. And when entering into arenas of weak volume, we were sometimes able to share in a surprisingly profitable trading environment. Unfortunately, avoiding strength, but attacking weakness cannot be done without knowing an instrument's strength or weakness. Without this knowledge, we enter the trading day not knowing the enemy; consequently, we take on risk by approaching the battlefield without a full array of defensive armament.

CHAPTER 13

Predictor Variables

Study the art of science.
Study the science of art.
Develop your senses.
Especially, learn to see.
Realize that everything connects to everything else.

—Leonardo da Vinci

The systems in this chapter are unlike earlier strategies because the focus of our trading decision is not derived from the instrument we are trading, but from a contributory variable.

This study utilizes the eurozone currency (EC) contract[1] as a leading variable for trading the ES (equities) contract as well as the GC (gold) contract. In implementing these systems, we are going to inspect two aspects of the euro over 712 trading days: its 06:00 price, which varied from $1.1911 to $1.5121, along with its price direction from 06:00 to 09:00.

Although we are investigating two commodity contracts, they each have many derivatives. My favorite for the ES contract is the spiders (SPY), since the ES contract has a strong correlation with the cues (QQQ) as well as the Russell 2000 (IWM); they are good trading alternatives.

The other dependent variable is the GC contract. It has its share of alternatives with less expensive multipliers, but for those more receptive to gold funds, there are two popular replacements: GLD at $167.35 averages

[1]The euro is a foreign exchange product, with a trading class 6E, its currency is the USD, and trades with a multiplier of 125,000 (there are various symbols depending on your trading platform). It is the official currency of the eurozone and its universal symbol is €, code = EUR.

12.2 million shares per day; however, IAU is one-tenth the price ($16.80) with half (6.1 million shares) the daily trading volume (using February 17, 2012).

Setting the Stage

This analysis takes place from March 1, 2009, to December 1, 2011; therefore, it captures strong rallies for the two dependent variables. The ES contract ($50 multiplier) with its lowest 06:00 price coming on March 9, 2009, at $677.00; from there it ran to its highest price of $1,368.00, on May 2, 2011.[2] The GC contract fell to its lowest price ($872.60) on April 20, 2009, but rose to $1,899.40 on September 5, 2011.

The ES contract (Figure 13.1) starts this study at a price of 718; in 712 trading days it rises 626 points, finishing at 1,244.

One thing we want to know is how to avoid those days when economic news sends investors from equities flocking to the safety of risk-averse investments. In this study, the theoretical groundwork for the onset of a nasty correction was brought on by the fiscal woes of those countries on the periphery of the European Union; conversely, when at the brink of

FIGURE 13.1 The ES contract rises steadily to 1,200 before a soft setback; thereafter, it soared to 1,368 before hitting strong headwinds.

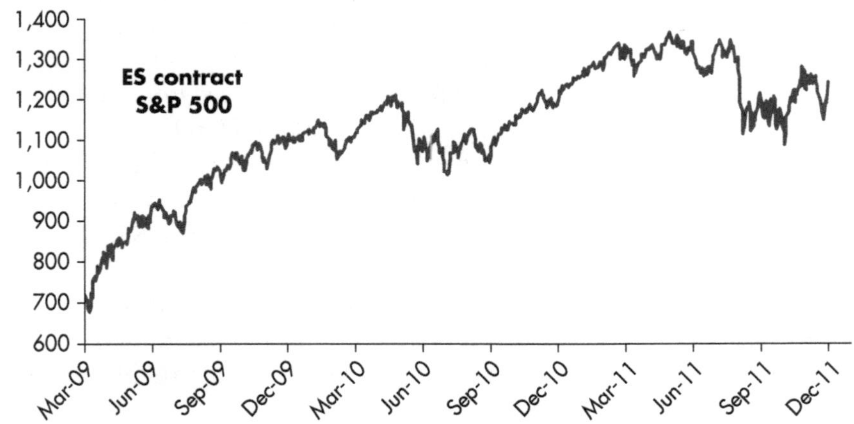

[2]The ES contract is an equities contract; it represents the mini version, but is a more active trading component of the S&P 500.

FIGURE 13.2 This study begins with the GC contract at $952.30; it rises steadily, without many setbacks to $1,899.40 (06:00 price) before it plunges $192.10 in 15 trading days during the fall of 2011, finally recovering some of these losses by closing at $1,754.30 after these 712 trading days.

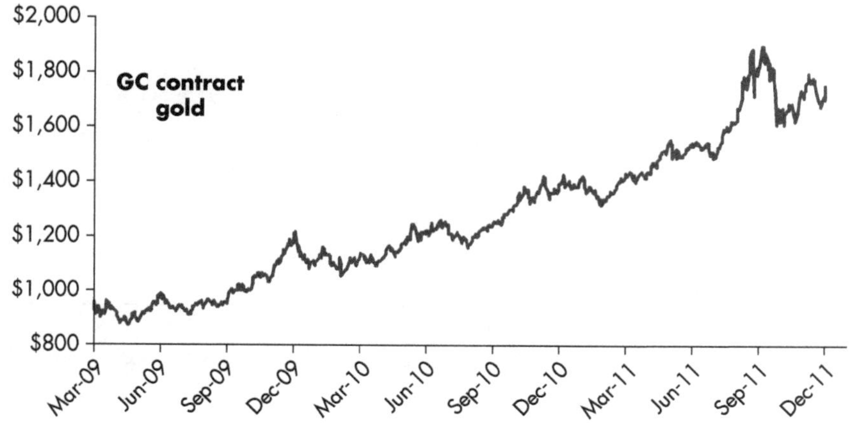

bankruptcy any indication of a cooperative transatlantic solution was responsible for a single-day rally in the equities market.

Climbing seamlessly (Figure 13.2), except for the perceptible pullback in the fall of 2011, this precious metal had relatively small slips. Tarnishing its progress, however, was an abrupt $192.10 fall in 15 trading days. This free fall is somewhat disturbing because it shows how susceptible gold bugs are to these bungee drops when holding a position in this commodity.

Background of the Predictor Variable

According to the economists, the European sovereign fiscal crisis has been largely responsible for massive market swings; the fallout from this crisis often lies squarely on the euro; therefore, we start this investigation by using the euro (EC contract) as our contributory variable.

The EU central banks' problem lingers as an unbroken volley of confidence-restoring measures for these transatlantic economies has been unsuccessful. The solution remains elusive, as there appears to be no magic wand. As the instability in this region continues to make market headline news, it has been partially responsible for the price direction of our two response variables.

In this investigation, we are exploring two aspects of the euro. We begin with an analysis of the 06:00 to 09:00 price change in this contributory

FIGURE 13.3 The EC contract (euro) appears to be trading in a restrictive range. This has been a fractious currency with aggressive selling followed by a long trending upturn with relatively minor setbacks.

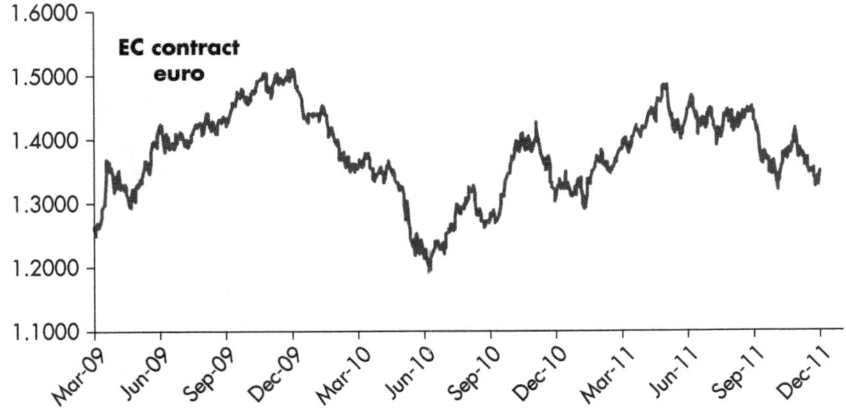

variable. More specifically, we want to know how a rise/fall in this currency within these three hours impacts the two response variables when trading from 09:00 to 15:00. After exploring this issue, our attention focuses on the actual (06:00) price of this currency contract. For example, do the response variables perform differently when the euro is below 1.3000 in comparison to a price above 1.4000?

The dates of this study are from March 1, 2009, until December 1, 2011; it covers 712 trading days.

Figure 13.3 is the 06:00 price of the contributory variable for this study.

After climbing steadily, the price of the euro slips from $1.50 to slightly below $1.20 before regaining strength. In the spring of 2011, it begins making lower peaks, finally falling to a price slightly above $1.30. The question remains, how does the price of these two response variables behave in these diverse settings?

Before commenting on the contributory influence of this currency, it is best to glance at the euro along with the price movements of the two response variables: the E-mini S&P 500 (ES) contract (see Figure 13.4) and the gold futures contract (GC) (see Figure 13.5). By themselves, using the 06:00 price, these two response variables have a strong correlation ($r = .756$). The correlation between this currency contract and the equities contract is not as strong ($r = .208$).

The pattern of these two contracts has some variation. At the start of the bull market both strengthen (March 2009 to December 2009), but then

FIGURE 13.4 Despite the weak correlation (r = .208), with the exception of March 2010 to January 2011, these two variables appear to move in tandem; this forms the theoretical basis for our analytical assumptions.

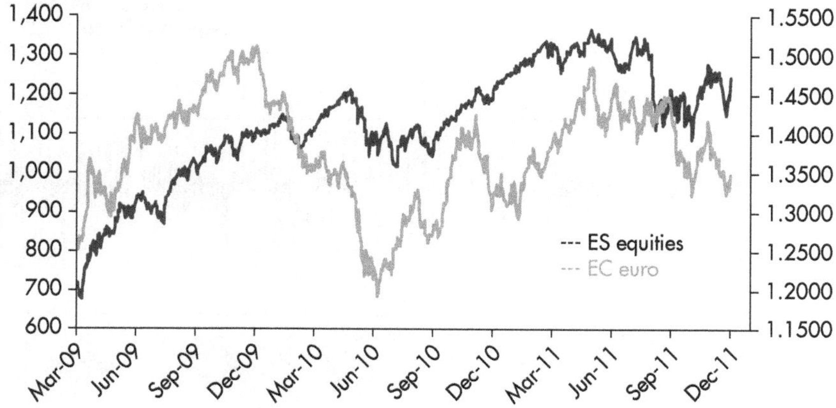

FIGURE 13.5 The price of the gold (GC) contract rises steadily regardless of the direction of the euro (EC) contract.

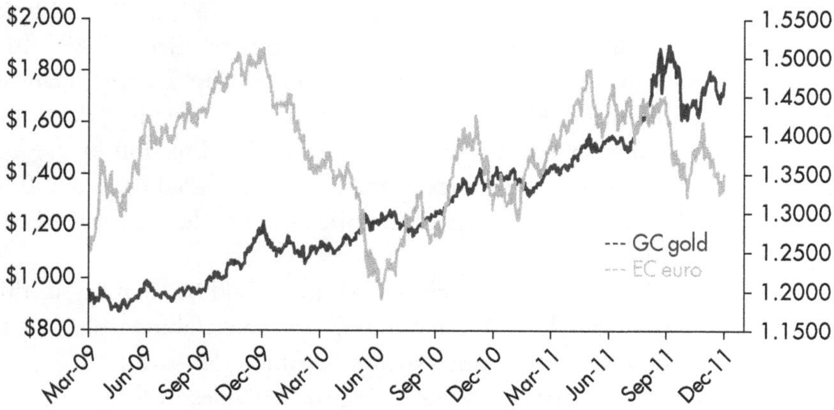

the euro begins a long sharp slide to its lowest price (1.1917). With this downward move, the price of equities stalls. As this currency rebounds, equities, at first, delay their upward movement until September 2010; thereafter, both contracts strengthen again. As the euro starts to weaken (May 2011), equities remain in a sideways pattern, finally falling below a triple bottom (August 2011). Starting in the fall of 2011, they begin tracing each other's movement.

FIGURE 13.6 This displays the early-morning price change for the EC contract. What will its impact be on the two response variables?

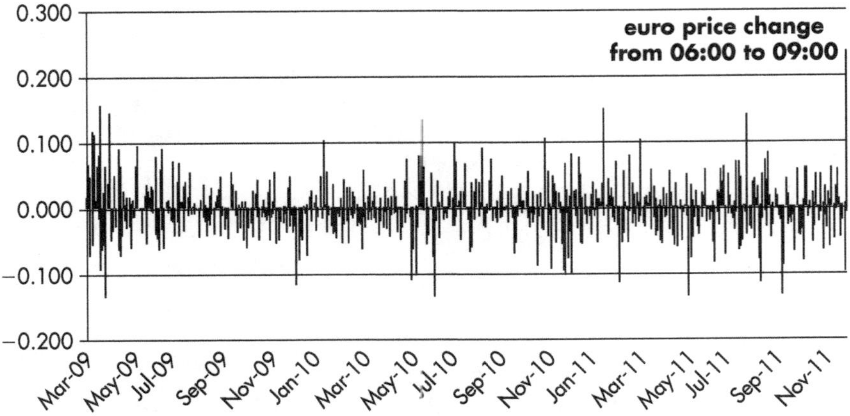

With its steady rise (Figure 13.5), the direction of the EC contract does not appear to covary with the price of gold. With basically no (r =.074) correlation between these two variables, it appears as if there is no predictive association.

After examining the course of this precious metal, it would appear that the correct strategy is to simply buy at its lowest price ($872.60) and hold tight, selling your shares when they attain their loftiest price ($1,899.40). Certainly, hindsight is perfect; however, we are taking a more realistic approach. We are not holding on to this position for 712 trading days, but taking aim at a much smaller target by using the price direction of the EC contract from 06:00 to 09:00 to forecast the direction of gold from 09:00 to 15:00. Figure 13.6 shows the range of the price changes for this three-hour early-morning setting.

As the euro rises strongly (March to December 2009), volatility in this three-hour setting subsides. With the onset of a currency falling from a price of $1.50 to below $1.20, these price swings become more erratic.

Below are the abbreviations representing the variables in this study:

es69	ES contract from 06:00 to 09:00
gc69	GC contract from 06:00 to 09:00
ec69	EC contract from 06:00 to 09:00
es915	ES contract from 09:00 to 15:00
gc915	GC contract from 09:00 to 15:00
ec915	EC contract from 09:00 to 15:00

TABLE 13.1 The descriptive statistics during the 06:00 to 09:00 trading span for the three commodity contracts. Unlike the performance gains showing the flight of the 06:00 price in the earlier charts, these three hours do not assist in lifting equities or the precious metal contract.

Results of Trading from 06:00 to 09:00 for the Three Commodity Contracts								
n = 712	**Min**	**Max**	**Adv**	**Dec**	**Ties**	**APT**	**Sum**	**Stdev**
es69	–24.50	40.50	343	344	25	–.1387	–98.75	4.783
gc69	–40.20	39.20	343	363	6	–.1562	–111.20	6.881
ec69	–.0137	.0236	323	376	13	–.00023	–.1635	.00414

TABLE 13.2 These are the findings for the three commodities when trading from 09:00 to 15:00. The equities market produces a .3633 point APT; whereas, the yellow metal turns in a less impressive performance ($0.0410 APT). Can we improve upon these results by using the euro as our predictor variable?

Results of Trading from 09:00 to 15:00 for the Three Commodity Contracts								
n = 712	**Min**	**Max**	**Adv**	**Dec**	**Ties**	**APT**	**Sum**	**Stdev**
es915	–43.25	46.50	383	325	4	.3633	258.75	9.647
gc915	–74.50	51.70	388	320	4	.0410	29.20	10.686
ec915	–.0204	.0303	360	347	5	.00001	.0068	.00590

When trading in this 06:00 to 09:00 setting, the statistics (Table 13.1) portray a negative trading environment.

Although the earlier line charts clearly express upward trending response variables, these three hours do not characterize a positive landscape. A 98.75 point decline in the ES contract is accompanied by a $111.20 decline in the GC contract. Fortunately, this is not where our trading takes place; we are looking to the 09:00 to 15:00 time frame to produce revenue.

Table 13.2 shows the six hours (09:00 to 15:00) representing the findings of each response variable; going forward these descriptive statistics become our performance benchmark.

This is our challenge, to improve upon the strong 258.75-point advance (.3633 APT) in the equities contract; however, with a standard deviation at 9.65 points, expect unstable price swings. Surprisingly, the record of this precious metal contract has not been very positive, a $29.20 run in comparison to its strong profits in 712 trading days. Another concern is its $10.686 standard deviation; such a wide variation makes this risk/return quotient difficult to accept.

Eurozone Crisis

The euro crisis has offered sobering lessons, putting every investor in a risk-on, risk-off cycle. Amid concerns that there is no solution to fixing this fiscal morass, it has become a serious problem; failure to restore investors' confidence has been felt in the price of the eurozone currency.

A strengthening in the EC contract is seen as stabilizing the region's fiscal concerns; whereas a weakening currency underscores the growing fear in the fiscal ability of its members to repay outstanding obligations.[3]

The early-morning (06:00 to 09:00) price change in the EC contract serves as the predictor variable; whereas the response variables are the two variables trading from 09:00 to 15:00.

1. ES contract trading from 09:00 to 15:00
2. GC contract trading from 09:00 to 15:00

We customarily refer to a euro in terms of USD, such as: 1 € = $1.3500 USD.

When including the two response variables in this study, we can break our research hypothesis into four categories:

1. If ec69 price change > 0, this will increase the 09:00 to 15:00 price in the ES contract (es915).
2. If ec69 price change < 0, this will decrease the 09:00 to 15:00 price in the ES contract (es915).
3. If ec69 price change > 0, this will decrease the 09:00 to 15:00 price in the GC contract (gc915).
4. If ec69 price change < 0, this will increase the 09:00 to 15:00 price in the GC contract (gc915).

One way to verify the accuracy of this hypothesis is to break apart the ec69 (i.e., price change of the euro from 06:00 to 09:00) into two categories:

1. ec69 > 0 a rising euro from 06:00 to 09:00
2. ec69 < 0 a falling euro from 06:00 to 09:00

[3]This study uses the EC contract as the price for the official currency of the eurozone. (Most trading platforms use 6E as its trading symbol.) When the EC contract rises, its currency strengthens; at its highest price it takes more USD to purchase one euro; conversely, when this contract falls its currency weakens, at its lowest price it takes less USD to purchase one euro.

TABLE 13.3 On those 323 days in which there was an early-morning (06:00 to 09:00) price increase in the euro, taking a long position in these response variables at 09:00 until 15:00 had diverging results, producing a 315.25-point advance in the ES contract, but a $137 decline in the GC contract.

Euro > 0			**Trading from 09:00 to 15:00**					
n = 323	**Min**	**Max**	**Adv**	**Dec**	**Ties**	**APT**	**Sum**	**Stdev**
es915	−29.00	27.75	175	147	1	.9760	315.25	9.407
gc915	−38.80	28.80	159	163	1	−.4263	−137.70	9.662
ec915	−.0204	.0303	176	145	2	.00044	.1414	.00587

TABLE 13.4 The results of trading these three commodities from 09:00 to 15:00 after an earlier price decline in the EC contract.

Euro < 0			**Trading from 09:00 to 15:00**					
n = 376	**Min**	**Max**	**Adv**	**Dec**	**Ties**	**APT**	**Sum**	**Stdev**
es915	−43.25	46.50	200	173	3	−.1356	−51.00	9.805
gc915	−74.50	51.70	219	154	3	.3210	120.70	11.593
ec915	−.0191	.0207	177	196	3	−.00033	−.1259	.00594

When the currency strengthens (euro > 0) in these three early-morning hours, in the 323 trading days during the 09:00 to 15:00 six-hour span, there was an inverse relationship between the two response variables (Table 13.3). The summary result for the equities was positive (315.25 points); whereas, the impact on gold was negative (−$137.70).

The effect of this currency rising three hours before taking a long six-hour position in the ES contract resulted in a .9760 APT profit in 323 days (175-147-1), this compares favorably to the .3633 APT with 712 trading days; consequently, it supports our hypothesis.

Furthermore, these results verified our hypothesis stating that a strengthening eurozone currency would decrease the price of gold, as this precious metal commodity took a beating, by falling $137.70 in these 323 trading days (−$0.4263 APT).

After experiencing weakness in the early-morning hours, does this currency produce an opposite reaction in our two response variables (Table 13.4)?

In contrast to a rising currency, these response variables reacted differently. A weakening of this currency (euro < 0) in these three hours (06:00 to 09:00), was responsible for a 51-point decline in the ES contract, but an

TABLE 13.5 After splitting trading in the euro in the earlier three-hour session into either a rising or falling category, notice the performance sign changes in the three commodities, which is indicative of a substantive predictor variable.

	EC 06:00 to 09:00	
Summary Scores 09:00 to 15:00	Euro > 0	Euro < 0
	n = 323	n = 376
es915	315.25	–51.00
gc915	–137.70	120.70
ec915	.1414	–.1259

advance of $120.70 in the GC contract; this reinforces our earlier convictions about our research hypothesis.

A summary of these two early-morning (06:00 to 09:00) currency conditions is found in Table 13.5.

These findings support our hypothesis because of the differences found when we split the earlier currency contract into a situation of rising/falling price direction. The es915 had a 366.30 absolute point difference; whereas, the GC contract had a $258.40 absolute point difference. The absolute difference in the independent variable between the two categories was $0.2673. Certainly, these findings demonstrate statistical significance.

Any performance discrepancy occurs because of the 13 three-hour sessions in which the ec69 =.0000; therefore, they are not part of ec69 > 0 or ec69 < 0 calculations.

In the past two years, the faintest suggestion of an epochal collapse in sovereign fiscal credit has produced a panic response, taking down companies over mounting concerns for the welfare of the equities market. Since our analysis is showing an inverse relationship, a weakening of currency prices appears to brighten the prospects for gold bugs.

Outlying Scores

With a strong downturn in the early morning price of the euro, will it take down equities, but spark a rally in gold?

The analysis in Table 13.6 tracks the two contracts from March 1, 2009, until December 1, 2011

Not surprisingly, when we run a study of the 72 weakest declines (Table 13.7) in the EC contract's fall (this entails 10 percent of the scores,

TABLE 13.6 These are the percentile scores for trading the EC contract between 06:00 to 09:00.

Percentile Scores	Euro 06:00 to 09:00
.95	.00644
.90	.00479
.80	.00260
.50	–.00030
.20	–.00320
.10	–.00499
.05	–.00635

TABLE 13.7 This represents the 72 worst scores (10th percentile) of trading by the EC contract during the three hours from 06:00 to 09:00.

Euro < –.00499	Trading from 09:00 to 15:00							
10th Percentile	**Min**	**Max**	**Adv**	**Dec**	**Ties**	**APT**	**Sum**	**Stdev**
es915	–43.25	24.25	35	37	0	–1.15	–82.50	11.90
gc915	–37.70	27.60	46	25	1	1.64	118.20	11.60

representing a decline <–.00479), equities fell −82.50 points; however, the rally in the GC contract was massive ($1.64 APT with a $118.20 return in these 72 trading opportunities).

The =PERCENTILE(range of 712 days,.10) function reports 10 percent of the scores (<–.00499) in this analysis.

Of course, if the 72 worst scores deliver value, can we gather more meaningful information about the early-morning movements of this currency by investigating those scores from the 5th percentile?

The =PERCENTILE(range of 712 days,.05) reports 5 percent of the scores (<–.006345)

=IF(ec69 cell value <–.006345, ec69, "")

This pertains to those qualifying scores with ec69 <–.006345. This statement is asking for the 36 steepest declines of the euro within these early morning hours.

A scattergram is a handy device, but considering there are 712 – 36 days of blank spaces in the performance column, how do you draw one? More specifically, how do you get the 36 scores in the column with the ec69 information along with the corresponding results of the gc915 response variable? One way to capture these 36 scores is by using the filtering function (it is located in the View ribbon and has the shape of a funnel); however, remove the check in the "blanks" space (Figure 13.7).[4]

Figure 13.8 is scattergram of the 36 scores of the ES equities contract starting at a <−.006345 change in the euro.

FIGURE 13.7 After using the filtering function, uncheck the blank box to capture the necessary performance scores.

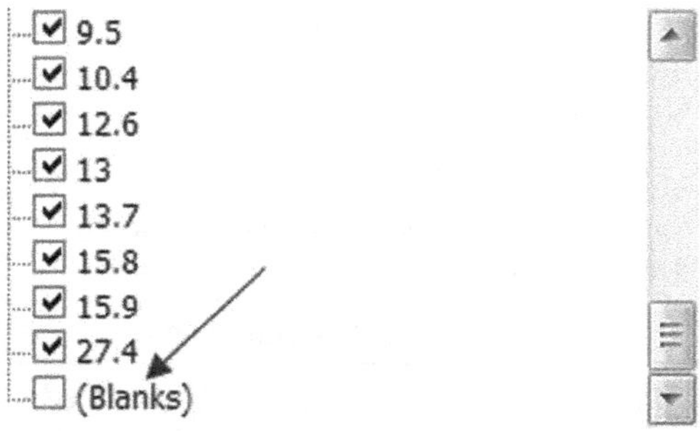

FIGURE 13.8 This is a scattergram showing the steepest declines (5th percentile) of trading by the euro (EC contract during the three hours from 06:00 to 09:00) applied to the ES equities futures contract trading from 09:00 to 15:00.

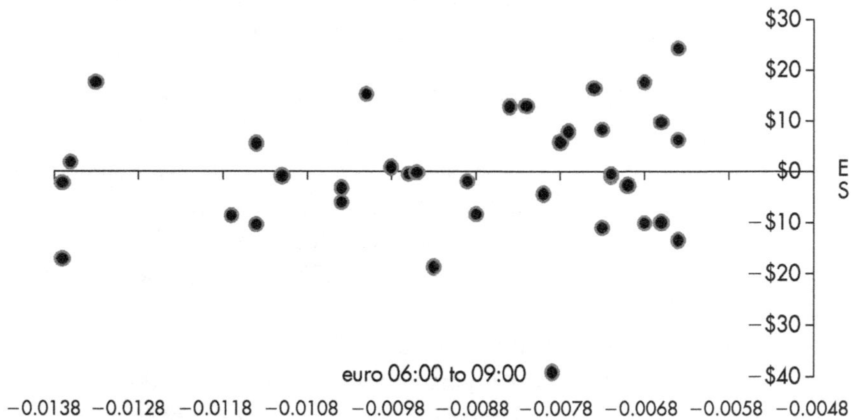

[4]Another approach, though it takes more steps, is to us the IF statement using <> "" as the true response.

FIGURE 13.9 This is a scattergram that includes the steepest declines (5th percentile) of the EC contract during the three hours from 06:00 to 09:00; they are applied to the GC gold contract trading from 09:00 to 15:00.

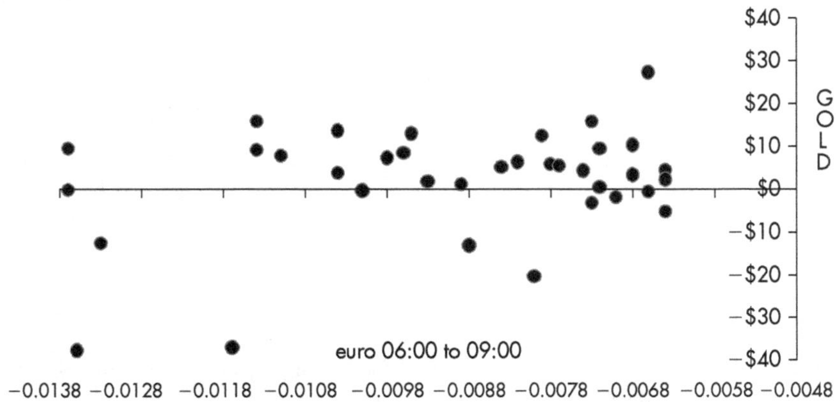

When the euro falls <−.006345 (36 scores), the ES contract trading from 09:00 to 15:00 gave back 9.25 points in 36 sessions (−.2570 APT). The largest loss (−39.25 points) was responsible for most of this setback.

Always take notice of those outlying scores with the largest declines. In this setting, they did not put unnecessary strain on the price of equities, but each instrument responds differently. We turn next to a scattergram of a weakening currency with the worst 36 scores, but use the GC contract as our dependent variable (Figure 13.9).

When scores fall in this 5th percentile, the 36 steepest early morning declines in the euro brought the gleam back to gold, with $74.20 in profits (a $2.06 APT advantage). In this case, however, the five biggest outlying currency scores were responsible for two $30-plus losses.

Price Brackets

Another aspect for us to cover is the price of the euro. Certainly, an early morning price change by itself has been a meaningful predictor; however, how does this performance differ when the eurozone currency is relatively strong (at a price above $1.4000) or relatively weak (at a price below $1.300)?

Before running the analysis, below are the frequencies of the EC contract at an opening price of 06:00 (Tables 13.8a and 13.8b).

TABLE 13.8a The frequency of trading days among six pricing categories for the EC contract.

Euro Price at 06:00	Coding of Category	Number of Trading Days
<1.2500	1	34
<1.3000	2	70
<1.3500	3	129
<1.4000	4	194
<1.4500	5	196
≥1.4500	6	89
SUM		712

TABLE 13.8b This illustration mixes the dates for the purpose of demonstrating the =IF statement to produce the 06:00 pricing categories (CAT) for the EC contract.

	A	B	C	D	E	F
1	Date	ec6	ec69	es915	gc915	CAT
2	12/01/11	1.3493	–.0009	1.50	–3.70	3
3	11/09/11	1.3675	–.0061	–19.00	–24.10	4
4	09/05/11	1.4123	–.0020	–9.25	13.30	5
5	08/18/11	1.4396	–.0031	–29.25	8.60	5
6	08/18/10	1.2901	.0010	3.25	3.90	2
7	06/01/10	1.2130	.0052	11.75	–2.10	1
8	01/12/10	1.4504	–.0038	–2.25	–17.50	6

By taking random samples of dates, we can show how to write a categorical response in the cat column (F column):

CELL "F2"
=IF(B2<1.25,1,IF(B2<1.3,2,IF(B2<1.35,3,IF(B2<1.4,4,IF(B2<1.45,5,6)))))
CELL "F3"
=IF(B3<1.25,1,IF(B3<1.3,2,IF(B3<1.35,3,IF(B3<1.4,4,IF(B3<1.45,5,6)))))
CELL "F4"
=IF(B4<1.25,1,IF(B4<1.3,2,IF(B4<1.35,3,IF(B4<1.4,4,IF(B4<1.45,5,6)))))

TABLE 13.9 Descriptive statistics of the ES contract (09:00 to 15:00) within each of the six categories using the 06:00 price of the EC contract.

09:00 Price of Euro	n	Mean	Sum
Lowest to 1.2499	34	−1.846	–62.75
1.2500 to 1.2999	70	.639	44.75
1.3000 to 1.3499	129	1.448	186.75
1.3500 to 1.3999	194	.161	31.25
1.4000 to 1.4499	196	.188	36.75
1.4500 to highest	89	.247	22.00
ES Summary	712	.363	258.75

The performance of equities by currency pricing category is shown in Table 13.9.

This shows the performance of the equities contract within the six currency pricing categories. In the 34 days with the 06:00 price of the EC contract below 1.2500, equities fell 62.75 points; however, the other five categories were in the black.

When at a price of 1.30 to 1.35, the ES contract amassed 186 of the 258 points; however, when the 06:00 price was above 1.35, the gains were less impressive.

Table 13.10 displays the performance of the ES contract, but separates these results according to the 06:00 to 09:00 price movement of the euro. Clearly, a long position from 09:00 to 15:00 in the equities market after a rising currency (euro > 0) was the best choice.

This factorial design examines the performance of the ES contract from 09:00 to 15:00, within the six pricing categories at 06:00 by the performance of the EC contract when this currency is stronger (euro > 0), weaker (euro < 0) or in the 13 days in which there is no price change (euro = 0) from 06:00 to 09:00.

An evaluation of the early-morning price differences show a wide disparity between a rising euro, with a 315.25 point advance, and a falling euro, with a 51 point decline; moreover, the largest difference among the categories was 1.25 to 1.30 and 1.35 to 1.40.

A cylinder chart (Figure 13.10) portrays these differences. With the exception of the weakest category (< −1.2500), an advancing currency (euro > 0) creates a positive score for the other brackets.

FIGURE 13.10 With the exception of the weakest category, a strengthening of the European currency (euro > 0), when trading within the hours of 06:00 to 09:00, generates more profits for this equities contract.

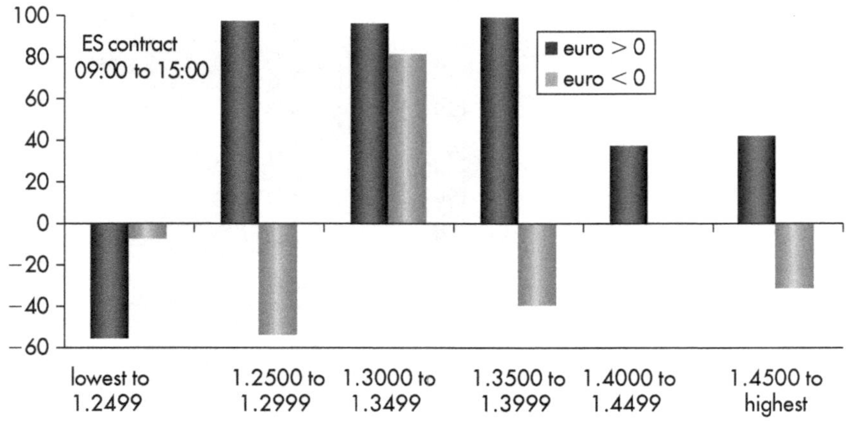

FIGURE 13.11 The gray line traces the running summary of equities when the early-morning EU currency strengthens, that is, the euro rises in price between 06:00 to 09:00. After reaching 1.50, the steep unrelenting drop has little impact on equities.

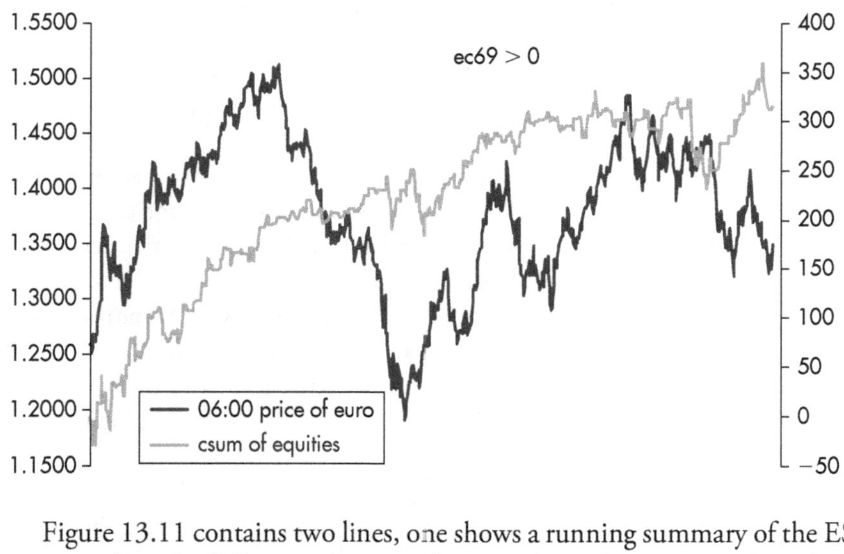

Figure 13.11 contains two lines, one shows a running summary of the ES contract when the EC contract strengthens in the early morning; the other, follows the 06:00 price of the EC contract.

A relentless downward drop of the EC contract holds equities at a standstill. Most apparent is the quick getaway from the starting gate, but as the currency falls below 1.5000, it reverses direction. This steep drop, pushing the EC contract to its lowest price, did not reflect negatively on equities, as the currency strengthens, equities slowly rise to their highest cumulative sum before slightly tailing off at the conclusion of this study.

The daily price of the EC contract, disguises its effect on the equities market. Unfortunately, when using a predictor variable, most pundits consider a strong correlation between instruments as an absolute requirement for success. Nevertheless, in spite of the weak correlation (r = .208) between these two variables, when this currency strengthens after a 06:00 price of $1.2500, the equities contract from 09:00 to 15:00 was capable of making some impressive gains (315.25 + −55.50).

The Effect of the Euro on Gold

The 712-day performance of the GC contract by categories can be seen in Table 13.11.

This shows the performance of the precious metal contract within the six currency pricing categories. Gold certainly did not sparkle when the 06:00 price of the EC contract was 1.3000 to 1.3499; however, there were some bright spots, but with a $29.20 advance in 712 trading days, expectations were low. When the currency starts the day above 1.3500, gold was more likely to go up in price.

TABLE 13.10 Descriptive statistics of the ES contract (09:00 to 15:00) within each of the six categories (EC 06:00 price) by price direction of the EC contract from 06:00 to 09:00. Essentially, we are using price as a predictor variable by putting an emphasis on this currency's direction during the early morning hours.

	Euro > 0		Euro < 0		Euro = 0	
09:00 Price of Euro	**n**	**es915**	**n**	**es915**	**n**	**es915**
Lowest to 1.2499	18	–55.50	16	–7.25	0	0.00
1.2500 to 1.2999	43	97.00	26	–53.75	1	1.50
1.3000 to 1.3499	63	96.25	63	81.25	3	9.25
1.3500 to 1.3999	89	99.00	102	–39.50	3	–28.25
1.4000 to 1.4499	79	36.50	113	0.00	4	0.25
1.4500 to highest	31	42.00	56	–31.75	2	11.75
ES Summary	323	315.25	376	–51.00	13	–5.50

TABLE 13.11 Descriptive statistics of the GC contract (09:00 to 15:00) within each of the six categories using the 06:00 price of the EC contract.

09:00 Price of Euro	n	Mean	Sum
Lowest to 1.2499	34	–.856	–29.10
1.2500 to 1.2999	70	.820	57.40
1.3000 to 1.3499	129	–.694	–89.50
1.3500 to 1.3999	194	.274	53.20
1.4000 to 1.4499	196	–.045	–8.80
1.4500 to highest	89	.517	46.00
GC Summary	712	.0410	29.20

Since the profitability of these categories skips a bracket, it inspires less confidence in the results; therefore, I would monitor them carefully before parting with my finances. The cautious inference is not in the procedure but in trading this particular instrument. When evaluating a different commodity, it is best to run this procedure before arriving at any hasty conclusions.

Price Direction within a Category

Next, Table 13.12 examines the performance of the GC contract from 09:00 to 15:00, within the six pricing categories by the 06:00 price of the EC contract. The pricing categories reflect a stronger (euro > 0), weaker (euro < 0) as well as the 13 days in which there was no price change (euro = 0) within the trading hours from 06:00 to 09:00.

In the earlier presence of a rising euro, the price of gold was unable to advance, falling –$137.70 in 323 trading days; however, in 63 trading days, the 1.3500 to 1.3999 category was responsible for −136.10 of this loss.

At a price below 1.3500, the 06:00-to-09:00 price direction of this currency was instrumental in producing contrasting results. This response variable (gc915) fell back badly, losing $192.10 in 124 trading days when the euro was strengthening (> 0), but ran up $100.90 in 105 trading days, after experiencing weakness (< 0). Although these findings found statistical significance among some aspects of this study, it is still our task to inspect the reliability of these numbers in a more recent trading setting.

FIGURE 13.12 When the 06:00 price of the euro was below 1.3500, along with an early-morning price advance, these two conditions resulted in a $192.10 drop in the price of gold (gc915).

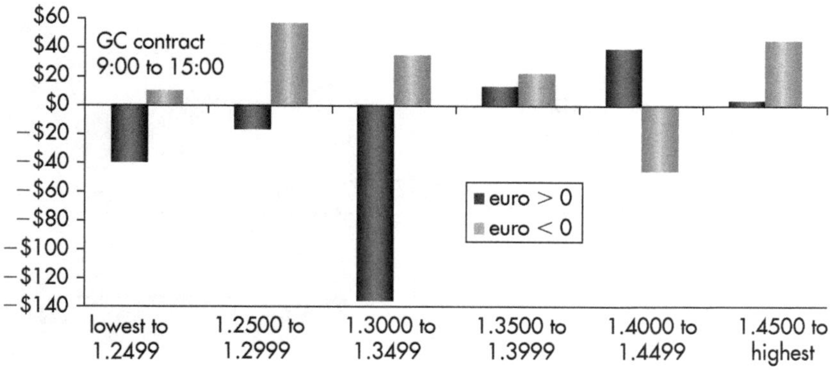

A weaker currency (euro < 0) produced five positive performance categories, albeit small price changes, with the most favorable one from 1.25 to 1.30.

Clearly, the cylinder chart (Figure 13.12) shows how a rising euro deflates gold prices when the euro is below a price of 1.35.

When in the earlier presence of a falling euro, in 376 trading days, there was a $120.70 appreciation in its 09:00 to 15:00 setting, producing positive results in five of the categories, with the one losing effort coming from the 1.4000 to 1.4499 category.

TABLE 13.12 Descriptive statistics of the GC contract (09:00 to 15:00) within each of the six categories (EC 06:00 price) by price direction of the EC contract from 06:00 to 09:00.

	Euro > 0		Euro < 0		Euro = 0	
09:00 Price of Euro	**n**	**gc915**	**n**	**gc915**	**n**	**gc915**
Lowest to 1.2499	18	−39.40	16	10.30	0	.00
1.2500 to 1.2999	43	−16.60	26	56.30	1	17.70
1.3000 to 1.3499	63	−136.10	63	34.30	3	12.30
1.3500 to 1.3999	89	12.90	102	22.10	3	18.20
1.4000 to 1.4499	79	38.90	113	−46.30	4	−1.40
1.4500 to highest	31	2.60	56	44.00	2	−.60
GC Summary	323	−137.70	376	120.70	13	46.20

FIGURE 13.13 This is the running sum of the GC contract (csum of gold) when this currency's 06:00 price is within 1.30 to 1.3499 and advances in the 06:00 to 09:00 setting. The primary axis (black line) shows the 06:00 price of this EU currency over the 712 trading days (March 2009 to December 2011).

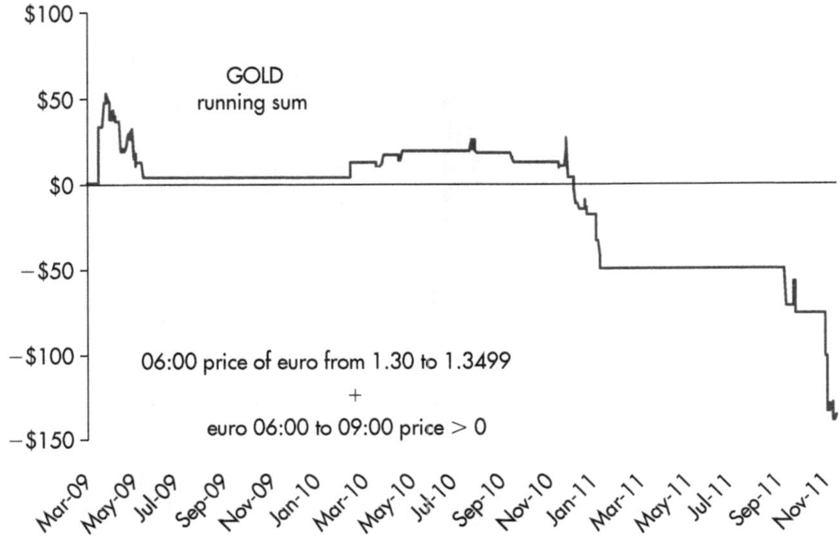

Figure 13.13 is the line chart showing the running summary of this $136.10 loss on those days in which the currency strengthens when it starts the 06:00 session between a price of 1.3000 to 1.3499.

Summary

As always, there are few absolute rules, but there are guidelines when using predictor variables. For instance, when the findings from our analysis contain less volatility, it produces more reliability in our forecasting; therefore, our investigation requires less back testing.

The inclusion of more variables often reduces the error term, which produces a more accurate representation of future prices. The rub is, when the study contains more variables it often necessitates more cases to justify confidence in our findings.

You can strengthen a study's predictive ability by including two independent variables. They will augment your predictive accuracy by allowing you to see how these variables working together give you a fuller picture of your response variable.

Technicians make a compelling case for taking a position on the basis of previous price patterns; nevertheless, there is a paucity of work done on how a leading indicator influences the price of the instrument you are trading. This is unfortunate because these contributing factors often drain the power from your most dependable indicators. Pundits may disagree over the efficacy of these leading variables because their influence does not hold steady; within a shifting economic landscape, the variable possessing the biggest impact over a commodity does not always maintain celebrity status—it can take many weeks, but eventually another contributory variable comes along and supplants it in importance.

Remember, numerous factors affect market movements; therefore, trading information is never free from the entanglement of other variables. The precise amount of influence it has over our response variable constantly changes. Before long, another contributory variable will come along and easily overshadow the current one.

With many prospects circling about, the process of rejecting those variables with less predictability becomes a daunting task; however, with experience it becomes easier to recognize these extraneous forces.

CHAPTER 14

Cross-Hedging Strategies

If a man will begin with certainties, he shall end in doubts; but if he will be content to begin with doubts, he shall end in certainties.

—Francis Bacon

Most traders perform best in a bullish setting; however, they suffer losses when equities markets confront a downturn. Adopting a cross-hedging strategy is particularly good for those individuals who have difficulty timing the direction of the market, but fare better at stock picking good plays over bad.

This strategy pits two forces against one another. For instance, given two instruments, you want two opposing trading positions: taking a long position in the one with the better probability of success and shorting the one that is likely to underperform.

Furthermore, for those traders applying this strategy, it is the perfect remedy when the market suffers a series of heart-stopping down days, without putting your capital in harm's way; this takes the worry away from participating in a market on the skids.

When you are not playing this strategy, you can select stocks with better performance records. Nevertheless, long positions in a bearish trading environment are going to be unprofitable. This strategy insulates you from the vagaries of the market because you can produce positive results in a bullish, bearish, or sideways environment; however, without a good stock-picking system, the possibility of steady losses is a realistic concern.

As you will see, when attempting to construct a cross-hedging strategy, an analysis of different instruments often maximizes our trading prospects. In fact, searching for these cross-hedging plays frequently results in uncovering more trading prospects for conventional trades, such as simply taking long or short positions in those instruments under investigation.

We begin by developing a cross-hedge among the popular trading indices. In order to make their designation easier to reference, the monikers are given with a short description.

Nickname	**Symbol**	**Index**	**Trading Class**
spiders	SPY	S&P 500	large cap
small caps	IWM	Russell 2000	small cap
cues	QQQ	NASDAQ 100	technology

As we go forward, with experience we can increase the complexity of our designs by including more instruments in this strategy.

This study has two approaches to trading. For example, say your analysis favors the performance of the spiders over the cues; in response, you would take a long position in the spiders together with a short position in the cues. More likely, however, by mixing these index funds you will discover more percentage plays. Under these circumstances, instead of cross-hedging, you would simply take either a long or short position.

Size of Position

In order to remove the influence of the market, it is important to give each position approximately the same weighting. How do you produce this comparable outcome? Your first reaction might be to simply balance the shares by their stock price. For example, when pitting two companies against one another, say the better one is at \$20, the other at \$10. It would make sense to buy 100 shares (100 × \$20) in the company you favor, but take a 200 share (200 × \$10) short position in the company with a less promising prospect for success.

On a price basis, holding the long position does not always produce income. For instance, the following combination of positions results in a \$4 loss.

A 100 share long position at \$20, advances \$0.20 = \$20 profit, but 200 shares short on a \$10 company with a \$0.12 daily advance produces a \$24 loss. Consequently, we are looking for your long position to outperform your short position on a percentage basis. Once we accomplish this, we can have a profitable outcome despite the movements of the market.

TABLE 14.1 This reports the average opening price over 300 trading days.

ETF	Mean Score	Stdev
SPY	125.86	6.30
IWM	76.51	5.87
QQQ	55.68	1.65

Nevertheless, selecting a comparable allotment of shares between these two companies is not an easy task. The price of an instrument is a good beginning, but other factors, such as the volatility among instruments should influence your decision

Pricing Dissimilarities

This study contains 300 trading days and runs from October 8, 2010, to December 15, 2011

The 300-day average opening price for these three instruments can be seen in Table 14.1.

The breakdown of price among the indices is as follows:

SPY/IWM = 1.65
SPY/QQQ = 2.26
IWM/QQQ = 1.37

The easy approach is for us to work around this premise:

100 shares SPY = 165 shares of IWM
100 shares SPY = 226 shares of QQQ
100 shares IWM = 137 shares of QQQ

This appears convincing; still, using price by itself is a good, but an imprecise measure. You can achieve greater accuracy, however, in producing symmetry in the buying/selling share allocation among instruments by assessing their volatility.

Going forward, there are many possibilities, but in applying this strategy, my focus is on the daily percentage change in price. We begin with three line charts (Figure 14.1) demonstrating daily percentage price change differences among the three indices.

FIGURE 14.1 The 300-day running summary for the three indices in the daily trading session.

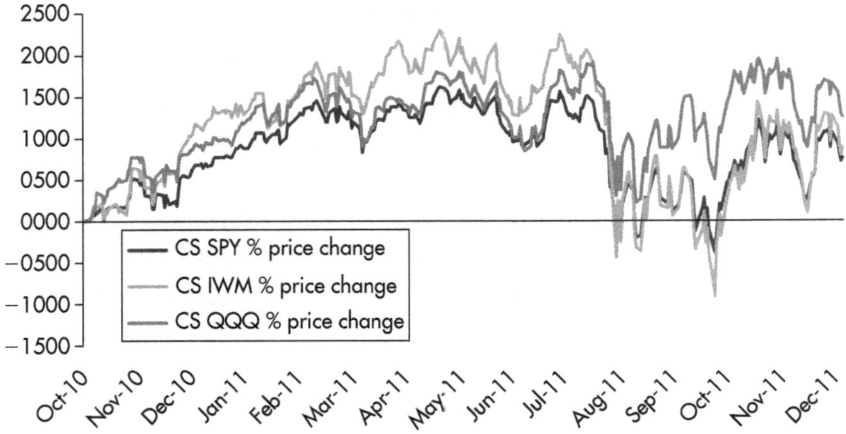

PC = ((Closing price (t_{-0}) − closing price (t_{-1})) / closing price (t_{-1}))

This is a preliminary investigation of the running daily percentage change performance among these three funds. The gaps between the lines demonstrate the viability of this cross-hedging strategy, the wider the spacing among funds, the more opportunity. Early on, the largest opening is in the small caps (IWM); however, in the fall of 2011, the spiders produce the widest separation.

We begin by turning our attention to an environment with a more extensive trading setting. In order to do this, it is necessary to make an assessment of these three funds with two-way combinations:

Daily Comparison

SPY-IWM
SPY-QQQ
IWM-QQQ

After completing this process, draw a running summary of these combinations. The purpose of this assignment is to uncover trending patterns.

Figure 14.2 begins a daily comparison of the large-cap spiders (SPY) against the small cap index of 2,000 stocks (IWM).

In the fall of 2010, the line chart between the SPY-IWM combination declines. Since we are subtracting SPY from IWM, a dropping line indicates

FIGURE 14.2 The daily percentage price change contrast of the spiders with the small cap index. The spiders underperform until April 2011, after plunging again to a familiar bottom; they battle back with a strong double-digit rally, but finally slip back in the fall of 2011 holding at a 2 percent percentage change loss to the small caps.

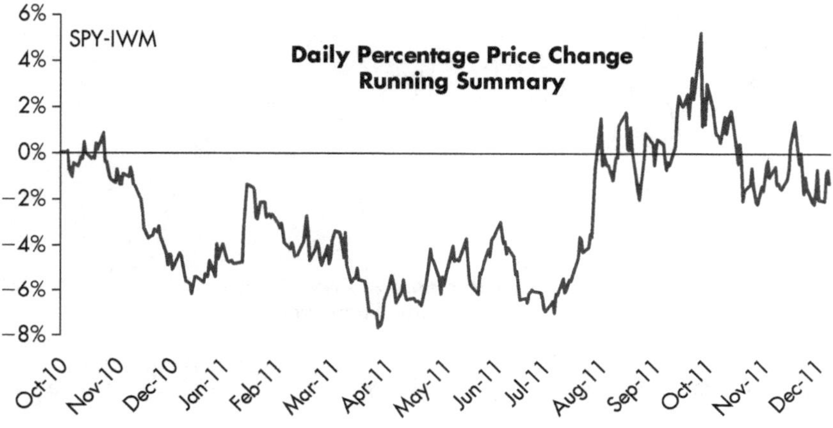

TABLE 14.2 The line chart (Figure 14.2) between the SPY-IWM descends because the spiders underperform the small caps by this margin. The percentage daily price advance extends from October 8, 2010, to December 15, 2011.

SPY	7.46%
IWM	8.73%
QQQ	12.47%

weakness in the spiders. After heading down to −.0618 on December 15, 2010, the spiders rally, but fall back below this earlier bottom. These prominent spikes persist; until July 13, 2011, when the spiders briefly drop below −6 percent, before making a strong recovery over the breakeven line. Once spiking above 5 percent, the spiders fall back, finally holding firmly at a multiple bottom of −2 percent.

In order to make this system work, your agility in acting on this cross-hedging opportunity after July 11 is critical.

Before moving on, the running summary of the daily percentage return of these indices represents a positive trading environment with the cues possessing the best percentage gain (Table 14.2).

Figure 14.3 is a running summary of the difference between the daily percentage price changes within the SPY-QQQ combination.

FIGURE 14.3 The running summary of the SPY – QQQ combination. After meandering in a restrictive trading environment, in July 2011 the spiders underperform, but regain their footing in the fall of 2011.

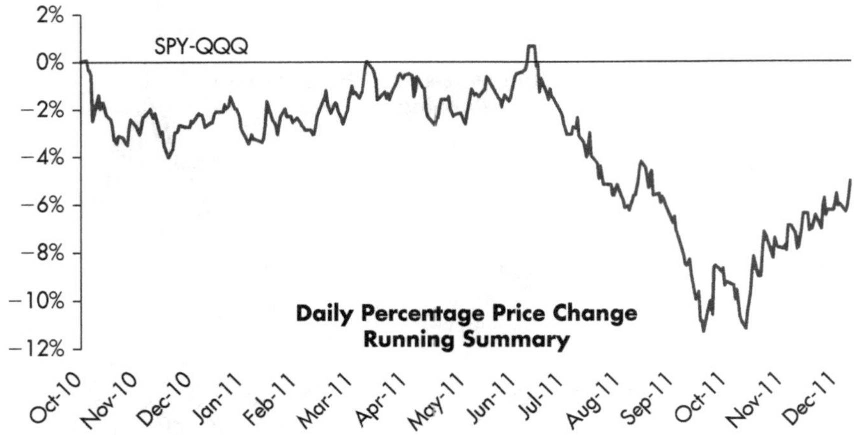

FIGURE 14.4 The confrontation between the IWM-QQQ indices offers opportunity for some productive cross-hedging trades.

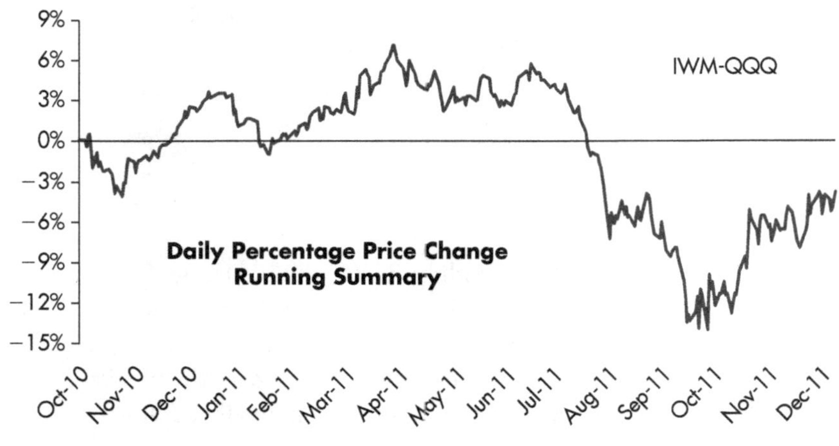

Whenever there is an acute drop (July 2011 to October 2011), it presents a cross-hedging play by buying shares in the cues but selling shares in the spiders. Market technicians may differ in the trigger for this hedge, but once the spiders fell below their previous bottom (around −4 percent), the slide was relentless. The spiders, however, apparently were oversold as they put on a strong year-end rally.

TABLE 14.3 The descriptive statistics for the overnight session give a slight advantage to the small caps.

n = 300	Min	Max	Adv	Dec	Ties	$ Sum	$ APT	$ Stdev
SPY	−3.47	3.44	155	144	1	3.34	.0111	1.024
IWM	−2.83	2.90	160	138	2	4.64	.0155	.763
QQQ	−1.65	1.46	153	145	2	3.34	.0111	.447

TABLE 14.4 Descriptive statistics for the regular trading session over these 300 days (October 11, 2010, to December 15, 2011). The small caps, finishing with a $2.22 decline, were not able to keep pace with its rivals.

n = 300	Min	Max	Adv	Dec	Ties	$ Sum	$ APT	$ Stdev
SPY	−4.65	4.07	162	137	1	$2.31	.0077	1.141
IWM	−3.89	4.47	158	141	1	−$2.22	−.0074	1.025
QQQ	−1.81	1.72	156	143	1	$1.65	.0055	.573

The third combination pits the small cap index against the cues (Figure 14.4). Again it offers enough variation to make some interesting long-term trades. The small caps start strongly; hold their own in the spring of 2011, but fall to a 14 percent deficit, before they begin to take back some ground from the cues.

These steady trends provide enough firepower to successfully play this cross-hedging strategy. The small caps have the early advantage, but with a strong rally in the cues around July 2011, a cross-hedging strategy, until the fall of 2011, was an effective play. Thereafter, the small caps regain their dominance over the cues as they drift toward the breakeven line. Some similarities exist between the two combination charts with the cues (SPY-QQQ + IWM-QQQ), particularly, in the breakdown from July to September 2011, as well as the year-end recovery.

Before assessing this strategy, run an analysis showing the differences between the two trading sessions. Table 14.3 shows the price change $ summary scores of the three indices when trading in the overnight session. A review of the overnight statistics offers the investor a sterile forecast as there appear to be no restrictive plays. This can be seen for the regular session (Table 14.4) and the daily trading session (Table 14.5).

In these 300 trading days the small cap index has a small performance advantage in the overnight session. This difference fades, however, in the regular trading session.

TABLE 14.5 Descriptive statistics on the daily price change of the three indices. In percentage terms, the cues were the best-performing fund.

Daily Trading Session									
n = 300	**Min**	**Max**	**Adv**	**Dec**	**Ties**	**$ Sum**	**$ APT**	**% Sum**	**$ Stdev**
SPY	−7.82	5.22	167	133	0	$5.65	.0188	.0746	1.641
IWM	−6.21	4.34	163	137	0	$2.42	.0081	.0873	1.359
QQQ	−3.24	2.44	162	135	3	$4.99	.0166	.1247	.765

The separation of an instrument from the pack provides us with a long-term trading advantage. This, however, is a small representation of how we can make our trading decisions.

Outlying Scores

This series of statistics questions the effectiveness of excessive performance scores between two indices. Basically, we are seeking a cross-hedging opportunity when there is an aberrant price difference among indices. For instance, if the spiders come away with a daily percentage gain, but the other two indices have difficulty ending the day in the plus column, would it seem reasonable to buy shares in the underperforming indices but short the spiders?

The focus of the previous study was on the running summary performance between two indices. We were looking for trending patterns for a cross-hedging strategy. This system functions more on daily positions, as the source of your trading decisions occurs from outlying differences between two indices.

These are the cross-hedging combinations among the three index funds:

Daily Hedging Combinations (closing price t_{-0} − closing price t_{-1}))

long SPY versus short IWM
long SPY versus short QQQ
long IWM versus short QQQ
short SPY versus long IWM
short SPY versus long QQQ
short IWM versus long QQQ

Amid these combinations we are looking to take a cross-hedging position on the basis of the 30 best/worst daily price change differences between two

TABLE 14.6 After converting the daily performance of these funds into a percentage-change score, we are investigating those outlying scores within each cross-hedging combination.

300 Trading Days	Daily Percentage Difference between Funds		
	SPY − IWM	SPY − QQQ	IWM − QQQ
10th percentile	−.0075	−.0058	−.0099
90th percentile	+.0085	+.0057	+.0087

indices. Since we are investigating 300 days, this represents 10 percent of the outlying scores.

=PERCENTILE (range of 300 scores,.10) = 10th percentile
=PERCENTILE (range of 300 scores,.90) = 90th percentile

For instance, after converting the daily price change into a percentage score, we are going to run an analysis on the 30 worst days in which the spiders underperform the small caps (SPY < IWM) as well as the 30 best days in which the spiders outperform the small caps (SPY > IWM).

Table 14.6 shows the differences in percentage terms between the three combinations.

Since we have 300 trading days, a 10 percent outlier gives us the 30 worst/best scores for each of the three cross-hedging combinations.

The 30 steepest declines (10th percentile) have a negative sign because the fund with the highest price underperforms its counterpart:

SPY < IWM by < −0.75%
SPY < QQQ by < −0.58%
IWM < QQQ by < −0.99%

The 30 sharpest advances (90th percentile) have a positive sign because the fund with the highest price overperforms its counterpart:

SPY > IWM by > 0.85%
SPY > QQQ by > 0.57%
IWM > QQQ by > 0.87%

Research Question: Using the 30 best/worst daily scores from the three hedging combinations, what performance inferences can be made about trading this strategy when there is a long versus short hedging opportunity?

TABLE 14.7 This displays the results of trading on the following day after the spiders underperform the small cap stocks. Despite the losses in this environment, the 2.23 percent daily decline in the cues was not as bad as the 8.31 percent daily loss in the small caps.

SPY − IWM < −0.75%	SPY	IWM	QQQ
30-day $ summary	−$6.69	−$5.66	−$1.34

TABLE 14.8 When the spiders perform badly in comparison to the cues, a short position was the best alternative; however, there were no cross-hedging prospects.

SPY − QQQ < −0.58%	SPY	IWM	QQQ
30-day $ summary	-$5.84	-$3.55	-$3.65

TABLE 14.9 In the 30 days the results are unspectacular; however, the analysis affords us a very slight hedging opportunity. In percentage terms, the 4.24 percent advance in the small caps has a decisive advantage over the −2.37 percent decline in the cues.

IWM − QQQ < −0.99%	SPY	IWM	QQQ
30-day $ summary	−$0.68	$1.80	−$1.57

TABLE 14.10 Taken together, these are the 90 days of results found by adding the daily summary scores within the three previous hedging combinations.

10th percentile	SPY	IWM	QQQ
Count	90	90	90
90-day $ summary	−$13.21	−$7.41	−$6.56

Basically, we want to know, when comparing two instruments, does an excessive daily price difference affect performance on the following trading day?

Thirty Worst Scores Daily Comparisons

Table 14.7 shows the daily results of the lowest 10 percent (30 worst scores) for each of the three cross-hedging combinations.

The findings for the three possible combinations are contained in Table 14.8 (SPY − IWM), Table 14.9 (SPY − QQQ), and Table 14.10 (IWM − QQQ).

TABLE 14.11 Thirty-day performance results for the three index funds, after the spiders outperform the small cap stocks by 0.85 percent.

SPY – IWM > 0.85%	SPY	IWM	QQQ
30-day $ summary	$5.69	$6.84	$2.12

FIGURE 14.5 The results of trading on the following day, after the spiders strongly outperform the small cap index. This column chart shows the next-day performance of the cues (gray vertical line) versus the small cap index (black vertical line).

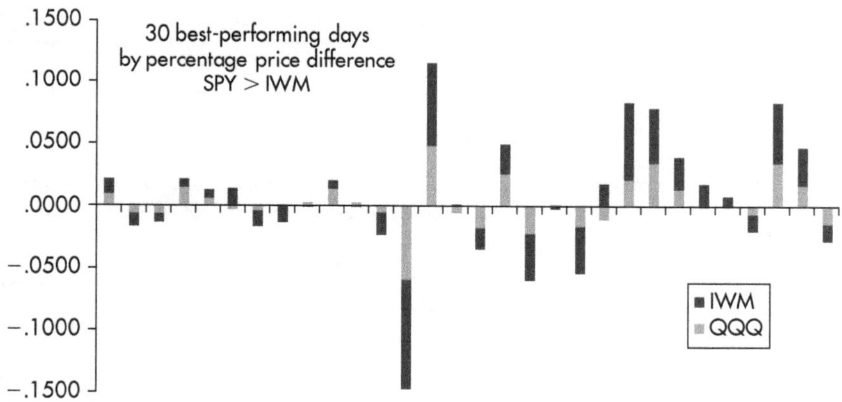

Most noteworthy were the heavy daily declines among these indices; going forward, we definitely want to monitor this meaningful performance pattern.

Thirty Best Scores Daily Comparisons

Below are the three cross-hedging combinations with the results of the 30 best scores (residing at or above the 90th percentile); that is, the scores with the greatest price differences for each of the three combinations.

Table 14.11 displays the 30 best scores on a daily basis using the SPY-IWM hedging combination.

After losing ground to the spiders, the small caps were the best performing index. With a $6.84 profit, it had a 6.54 percent (11.96% – 5.42%) advantage over the spiders and a 7.61 percent (11.96% – 4.35%) advantage over the cues.

Given the results of the SPY-IWM combination, the chart (Figure 14.5) depicts the daily percentage difference between the small caps (11.96 percent)

TABLE 14.12 After another thrashing by the spiders, the 30-day return of these indices was positive. Given these 30 days, the small caps again were the best percentage performers, rising $6.25 on the following trading day.

SPY – QQQ > 0.57%	SPY	IWM	QQQ
30-day $ summary	$8.60	$6.25	$2.92

TABLE 14.13 When the small caps have a big day, it was a good hedging opportunity. On the following day, the cues beat the small caps by $5.40 in these 30 days.

IWM – QQQ > 0.87%	SPY	IWM	QQQ
30-day $ summary	–$3.95	–$4.94	$0.46

TABLE 14.14 The summary results for the previous three hedging combinations were positive; the 8.57, 13.32, and 9.96 percent were the respective results of the SPY, IWM, and QQQ.

90th Percentile	SPY	IWM	QQQ
Count	90	90	90
30-day $ summary	$10.34	$8.15	$5.50

versus the cues (4.35 percent). The more recent dates (right side) display more volatility, with the small caps (black portion) taking a bigger share of the profits.

On a daily basis, Tables 14.12, 14.13, and 14.14 display the 30 outlying performances for the hedging combinations in this investigation.

In reference to excessive price differences among the indices, when the spiders outperformed their counterparts, the next trading day was positive; conversely, when they underperformed, the next trading day was negative.

Depending on the time frame, a comparison of these three indices is likely to offer different results. In comparing these two studies the earlier strategy using a line chart of the cumulative performance difference is better at producing a more conventional cross-hedging strategy. And since we are searching for trending patterns, trades are over a series of consecutive days or weeks. This is unlike the previous study because they do not consider trending patterns. The source of our trading action is on a daily basis, and its action is derived from taking a long or short position.

TABLE 14.15 Calculating the percentage share of volume for these three ETFs.

Date	V SPY	V IWM	V QQQ	VSUM	% SPY	% IWM	% QQQ
12/15/2011	198,559,039	50,080,310	58,674,911	307,314,260	.646	.163	.191
12/14/2011	237,738,827	77,673,450	63,657,276	379,069,553	.627	.205	.168

Widening the outlying scores produces a system overflowing with trading action; nevertheless, because of its unimpressive record, it does not qualify as a restrictive trading system because we are reducing our percentage of success. The inclusion of another predictor variable will often rectify this shortcoming.

Trading Volume as an Indicator

Trading volume generally contributes favorably as a predictor of price movements. Can a study using trading volume among the indices produce a cross-hedging opportunity?

We can run this analysis by measuring the daily volume of an index fund against the sum of all three indices. (A demonstration of this calculation can be seen in Table 14.15.)

Note that this calculation uses the daily proportion of trading volume among the three exchange-traded funds (ETFs). After calculating the daily percentages take the 300-day average score by using the =AVERAGE function.

SUM = the daily trading volume of the SPY + IWM + QQQ
VSUM = (volume SPY + volume IWM + volume QQQ)/3

Next, we have the percentage daily volume share of each index:

VOLUME SPY/vsum = vspy
VOLUME IWM/vsum = viwm
VOLUME QQQ/vsum = vqqq

Table 14.16 provides the statistics for the 300 trading days (October 11, 2010 to December 15, 1011).

The question is, what if one ETF grabs the lion's share of trading volume in a single trading day? More specifically, what happens when these instruments are one standard deviation above their average percentage share?

TABLE 14.16 The spiders capture nearly 61 percent of the daily trading volume among these three indices; therefore, they hold the largest percentage share. Although the two other instruments are not as active, they each represent about 19 percent of the daily trading activity.

300 Days	Percentage Daily Volume	Stdev Volume	1 Stdev above the Mean Score
SPY	.609	.043	.652
IWM	.192	.029	.221
QQQ	.199	.038	.237

TABLE 14.17 Results of the overnight session when the percentage volume of the index funds closes the trading day one standard deviation above its mean score. With the small caps exhibiting strong volume, the overnight session turns down; conversely, when the other two indices take on this leadership role, the return is positive.

		Overnight Trading Session		
Stdev above Mean	**n**	**SPY**	**IWM**	**QQQ**
SPY > 65.2%	46	\$5.59	\$3.53	\$2.07
IWM > 22.1%	44	−\$4.52	−\$3.23	−\$1.92
QQQ > 23.7%	49	\$3.29	\$3.50	\$2.83

Unlike most volume estimates, which strictly focus on the comparison of today's volume against a specific reference point, we are working with comparative volume among a collection of different instruments; consequently, we are measuring the performance of the overnight session when the percentage volume score for one of the three indices (VSPY, VIWM, or VQQQ) closes the trading day with its activity one standard deviation above its mean score (Table 14.17).

After a day in which the spiders consume > 65.2 percent of the volume, in these 46 trading days, they produce the strongest gains in the overnight session. When the cues qualified by exhibiting strong volume, the performance of the overnight session when trading these index funds was positive. Among them, the cues had the most attractive percentage play.

The small price differences across these volume categories do not fully support a cross-hedging strategy.[1] Given the three volume categories, the

[1]Given that we are restricting performance to the overnight session, it does constrain our returns; more opportunity for a wider discrepancy in price will occur when we expand our trading horizon.

TABLE 14.18 When separating the percentage volume leaders by either an advancing or declining regular trading session, the U.S. dollar summary discrepancies were most apparent when the small caps were most active.

% Share of Daily Trading Volume		**Overnight Trading Session**		
Is 1 stdev above 300-day mean	**n**	**SPY**	**IWM**	**QQQ**
SPY				
RTS of SPY > 0	20	\$1.25	\$0.63	\$0.14
RTS of SPY < 0	26	\$4.34	\$2.90	\$1.93
Summary	46	\$5.59	\$3.53	\$2.07
IWM				
RTS of IWM > 0	21	\$0.60	\$0.79	\$0.24
RTS of IWM < 0	23	−\$5.12	−\$4.02	−\$2.16
Summary	44	−\$4.52	−\$3.23	−\$1.92
QQQ				
RTS of QQQ > 0	25	\$2.15	\$2.61	\$1.75
RTS of QQQ < 0	24	\$1.14	\$0.89	\$1.08
Summary	49	\$3.29	\$3.50	\$2.83

cues give us the best opportunity, considering 100 shares of the spiders = 226 shares of the cues, this (\$3.29 to \$2.83) combination became our best hedging option. Meanwhile, when the Russell 2000 index receives most of the trading action, the numbers prove disappointing.

In following the standard procedure of separating an advancing from a declining regular session the breakdown is shown in Table 14.18.

Evaluation of SPY

When the percentage share of the spiders was over 65.2 percent, there were few hedging opportunities. The bulk of its gains came after a declining regular trading session.

Evaluation of IWM

When the percentage share of the small caps was over 22.1 percent, the 44 days of results were negative. Given this condition along with a negative

FIGURE 14.6 Given the strong volume in the small caps (IWM > 22.1 percent of VSUM) along with a declining RTS, the majority of these 23 overnight trades were facing down.

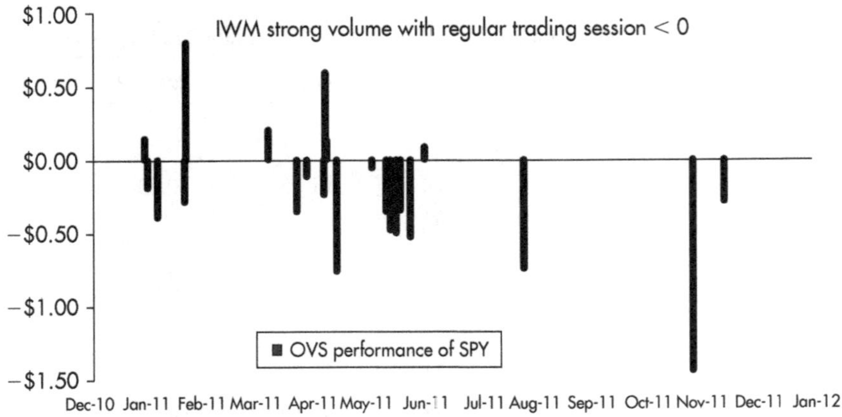

FIGURE 14.7 The small caps with a −$4.02 summary loss in the 30 overnight trading sessions are pointing down; however, there was less activity in recent days.

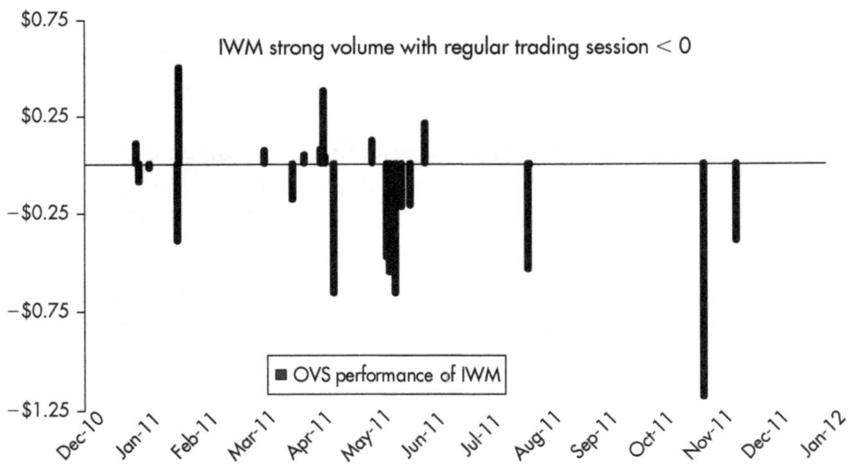

regular trading session, the overnight summary loss in 23 days was −$5.12 for the spiders, −$4.02 for the small caps, and −$2.16 for the cues.

Figures 14.6, 14.7, and 14.8 show the performance of these 23 days, in which the small caps were able to capture over 22.1 percent of the daily trading volume together with a declining regular trading session.

The directional patterns show the reciprocal relation among these three indices. Given similar pricing patterns, the spacing between them is close-

FIGURE 14.8 An evaluation of the overnight trading session of the cues does not differ from the other two indices; that is, the directional patterns are alike.

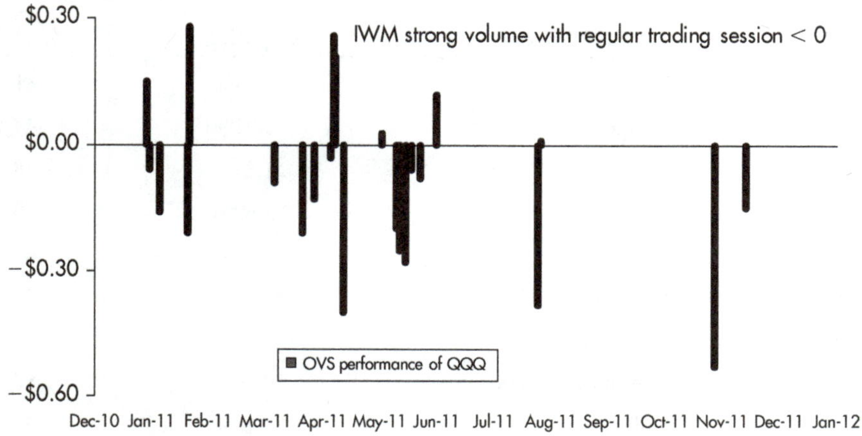

fitting; this offers us a very narrow margin of success. When trading a long trending pattern, if an opportunity arises—such as the small caps presenting themselves as the percentage leader along with a falling regular trading session—we would simply put more emphasis on taking a short position in the instrument demonstrating less success.

Evaluation of QQQ

When the percentage share of the cues was over 23.7 percent, the summary results were positive for both sessions. And it offered us the most attractive cross-hedging prospects as the cues held up fairly well against its rivals. An advancing regular session had a slight performance advantage over a declining one; however, the cues, in these 30 days, on a percentage basis were the performance leaders.

Of course, combinations of hedging possibilities abound. We can incorporate the different aspects of these past studies to construct more trading systems. The next study focuses on making decisions by using a comparison technique to construct a running summary.

Comparative Cross-Hedging System (CXS)

This study concentrates on the sector funds in the SPDR family (Table 14.19); however, this takes on a different cross-hedging approach from the

TABLE 14.19 These are the sectors representing the spiders. It consists of 500 companies; the largest weighting of these nine sectors arises from the technology sector. On April 30, 2012, its main contributor was Apple Inc., with 18.46 percent of this sector's weighting.

ETF	SPDR Sector	Weighting	Stocks
XLF	Financial	14.14%	81
XLE	Energy	12.01%	43
XLK	Technology	21.89%	78
XLB	Materials	03.69%	30
XLI	Industrials	10.96%	61
XLV	Health care	11.80%	52
XLP	Consumer stables	11.11%	42
XLY	Consumer discretionary	10.76%	80
XLU	Utility	03.66%	33
Sum	January 15, 2012	100	500

earlier ones in this chapter. Besides pitting different sectors against one another, it uses a comparative cross-hedging (CXS) approach; that is, it relies on one instrument—usually an equity index—to make a comparison with another instrument or between two or more instruments.

This study uses the spiders as a counterbalance to establish a baseline performance between instruments. For instance, if the spiders produce a daily percentage change of 1.00 percent, and a sector fund has a percentage gain of .80 percent, it receives a comparative change score of 1.00 − .80 = +.20. In a situation in which a sector has a percentage gain of 1.20 percent, it receives a comparative change score of 1.00 − 1.20 = −.20.

CCS = percentage daily change of spiders − percentage daily change of sector fund

Weaving a Strategy

This study examines the sector funds in the SPDR from August 12, 2009, to December 30, 2011 (603 trading days). These sector funds have complete transparency. By going to the www.sectorspdr.com, you can obtain a comprehensive listing of all 500 companies within its nine sectors.

FIGURE 14.9 With the financial sector experiencing a wave of selling as it racks up losses, this has been an attractive short play.

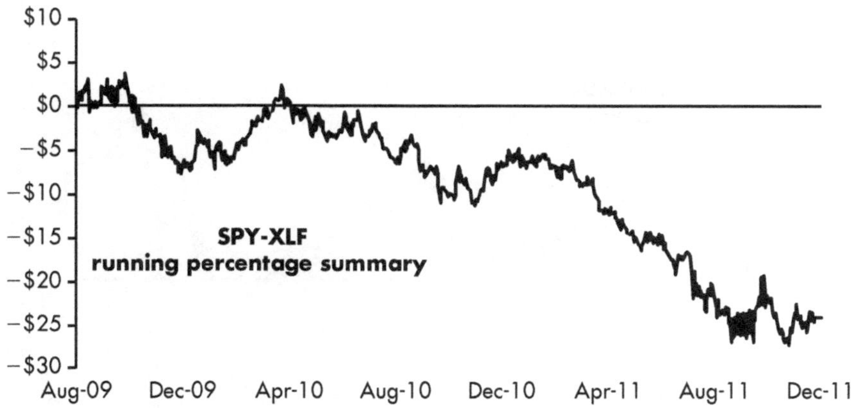

FIGURE 14.10 Early on, for about 200 trading days, the energy sector was a good downside play, but it snapped out of its doldrums running past a $20 cumulative profit before hitting resistance and backing down by making lower highs with a September 19, 2011, lower low.

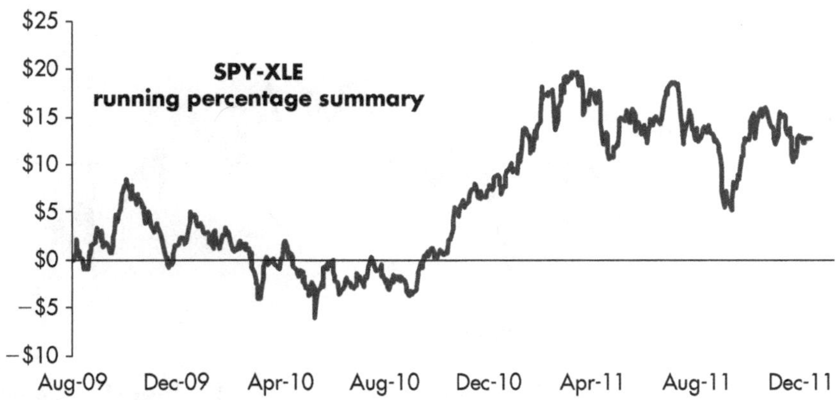

The comparative line charts in Figures 14.9 to 14.18 show the cumulative change scores on a daily basis; again we are subtracting the percentage change score for each sector against the spiders.

Some of this sector's funds have very long trend lines. When trading this system, success is derived from taking opposite positions in sectors moving in contrasting directions within the same time sequence.

FIGURE 14.11 The technology sector was a good channel play as it ran to a triple top before breaking above resistance. Most notable, however, were the multiple bottoms at around a −$2 deficit, which appears to have been the impetus behind a strong rally before sliding back down.

FIGURE 14.12 The basic materials sector has seen a $16 range; it has tremendous fractiousness as there was considerable indecisiveness. This was a particularly good hedge against gold (IAU).

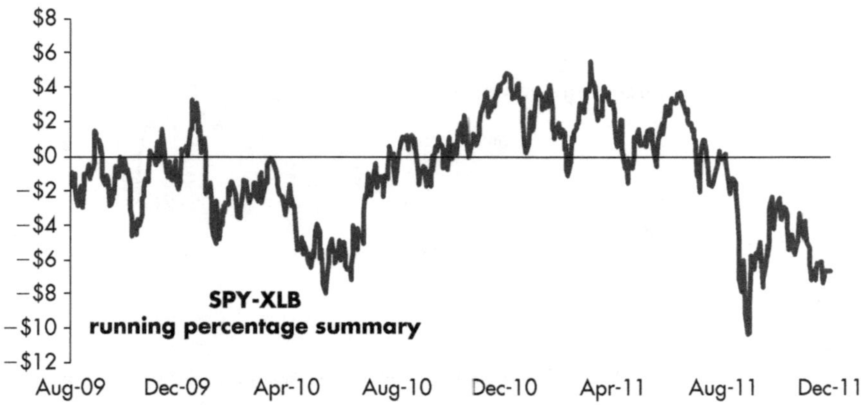

Since XLF is holding mostly banking stocks (Figure 14.9), this makes a perfect short because this sector has been battered by what some people believe to be casino capitalism. Once this ETF, which routinely averages 100 million shares per day, drifts lower, it becomes a pure short play. The party may be over, as it has been touching bottom at a summary loss of around $25; therefore, it remains to be seen if it will rally or break below recent support.

FIGURE 14.13 The industrials were a perfect play at about 200 days before bumping up against resistance; the slide lasting about 125 days took this sector back down to early support (late summer, 2010) before launching another rally.

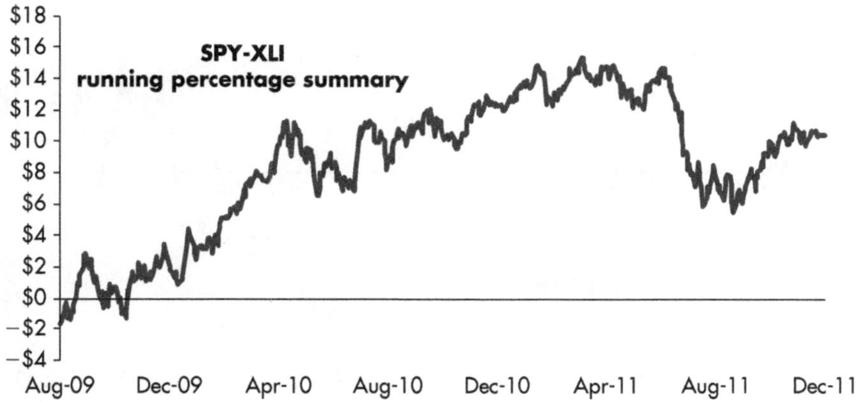

FIGURE 14.14 After a sickly start, the health care sector made a miraculous recovery in the spring of 2011, but it was unable to spurt above the breakeven point.

Once the technology sector turns on its high beams (Figure 14.11), it manages to make an explosive run before relinquishing its powerful gains.

An electrifying performance, in that, when XLU was moving down—these moves were long, sharp movements; conversely, when XLU was advancing, the two upward movements at $15-plus and $20-plus advances, were excellent buys. Going forward, follow the progress of its upward march, as it continuously encounters headwinds at breakeven, giving us a decisive sell sign.

FIGURE 14.15 The sector comprising consumer staples appears to follow along with the health care sector, but it was capable of piercing through the August 2010 previous high of $4.00 where it is still hovering.

FIGURE 14.16 The consumer discretionary sector offers a picture-perfect setting. Early on it deserves attention as an attractive buy against its competitors.

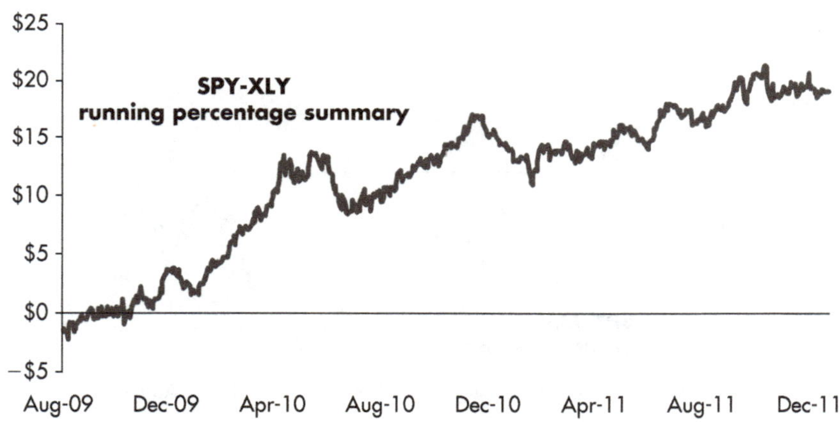

Convergent/Divergent Methods

With a basket of companies representing a sector fund, diversification of these companies puts the correlations among them on the strong side. With a strong positive relationship, we have a quandary over two hedging alternatives. Knowing the existing relationships among the sectors either construct a strategy by hedging two sectors with the highest correlations against

FIGURE 14.17 The utilities sector, because of its long decisive moves, was a good cross-hedging strategy.

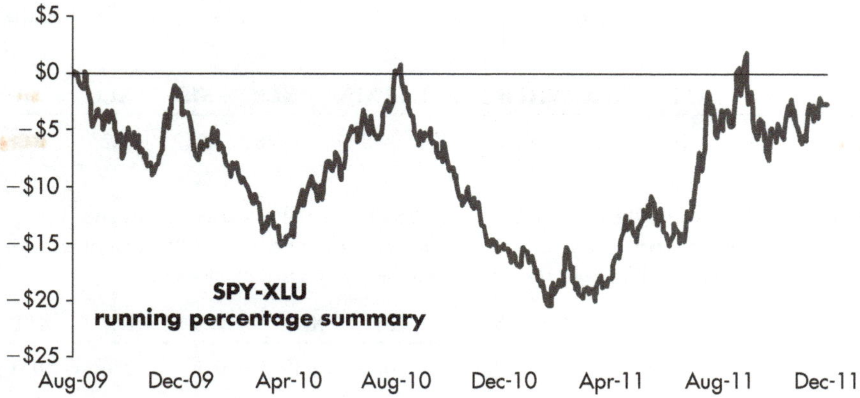

FIGURE 14.18 A slow start, with a run in April 2010, completing the year without breaking past a cumulative sum of $20. In 2011, this precious metal fund rallied as countries were buying it as an investment haven; before losing its sparkle, it pushed its way to $60 in August 2011.

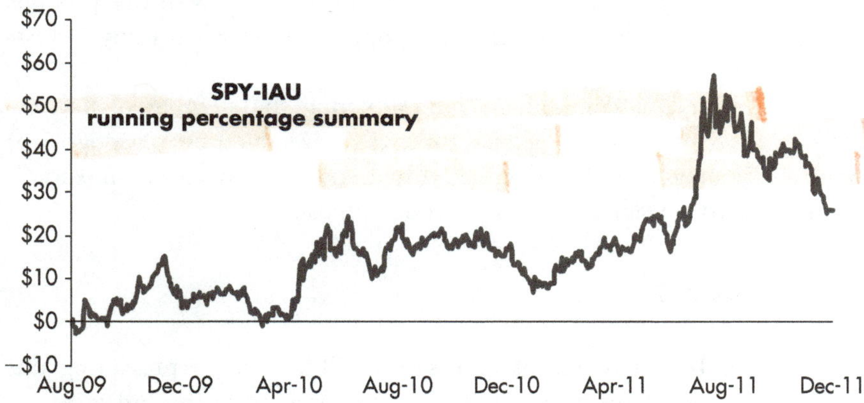

one another, or take aim by having the best-performing sectors compete directly against the worst performing sectors.[2]

Next we run the correlations of the percentage daily change of the spiders against each of the nine sector funds. We are including the gold fund (IAU)

[2]Naturally, there are numerous cross-hedging strategies when trading these sectors; therefore, it would take a thick book to adequately cover this topic.

TABLE 14.20 A percentage daily price change correlation score among 603 trading days from August 12, 2009, to December 30, 2011, between the spiders against the other ETFs. The utility sector has the lowest correlation (.823) with the spiders; however, the gold fund (IAU) does not share a strong correlation with the spiders or any of the other sector funds in the S&P 500 index.

	XLF	XLE	XLK	XLB	XLI	XLV	XLP	XLY	XLU	IAU
SPY	.928	.919	.945	.928	.964	.899	.878	.947	.823	.106

TABLE 14.21 Notice the minor relationships between the SPDR sector funds and gold (IAU). In running the percentage daily price change correlations of the SPDR sector funds with gold over these 603 trading days, there appears to be a very small relationship.

	XLF	XLE	XLK	XLB	XLI	XLV	XLP	XLY	XLU
IAU	.062	.200	.093	.238	.100	.080	.073	.056	.081

as part of our analysis. Table 14.20 shows the correlations of the spiders with the sectors representing the 500 companies in this popular index.

Table 14.21 reports the correlation of the sector funds with IAU.

Because this gold fund has practically no correlation with this precious metal, it creates an abundance of trading opportunities when using a cross-hedging strategy.

The four major components for estimating the strength of a cross-hedging strategy are (1) frequency of action, (2) duration of action, (3) intensity of action, and (4) repetitive patterns. Of course, your success depends on your readiness to act on your suppositions.

SPY versus XLF

XLF (Figure 14.19) is one of nine sector SPDR funds representing this popular index. Its percentage holding varies greatly; when this index regains its strength, it could control over 20 percent of the weighting of these 500 companies in the S&P 500. With an average daily trading volume of 98.821 million shares, it usually follows the spiders (SPY) on the daily leader board; therefore, the difference between the bid/ask price is often one penny, and, for our purposes, it is an easy stock to short.

This study contains 2,040 trading days and runs from January 2, 2004, to February 8, 2012.

The line chart displays the progression of XLF, as it exhibits three dissimilar pricing cycles. After trading in a restrictive environment for nearly

FIGURE 14.19 The line chart demonstrates this sector's daily price change over the past eight years.

three years, it makes two tries at surpassing a price of $40. Unsuccessful, it takes a precipitous plunge to its lowest price; thereafter, it shows some improvement. Since 2010, however, it has been contending with a $12 supporting price.

Going forward, this sector fund does not appear to offer us any promising prospects, but in a prosperous environment, it does offer us a good shorting opportunity because it underperforms most sector funds.

There are many trading combinations among sector funds; this one has the spiders competing against the finance sector. It has us exploiting a percentage mismatch in the daily performance between these two funds. Since it can go in either direction it gives us two contrasting research questions.

In either case we are looking for a daily percentage price change in which these two funds have a ± percentage difference. After a day in which the SPY outperforms XLF, is a long XLF versus a short SPY position a good play? After a day in which the XLF outperforms SPY, is a long SPY versus a short XLF position a good play?

The dates observed are September 28, 2009, to March 9, 2012.

SPY from $106.32 to $137.57 = +$31.25
XLF from $15.08 to $14.89 = −$0.19

The average 617-day price was $120.14 for the spiders in comparison to $14.69 for XLF. This ($120.28/$14.72) produces an 8.17 per share adjustment, which equates to a 100-share position in the spiders against an 817-share position in this sector fund.

FIGURE 14.20 The companies representing this finance sector appear to be trading in a constrictive range.

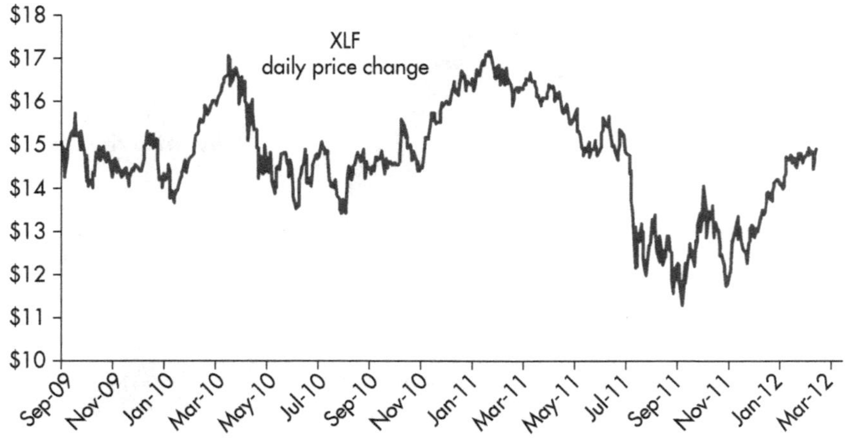

TABLE 14.22 The summary statistics of taking a 100-share long position in the spiders alongside an 800-share short position in the sector with a broad range of financial service firms.

	SPY +100 Shares	XLF −800 Shares
Trading Days	617	617
$ Sum	$3125	$152
$ APT	$5.065	$0.246
Adv	346	293
Dec	270	312
Win%	.561	.475

Figure 14.20 covers the daily price changes from September 29, 2009 to March 9, 2012 for the XLF sector fund; however, Figure 14.9 shows a running summary of the comparative price change between these two funds from August 12, 2009, to December 30, 2011.

Despite the large performance disparity between these two funds (Table 14.22), will this cross-hedge offer us a meaningful return? Because of this wide, $30+ difference, this study requires a different analytical approach.

Over these 617 trading days a comparative cross-hedging position provides us with $2,973 in profits ($3,125 − $152).

After an excessive daily price change between these two funds, is there a cross-hedging performance advantage on the following trading day? After

TABLE 14.23 These are the results of holding a 100-share long position in the spiders and an 800 share short position in the XLF sector fund. This study clearly demonstrates diverging performance results between the two trading parameters.

Cross-Hedge: SPY + 100: XLF − 800	**Summary Results**	**SPY > XLF by +1 Percent**	**SPY < XLF by −1 Percent**	**Trading Days within ± 1 Percent**
Trading Days	617	60	57	500
$ Sum	$2,973	$6,669	−$3,624	−$72
$ APT	$4.82	$111.15	−$63.58	−$0.14
Adv	329	39	23	267
Dec	287	21	34	232
Win%	.533	.650	.404	.534

computing a daily percentage price score for these two funds, subtract the SPY from XLF.

Next, create two columns, one for when the spiders have a > +1 percent advantage, another for when they have a < −1 percent disadvantage.

The contributory variable: When the daily percentage difference between these two sector funds is either > +1 percent or < −1 percent.

The response variable: A 100 share long position in SPY together with an 800-share short position in XLF.

When either condition exists, take both positions at the closing bell; hold this position until the closing bell on the following trading day.

SPY > XLF by +1 percent

Although each combination offers a small percentage of trading opportunities, there was a strong percentage of success when taking a 100-share long position in the spiders with an 800 short in the financials when the spiders have a percentage advantage.

SPY < XLF by −1 percent

On the day when the spiders underperform (Table 14.23), this trading position produces negative results (−$63.58 APT, with a 23-34 record). In order to produce positive results we have to reverse these positions by taking a short position in the spiders with a long position in the financials.

Of course, knowing the performance of these two instruments, holding long in the spiders was the best strategy, but we cannot trade the past. This was another profitable restrictive trading system, with few plays but an auspicious performance record.

Summary

Although this strategy has been around, it receives little attention. Since it has become easier for us to short the market (especially when trading the ever-growing family of ETFs), there should be a place for it in your everyday arsenal of trading systems.

In fairness, consider this chapter an introduction to using cross-hedging strategies. In order to address the combinations, complexities, and recommendations to adequately cover the topic, the scope of an entire book is necessary, as this strategy presents tremendous opportunity for investors willing to hedge their bets.

CHAPTER 15

Formulating Trading Decisions

I haven't failed. I've just found 10,000 ways that won't work.
—Jimmy Durante, aka "The Great Schnozzola"

The emphasis of this chapter is on the process of making your trading decisions. It starts with controversy by questioning the benefits of using protective stop orders.

Prevent Excessive Bloodletting

Amid the consensus among market strategists to take a defensive stance, simply questioning the absence of a protective stop order invites criticism. Before addressing this contentious topic, would you accept the premise that although protective stop orders can be effective, they frequently misfire?

The primary reason for supporting the use of a backstop is to offset your position before a minor loss turns into a devastating setback. Besides insulating you from further loss, it does offer the psychologically calming effect of knowing that your exposure to loss is fixed.

Although the premise for minimizing loss appears to be a sensible strategy, the basis of this recommendation comes from subjective theory not empirical evidence. And so the discussion often skirts around this issue by giving us platitudes such as *never let a small loss turn into a big one.* Rather than accept this at face value, I prefer to construct a statistical model to quantitatively measure the profitability of these protective stop orders.

Although investment literature has us *cutting our losses* before a small loss grows into a painful experience, for the majority of active traders, would it be more profitable to simply *bite the bullet* or apply these defensive orders after taking an opening position?

In order to research this question, I am using the less-expensive way to invest in gold bullion.

IAU (iShares Gold Trust)[1] has less trading volume, but its price is approximately one-tenth the price of the GLD (SPDR Gold Shares).[2]

With an early-morning protective stop in place, the analysis focuses on three possibilities. First, the spiders never drop down below your stop-loss order; consequently, your long position remains active. Second, it falls below your stop order, this offsets your long position; however, its price continues on a forceful downturn, proving your decision to be good one. Third, it again falls below your protective stop, but this instrument recovers, rising way above your selling price, which is the most upsetting outcome of placing a stop order.

Before entering into this defensive order, run an analysis on this instrument's past performance with the prevailing market conditions. In this case, we confine our analysis to those days in which this precious metal byproduct opens with a loss of .005 percent. Consequently, if the opening price is at $20, we are looking for a loss at a price at or below $\$20 \times .995 = \$19.90$.

Given the above condition, we are restricting this analysis to the 20 minutes after the opening bell (from 09:30 to 09:50). Why are we using such a short time frame? In these 322 days, IAU has a daily average of 6.388 million shares, in these 20 minutes it generates 8.35 percent of its daily trading volume. As a result of this activity, we anticipate more volatility; therefore, more opportunity for our stop-loss order to fill.

Naturally, the effectiveness of using a backstop depends on many factors, such as the instrument, the distance of the stop price from its opening fill, the volatility of the current economic environment, the volatility of trading during the hours the order is active, how long the order will remain active, and the cost of trading commissions.

For the response variable, take a long position in IAU at the opening 09:30 price with a stop-loss order at .005 percent from this price. If there is no execution of the stop order by 09:50, we hold this position until 11:00.

---

[1]IAU is an iShares Gold Trust. It had a 10:1 split on June 24, 2010; this action was effective at increasing its liquidity. Not all downloading programs make the appropriate price adjustment in its historical pricing.

[2]September 14, 2011, opening price for GLD = $177.55; IAU = $17.80.

These are the questions we want to answer:

- What are the dates of this study?
  The study begins on the day after a 10:1 stock split, with an opening price of $12.08 on June 24, 2010. It runs 322 trading days to an 11:00 price of $15.70 on September 30, 2011.
- What is the frequency of an overnight decline of .005 percent for this gold fund?
  This fund qualified for a stop in 29 days (9.006 percent of the trades).
- In 29 days, the price fell below our stop loss. What was the performance difference between the 11:00 price minus the execution price for offsetting this long position at our stop-loss fill?

  The overall savings from applying a protective stop was −$0.336. Considering the cost of commissions, together with a less attractive selling price, especially in a fast-moving market, these 29 offsetting positions were unprofitable.[3]

Figure 15.1 measures the 29 stop-loss fills from their execution price to the 11:00 price. A negative score indicates the savings from placing a stop-loss order; conversely, a positive score reflects the benefits of not placing a protective order.

When using the stop-loss price as its starting point, there were few excessive declines. With the exception of the $0.39 decline, a protective stop was not a great option. Surely, there will be days when a single-day loss will exceed a dollar; this study suggests that it is better to simply take the good (such as the $0.41 bounce back) with the bad.

Although the desire to avoid a bloodbath is a natural response, being too defensive by obsessing about these losses can hinder long-term performance. Risk is part of the game. A healthy behavioral approach is to not carry around excess emotional baggage, but simply to accept your loss as the cost of doing business. Never, however, accept any losing position with resignation if you have not carefully done your homework.

Of course, these findings are specific to this gold fund, they are not indicative of how other instruments would react in this situation. Without

[3]This is generous, because it is giving us our stop-loss price, but in reality we are given a less attractive (often a penny) price for offsetting this instrument. For instance, at a 09:30 price of $16, the stop is at ($16 × .995) $15.92. In each of the 29 fills, my stop is at this price, but in reality we are getting a price below this estimate; consequently, the savings are on the liberal side.

FIGURE 15.1 This column chart shows the results of the 29 stop-loss fills. This is the performance difference between the .5 percent stop-loss price below the 09:30 price and this fund's 11:00 price.

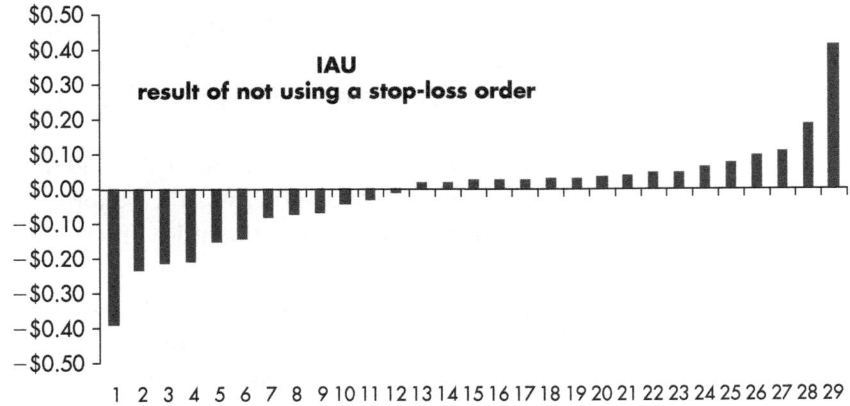

running the analysis, do not make assumptions, especially when you are comparing stocks from different sectors.

It is not that I am discouraging the reader from using protective orders; nevertheless, do not randomly place them without documenting an instrument's previous exposure to downside risk.[4]

Meanwhile, one safeguard automatically built into many of my systems arises from the duration of your system's exposure to a trading position, such as taking a long position at 09:00 but selling it at 11:00.

Trading with a Backstop

Consider using a protective order when you have the results shown in Table 15.1

Given these fictitious scores, a backstop is a good policy because a negative skew exists in these 40 scores. When there is an undesirable imbalance in outlying scores, a protective stop is a justifiable measure.

[4]I am referring to limit orders, stop orders, and triggers as well as bracket orders. In my book on emotional trading, there is an in-depth discussion on how to effectively apply these orders in different trading settings. Anthony Trongone, *Trading in the Footsteps of Sherlock Holmes: Balancing Probability for Successful Investing,* (Cedar Falls, IA: TradersPress 2010).

TABLE 15.1 Although this system provides a very appealing winning percentage, its losses are abysmal. Since the tenth percentile for these fictitious scores is at −$0.90, a protective stop-loss order is a smart preventive measure.

Adv	30
Dec	10
Avg	$0.30
10%	−$0.90
20%	−$0.60
50%	$0.10
80%	$0.30
90%	$0.50

Returning back to this inexpensive gold fund, but on a daily basis, is a protective stop a good alternative to simply holding on to the closing price?

In placing a long position in IAU (gold fund) at the opening bell will a protective stop-loss order be a profitable strategy when holding this position until the closing bell? Certainly a protective stop order is going to rescue us from some nasty days; the question is will this be a profitable strategy?

$$(16.00 \times .995) = 15.92$$

Dates observed were October 29, 2009, to March 15, 2012 (599 trading days). The response variable is as follows: A protective stop-loss order in IAU (gold fund) at .005 percent below the opening price. For example, when placing a protective stop at a price .005 percent below an opening price of $16.00, it would be set at a price of $15.92.

We are measuring IAU's performance difference given a stop-loss fill against its closing price. If the stop fills at $15.92 and the closing price is at $16.12, this strategy works against us because it has cost us $0.20.

When using a .005 protective stop, there were 280 fills, producing $2.10 in savings, with 112 favorable stops but 168 working against you.[5] Considering the commission cost, this was not a productive strategy.

[5]A stop works against you when the closing price finishes above your protective stop-loss order; a savings occurs when the closing price finishes below your stop order.

Although a stop-loss order at a price further from the opening price would trigger fewer fills, would it effectively reduce risk?

Would a stop loss at 1 percent below the opening price be more practical (e.g., with a $16 opening price × .99; the stop would fill at $15.84)? This less aggressive stop, gave us fewer fills, but these 104 fills cost us $1.71 with 57 days working against our protective order. What about lowering it to 1.5 percent? The results show 54 fills, costing us $1.60, with 28 days working against this defensive strategy; therefore a protective stop was unproductive when taking a regular session long position in this commodity ETF.[6]

Russell 2000 (IWM between 13:00 to 16:00)

This study traces the movement of the Russell 2000 (IWM). This system consists of two variables, its price from 11:00 to 13:00, as well as its trading volume. This investigation covers 303 trading days (July 1, 2010, to September 12, 2011).

In addition to framing a new study, my purpose is to appraise the effectiveness of accompanying my opening order with a protective stop order. In this investigation, I am extracting the highest 30 days by trading volume from the 303 days within this two-hour time frame. The response variable is trading in the small caps from 13:00 to 16:00 hours.

Does strong trading activity in these two midday hours (11:00 to 13:00) offer us a trading opportunity by taking a position at 13:00 until 16:00 hours? The dates are July 1, 2010, to September 12, 2011 (303 trading days).

After an evaluation of these three hours, it appears as if there are no tradable plays. The average return was $0.0057, giving us an advance of $1.73 in 303 trading days.

Before agreeing with this summary finding, we will assess the price range between these two midday hours by subtracting the difference between the highest − lowest price. The 11:00-to-13:00 trading range for the Russell 2000 (IWM) is $0.64. Certainly, this provides us with more information, but what about the quartile scores?

```
=QUARTILE($I$2:$I$304,1)  .40
=QUARTILE($I$2:$I$304,2)  .55
=QUARTILE($I$2:$I$30,3)   .77
```

[6]Remember that we are not considering the cost of commissions or receiving a less attractive selling price, which in this fund's case is generally one penny.

This gives us a wide berth for experimentation; nevertheless, it excludes the actual results from those days responsible for our trading decisions, that is, the 30 days with the highest trading activity.

Trading Volume between 11:00 to 13:00:

Average = 11.22 million shares
90th percentile = 17.60 million shares

In descending order, the 13:00 to 16:00 IWM performance of those 30 days with the highest trading volume between 11:00 to 13:00 were as follows:

Negative Scores	Positive Scores
−2.88	2.03
−2.36	1.07
−1.33	.85
−1.16	.61
−1.01	.57
−.63	.54
−.61	.49
−.54	.42
−.46	.34
−.43	.30
−.42	.29
−.34	.17
−.15	.01
−.13	
−.13	
−.03	
−.02	

With the results of trading the Russell 2000 index (IWM), the five worst declines produce a downside bias. This 13-17 record with the $0.165 average loss is weighing on the 303-day performance. When excluding these 30 days, the Russell 2000 returns $6.67.

FIGURE 15.2 After selecting the trading volume category, put your mouse on the Number Filters arrow. This will open the directional option display.

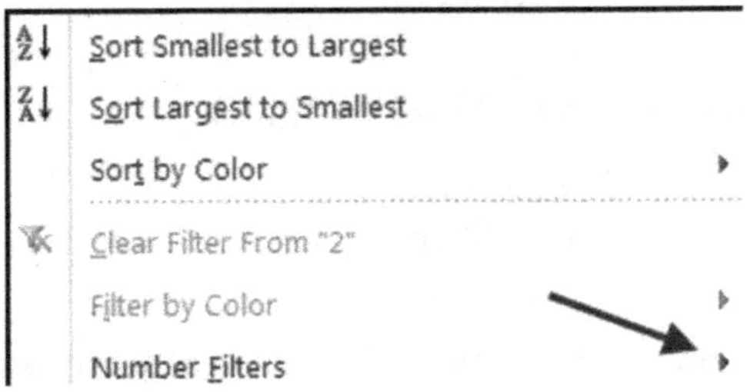

FIGURE 15.3 Select Top 10 . . . , from the column containing trading volume; it will produce the 10 highest scores.

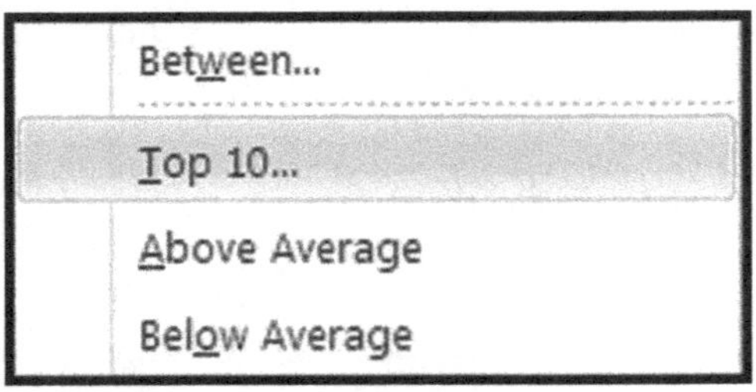

Whatever it takes in practice, be sure to put the filter function in your bag of tricks. The following illustrations show how to summon this analytical tool.

After selecting the filter command (funnel icon), this action will display a down arrow, click on the arrow in the column header you are investigating, trading volume (vm). Next, select the Number Filters side arrow to produce a selection of filtering commands (Figure 15.2). Reference the 30 days with the strongest trading activity, by selecting the Top 10 . . . (Figure 15.3); this will open another box of options.

Figure 15.4 illustrates two different procedures that capture the 30 highest-activity days for this small cap index in this setting.

Either of these filter commands will restrict your analysis to the 30 scores with the highest trading activity between 11:00 to 13:00 hours; be sure to maximize the usefulness of this function by experimenting with this option.

Perceptive readers will want to break down the analysis into smaller parts. In this case, we want to produce two categories, from those 30 days by

FIGURE 15.4 Selecting either option (30 items or 10 percent) will filter the 30 highest days by trading volume.

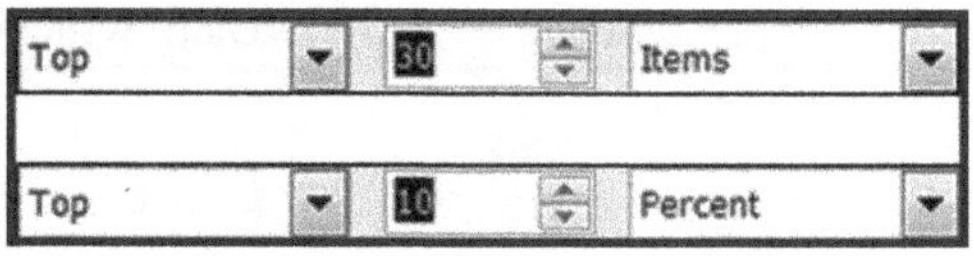

TABLE 15.2 These are the days with a loss < −\$0.50. The table includes the volume, the price change and the range between the highest − opening price (i.e., highest price between 13:00 to 15:00 minus the 13:00 opening price). After taking a short position, a protective (buy) stop at \$0.50 above the opening price would have offset three of these eight profitable down days.

Date	Op	Hi	Lw	Cl	Vm	Pc	Hi-Op
03/16/2011	78.81	78.93	77.76	78.27	44,162,773	−.54	.12
08/22/2011	65.74	65.93	64.88	65.13	22,704,047	−.61	.19
05/05/2011	83.44	83.97	82.41	82.81	33,661,258	−.63	.53
08/05/2011	72.34	72.90	70.91	71.33	43,137,747	−1.01	.56
08/02/2011	77.94	78.20	76.61	76.78	34,196,320	−1.16	.26
08/10/2011	67.36	68.83	65.87	66.03	60,195,494	−1.33	1.47
08/04/2011	75.01	75.16	72.59	72.65	50,963,500	−2.36	.15
08/08/2011	68.02	68.25	65.10	65.14	64,548,508	−2.88	.23

separating their earlier (11:00 to 13:00) performance into the following conditions:

- A positive session (price change between 11:00 to 13:00 > 0)
- A negative session (price change between 11:00 to 13:00 < 0)

With your participation in equities or commodities trading, completely circumventing risk is impractical; in the long run, being excessively cautious, without having the facts, is going to form an unhealthy behavior pattern.

In trading, losing is inevitable; embrace it as part of doing business. Particularly, because a loss can elicit great wisdom, if nothing else, it teaches us how enjoyable winning is; the trick, however, is not to make losing a habit.

TABLE 15.3 Each trader generates $500 in winnings; the difference is that some require making more trades.

Trader	Trades	Daily Winnings
A	4	$500
B	8	$500
C	16	$500
D	32	$500
E	64	$500
F	128	$500

Defining Success

Given the opportunity to make $500 a day trading, do you prefer to do this in 8 or 16 trades? Take a look at Table 15.3. Disregarding commissions, which trader would you prefer to be? Either way, after completing your trading day the profits are the same, but would you prefer cashing in on a few monster trades or a screen full of smaller ones?

In this case, finding the proper fit is an important consideration; that is, one that corresponds to your ability to handle risk. Trying to capture $500 in a few trades within a single trading day may be too risky for you. Since such winnings require a sizeable investment, perhaps it is beyond your risk tolerance.

The definition of success changes depending on your answer. With fewer trades you are sitting on the sidelines, patiently waiting for the big one; conversely, with more trades, you have a better winning percentage, but you are receiving less income per trade.

The distinction may seem small, but consider the following assumptions:

1. Attempting to make $500 on four trades in a single day requires heavy bets; you may not be comfortable taking this on. For instance, in poker, everyone has a comfort zone. Many players can profitably compete in games with a $1 to $5 ante, with raises hitting a maximum of $20 a hand, but if they were in a game with a $50 ante, with raises at $500, they would not perform as effectively because with more riding on the outcome, emotions are a destructive force. In such situations, even with a competitive hand, such high stakes might induce players to react by folding their cards prematurely.

2. When you are making more trades, you are closely following price movements. An increase in activity amplifies your susceptibility to emotionally driven trading. This is damaging because often you begin reflexively firing off trades without performing an analysis of the current trading environment; when this occurs you are likely to completely abandon your game plan. Impulsive trading may be profitable in a short-term setting, but in the long run any attempt to make exceptions to your philosophical style of trading is not in your best interests.

Of course, a payday of $500 is unattainable for traders with less proficiency. And for those with big pockets or for those who already possess the requisite trading skills, this is too paltry a sum. This leaves the majority of traders stuck somewhere between these extremes. The point is that each individual performs best within a reasonable target commensurate with his or her trading ability, upfront capital, and tolerance for risk.

In adopting this trading philosophy, it is best to put your attention on improvement. Of course, this represents honing a collective assortment of trading skills. As you continue to improve, the extrinsic rewards will follow. Never allow the extrinsic rewards to supplant your desire to expand your trading skills.

Staying in Your Comfort Zone

Certainly, there are ways in which you can mitigate risk without using protective stops; following are some helpful suggestions:

- Take a position with fewer shares (e.g., buy 100 shares of the spiders versus 1,000 shares).
- Decrease the duration of your trades (e.g., two hours versus six hours).
- Trade instruments with smaller price swings.
- Trade instruments with active volume, where the bid/ask spread is within a few pennies.
- Trade in a time frame with a history of demonstrating less volatility (e.g., between 11:00 and 15:00 versus 09:30 to 10:30 or 15:00 to 16:00).
- Give preference to those trading systems with a history of fewer adverse price swings.
- Do not participate in those time frames prior to the release of market-moving news (e.g., major economic reports, earnings release of bellwether companies, or announcements by the Federal Reserve).

- Trade less when confronting trading slumps; that is, when your confidence wanes because of a series of recent losses, tread softly until you get back on track.
- When you encounter a rough patch, do not make unreasonable adjustments. Avoid absolutes. For instance, *always using stops* or *never using stops*.
- Before placing bets on high-percentage systems, monitor their recent success. If they no longer demonstrate profitability, refrain from trading them.
- Be careful extrapolating beyond the confines of your analysis. For instance, suppose your position was reflective of taking a long position until the closing bell; if you hold this position after hours, it may backfire.
- Once you place an order, do not make any adjustments; remember the primary goal is not generating a few extra dollars from this existing order; the emphasis should never be on short-term monetary gain; after a few days, the success of a day full of trades becomes a cloudy memory.

Part of the reason these stop orders do not appear useful, is because we were making comparisons of the Russell 2000 index within a 120-minute time frame. Certainly, risk increases as you lengthen the duration; nevertheless, owning fewer shares will effectively reduce your exposure to loss. After all, the purpose of these protective orders is to allay your fears about suffering the emotional pain of losing money.

Surely, it is more work, but keep accurate records of your performance using these protective orders; it is the best way to track their usefulness. Make a dispassionate assessment of their effectiveness; are they actually increasing your performance?

Transitional Developments

Sometimes systems take you in different directions. When you are given conflicting signals, the process of sifting, weighting, and prioritizing the merits of each system separately is not easy. Most academics accomplish this by offsetting the two dissenting sides of this binary problem. If after taking these steps a winning decision is not apparent, postulate an alternative hypothesis; if you cannot make a decision before having to place your trades, inactivity becomes your best recourse.

There are those days when a system points us in a particular direction, but the facts are piling up against our decision. Say your system calls for a long position, but there remains blight on the economic landscape; are you still going to be placing bets on an upward-trending market?

Perhaps, your system is calling for a short position, but the fog over future prices is fast clearing. Are you still going to bet on falling prices? Will you still take a short position but with fewer shares? The answers to these questions do not come easy, because no two trading settings are alike. It is best to plan ahead before you are in this situation. Despite a positive or negative outcome, if you have done the necessary analysis, accept your decision as the best solution.

You do not want to be putting your energy on a *should have, could have* approach mentality. Put your emphasis on doing the analysis because wasting your energy on the past is unproductive; it should be focused on the future.

Once you set your sights on the wrong target, emotions are likely to govern your trading decisions. When this occurs, you will learn little about yourself, making it difficult to refrain from repeating the same mistakes.

Summary

There are times when the wisest decision is to let the market move without you. Although your emotions may make this difficult to implement, you do not want to force yourself into a trading decision. When the facts are inconclusive, step away from the screen—accept inactivity!

Remember, if you do your analysis before entering a position, despite putting the percentages on your side, failure is part of the equation. In experimenting with the construction of new systems, you may produce 10,000 ways that won't work, but this is often the path to sustainable success.

CHAPTER 16

Preparing for Success

There has never been any great genius without a spice of madness.
—Seneca, Roman philosopher

Success is contagious, but how do we get going? I would be remiss not to have a discussion on the roadblocks everyone confronts as active traders. In the course of a constantly shifting economic landscape, the requirements for success may vary, but some personal attributes never vary.

Confidence is probably the biggest contributor to success; it instills the motivational structure reinforcing our desire to ask questions about the market.

Anyone striving to attain loftier goals wants to know the reason for an upsurge in price, why it remains stagnant or runs to the downside. In other words, they are curious about how prices can influence future market direction.

Asking Questions

According to the historian Kenneth Clark, Leonardo da Vinci was "the most curious man in history." We used to speak of him as "a typical Renaissance man, but that was a mistake." He goes on to say: "The more we know about him, the utterly more ingenious he becomes." This is because da Vinci was "never satisfied with a single answer, always countering imaginary antagonists, he goes on asking the same question, again and again and again."[1]

[1]Kenneth Clark, *Civilisation: A Personal View by Kenneth Clark* (1969). This TV series was produced by the BBC, as a historical documentary; the statement is taken from the presenter's prefatory comments in his discussion of the segment called "The Hero as Artist."

Curiosity is certainly an important characteristic, but knowing what to look for is the gateway to knowledge. Taking your curiosity to such extremes may seem mad, but the distinction between making a success of trading or failing miserably can be as flimsy as the fine line between sanity and insanity.

Once you enter into a position, you have to accept responsibility for your decision. By skipping the analysis, however, you do not have to hold yourself accountable for racking up losses—in this way, you do not have to label yourself as a bad trader. We conveniently manufacture excuses, such as proclaiming that we are too busy or too tired.

Besides rationalizing our competency as traders, when we bypass the analysis, we often make things worse because this produces an environment conducive to making impetuous trades, and when things go badly, we transfer the blame squarely on external forces. Whatever your excuse is, modify your behavior—basically, it comes down to doing your analysis; if you cannot perform the work, make fewer trades.

Sticking by Your Analysis

Often the trading position our system recommends is far different from the one we actually make. Without having mastery over our emotions, there often is little correlation between your system's recommendations and the fills you receive. Seen from this perspective, you can turn a great trading system into a poor one. Trading is unlike horseracing. The market is continuously evolving, earlier action has a tremendous impact on the present, but the horses in earlier races do not impact the current race.

As a presenter at the Trading Expo New York, I applied this racing analogy to drive home this point. Reflecting upon my early days spent at the track, I can remember standing in the long line at the $10 window. There you are, racing program in your hand, glancing at the past performances of the field while keeping a respectful watch over the posting of the latest payouts for the horses in the upcoming race.

After digesting every statistic on every entry in the field, my system clearly had me betting on the 6 horse. But waiting in the wagering line, as the flashing payouts on the board keep changing—favoring some horses by raising their prospects at the expense of other horses in the race—you begin reassessing your horse's chances. Why is the 2 the favorite? Why is my horse not attracting more attention? As the line shortens, you spot more attractive candidates. The early morning line on the 3 was 12-1, but now he is at 3-1, the 4 has some good early speed, the 5 has recently won some class races in good company. As you move closer to the betting booth, you can hear those in line, shouting their bets "give me $20 on the 9 horse to win, $50 on the nose of the 5 horse!" Finally, at the window, it's your turn to bet and you shout, "Give me $30 on the 10 horse to win!"

What happened to your system?

Clearly, if you do not have the emotional stability to refrain from drifting away from trading your systems, you are putting yourself in an unwinnable situation. Whenever emotions take precedence over your analysis, they impede your success.

Money Management

Mastery over the markets is not the result of how many trades you place; it springs from the development of new strategies reflective of the current trading environment. As a person still learning his or her way, the best approach is to take a few positions in a minimum of settings, such as prior to the opening bell or after the closing bell. Demonstrate mastery over a few trading settings before moving on and expanding your horizons.

Strive to learn about yourself, but not by counting your winnings, because measuring performance is often the result of current market conditions. Advancing days increase, whereas declining days are responsible for a decrease in your account.

Most day traders put their focus on making a success of the current trading environment, but your yardstick for success should not be on the existing market conditions. That is why it is important to know how you perform in different trading settings. Do you profit, but underperform the market on a blowout day? Are you consistently capable of turning a profit after the market takes a slight loss? On a day when the market has a strong correction, can you contain your losses to one-third of what the market lost? For instance, when the spiders produce a 1.25 percent increase; your winnings are 0.50 percent; conversely, when the spiders have a slight loss, are you able to finish the day with a 0.25 percent gain. The latter, although less profitable, demonstrates more trading expertise; the former is more extrinsically rewarding, but less intrinsically motivating.

Counting your capital can be gratifying, but in an up market, it does not necessarily offer meaningful information about self-improvement.

In this business, commonly heard rules often deliver conflicting advice, such as take your profits or let them ride. Money management rules are to be taken seriously; however, they do not apply across all market conditions nor should they hamper your opportunity to take advantage of the current trading environment. For instance, would your trading account benefit by adopting the same money management rules in either a bull or bear market, or would it serve you better to devise different guidelines?

Trading Philosophy

You cannot achieve mastery if you cannot resist pecking away with your mouse. As soon as the market goes against you, there is a pressing desire to take action. It is terribly disruptive to routinely make exceptions to your way of trading. If playing the percentages becomes your trading philosophy, do not jeopardize your finances by entering into situations when the percentages are not in your favor. Remember, even a poor strategy with a basis in analysis is going to outperform a series of reflexive trades.

A few poor trading days can knock you off your perch. So how do you respond to this dent in your confidence? Trading has always been about fear; the fear of having a long position in a down market and the fear of missing a profitable opportunity. This fear often supplants our work, and with a downward moving market showing no sign of relief, we often abandon our game plan by selling the pain.

Of course, a few investment themes loom large, such as fostering your imagination. In the construction of a system, which will allow you to act on your supposition, structure the appropriate research design and react accordingly. Some confuse imagination with madness because it implies radical thinking, but in many ways it is simply the yearning for knowledge.

Practice patience! For instance, in snowboarding, no one begins by carving down the expert slopes; lifelong skills often come slowly. It takes a few seasons before you can race down the vertical trails and finish in one piece. When carving down the slopes, you have to focus on the terrain in front of you, not behind you. When you are actively trading, your concentration has to be on making future trades, not on reviewing past trades.

In the process, do not place yourself far from your comfort zone. Make sure your spills are controllable, come less frequently, and that you can recover from them with relatively minor pain; that is, keep your losses small so you can quickly return to the slopes.

Percentage trading is no different. Place yourself in a safe environment, ride cautiously, take it slowly; enjoy the process of learning. But along the way, remember that it is always better to be a deciding agent with constructive knowledge about the past than a pawn reacting to speculation about the future.[2]

In summary, progress comes from being curious, from doing your analysis and from making dispassionate and informed decisions. During this process, you will encounter many days holding within a comfortable trading range. And there will always be pockets of volatility; however, when confronting prices far from normalcy, be the one beacon of light in a sea of madness.

[2]Anthony Trongone, "Warning: Bear Traps," *Technical Analysis of Stocks & Commodities* (November 2011).

Technical Appendix

This appendix begins with a discussion on trading the most popular exchange-traded funds (ETFs), followed by instructions on downloading historical daily prices. There are some illustrations of how to utilize some of the more difficult Excel functions (such as using absolute references, drawing column charts, line charts with a trendline, and more examples of statistical functions). It also contains more information on moving averages and the solution to the charting problem in Chapter 1.

Trading the Spiders

Below is a discussion on the importance of using ETFs routinely as an everyday trading instrument.

SPY (known as "the spiders") routinely has an average daily trading volume in excess of 100 million shares, outpacing the market in the ETFs category. As the most active instrument, the spiders offer the best representation of investor psychology. Given their extremely active pre- and post-market trading volume, the spiders are an attractive trading choice, since they normally have just a penny difference between the bid and ask price. This liquidity is an important feature, because few instruments offer the investor a reasonable bidding price to buy or asking price to sell outside of the regular trading session.

This ETF allows investors to participate in the collective intraday performance of the 500 companies in this popular S&P 500 index; however, it trades with the precision of a single security. Besides tracking these companies, it has an almost perfect correlation with the S&P 500 futures, which offers us another advantage because you can actively trade this futures contract as a replacement for the spiders during the day or night. This mini-contract (ES) trades internationally, around the clock at dazzling speeds, with small differences between the bid/ask price.

In addition to these advantages, it also has complete transparency. You can obtain a comprehensive listing of these companies, which comprise two-

FIGURE A.1 Price movements of the spiders along with the ES contract.

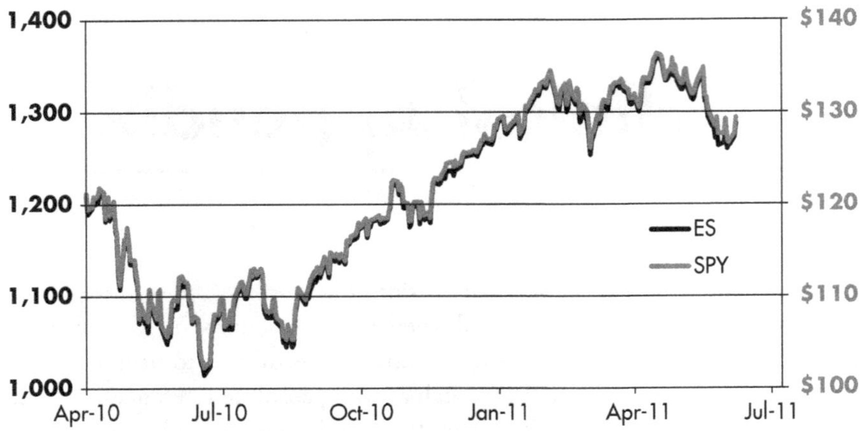

thirds of the total value of all U.S. stocks, by going to www.sectorspdr.com. A comparison of these two instruments can be seen in Figure A.1.

Trading the Cues

QQQ is also known as the cues. This immensely popular fund tracks the 100 companies in the NASDAQ-100 index. Because the cues track the prices of the companies in this index, they have an almost perfect correlation with the NQ futures. This allows you to actively trade this futures contract as a replacement for the cues during the day or throughout the night. Along with the spiders, this contract trades internationally, around the clock, with small differences between the bid/ask price.

Most companies in this index are household names, such as AAPL, MSFT, INTC, ORCL, GOOG, AMZN, NFLX, SBUX, CSCO, EBAY, COST, and YHOO. This PowerShares ETF is heavily into the information technology sector (67.93 percent). Apple, with the largest weighting, represents 17.24 percent of this index (as of March 8, 2012).

The cues have no exposure to the energy, finance, or utility sectors. Since they have active trading volume, they offer some outstanding advantages. With such vibrant activity, they normally trade with just a penny difference between the bid/ask price.

This liquidity is an important feature for both these ETFs because very few instruments offer the investor a reasonable bidding price to buy or asking price to sell outside of the regular trading session. In addition, these two ETFs allow investors to participate in the collective intraday performance of their respective indices by trading with the precision of a single security.

You can obtain a complete listing of the companies and their respective weighting on a daily basis by accessing www.invescopowershares.com/products/holdings.aspx?ticker=QQQ. With one click of your mouse, you can download these percentage weightings by company broken down by sector into an Excel worksheet.

Historical Daily Prices

Figures A.2 to A.6 provide some guidance on how to perform the steps necessary to download historical daily prices directly into an Excel worksheet.

Step 1: Enter symbol.
Step 2: Select Historical Prices.
Step 3: Change Start Date/End Date.
Step 4: Select Get Prices.
Step 5: Select Download to Spreadsheet.

FIGURE A.2 Enter the stock's symbol.

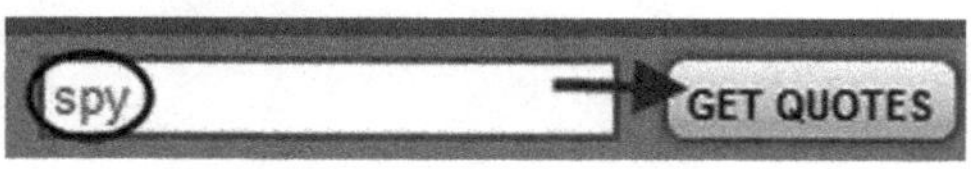

FIGURE A.3 Select "Historical Prices."

FIGURE A.4 Modify the starting and ending dates.

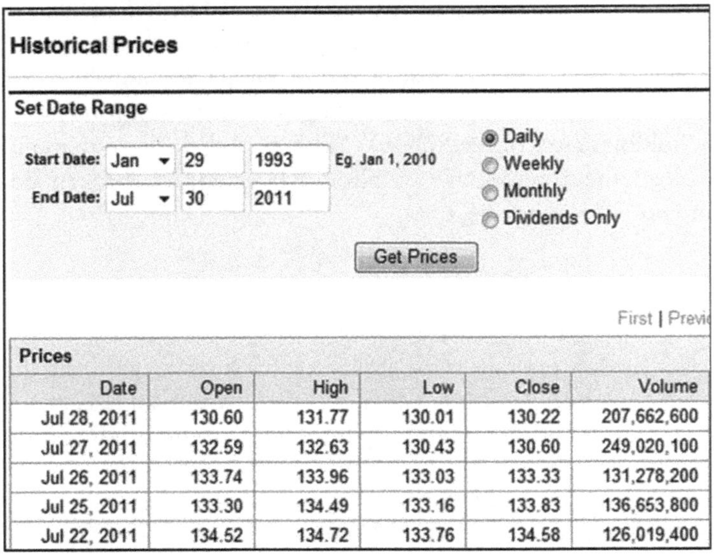

Historical Prices

Set Date Range

Start Date: Jan 29 1993 Eg. Jan 1, 2010

End Date: Jul 30 2011

Daily / Weekly / Monthly / Dividends Only

Get Prices

First | Previ

Prices

Date	Open	High	Low	Close	Volume
Jul 28, 2011	130.60	131.77	130.01	130.22	207,662,600
Jul 27, 2011	132.59	132.63	130.43	130.60	249,020,100
Jul 26, 2011	133.74	133.96	133.03	133.33	131,278,200
Jul 25, 2011	133.30	134.49	133.16	133.83	136,653,800
Jul 22, 2011	134.52	134.72	133.76	134.58	126,019,400

FIGURE A.5 After producing the dates, scroll down to highlight "Download to Spreadsheet."

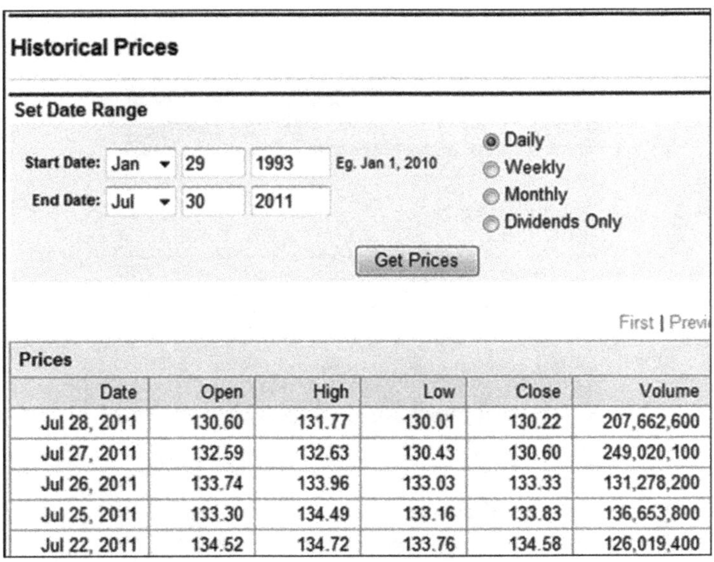

Historical Prices

Set Date Range

Start Date: Jan 29 1993 Eg. Jan 1, 2010

End Date: Jul 30 2011

Daily / Weekly / Monthly / Dividends Only

Get Prices

First | Previ

Prices

Date	Open	High	Low	Close	Volume
Jul 28, 2011	130.60	131.77	130.01	130.22	207,662,600
Jul 27, 2011	132.59	132.63	130.43	130.60	249,020,100
Jul 26, 2011	133.74	133.96	133.03	133.33	131,278,200
Jul 25, 2011	133.30	134.49	133.16	133.83	136,653,800
Jul 22, 2011	134.52	134.72	133.76	134.58	126,019,400

FIGURE A.6 Click on the download button.

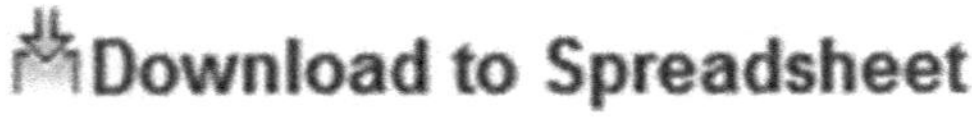

Relative versus Absolute Cell References

Unless you specify otherwise, the program uses relative references for cell addresses when you enter a formula, which allows the cell references to change after copying or dragging them down to another cell address.

When you want to keep cell references constant, you can either copy or drag the formula to a new location by using an absolute reference. By placing a dollar sign ($) in front of the column letter or row number, you freeze the cell reference. Performing this action preserves the structure of the original formula. Once you have your array in the equation, press the F4 function key, it will become a toggle switch rotating among four possible combinations:

=B2	remains a relative cell reference
=$B$2	both column and row become absolute references
=B$2	the column remains a relative reference, but the row becomes an absolute reference
=$B2	the column becomes an absolute reference, the row remains a relative reference

With certain functions this makes writing formulas infinitely easier. The =RANK.AVG function is one of them (Figure A.7).

By using the $ to capture the range scores, ranking the scores of GLD becomes a more expedient process.

As you pull your formula down the column, the range keeps adjusting down the "B" column; it does not keep the "B2:B9" range in place. You can, however, fix this by enclosing the range with "$" signs.

FIGURE A.7 Notice the $ signs.

	A	B	C	D
1	date	close	rank	
2	6/21/2011	150.76	1	=RANK.AVG(B2,$B$2:$B$9)
3	6/20/2011	150.03	2	=RANK.AVG(B3,$B$2:$B$9)
4	6/17/2011	149.94	3	=RANK.AVG(B4,$B$2:$B$9)
5	6/16/2011	148.97	6	=RANK.AVG(B5,$B$2:$B$9)
6	6/15/2011	149.12	5	=RANK.AVG(B6,$B$2:$B$9)
7	6/14/2011	148.67	7	=RANK.AVG(B7,$B$2:$B$9)
8	6/13/2011	147.77	8	=RANK.AVG(B8,$B$2:$B$9)
9	6/10/2011	149.24	4	=RANK.AVG(B9,$B$2:$B$9)

Drawing a Trendline

The process of drawing a trendline can be seen in Figures A.8 and A.9.

1. Click on the chart.
2. In "Chart Tools" select "Layout."

FIGURE A.8 Select the trendline icon.

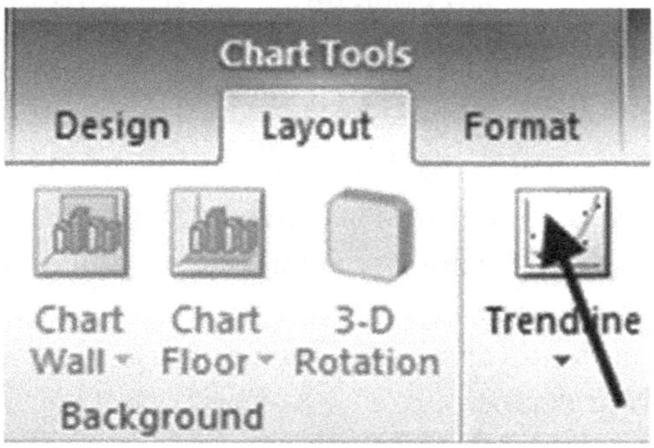

1. Select "Trendline."
2. Choose the "Linear Trendline" option.
3. Review the "More Trendline options . . . "

FIGURE A.9 Select one of the trendline options.

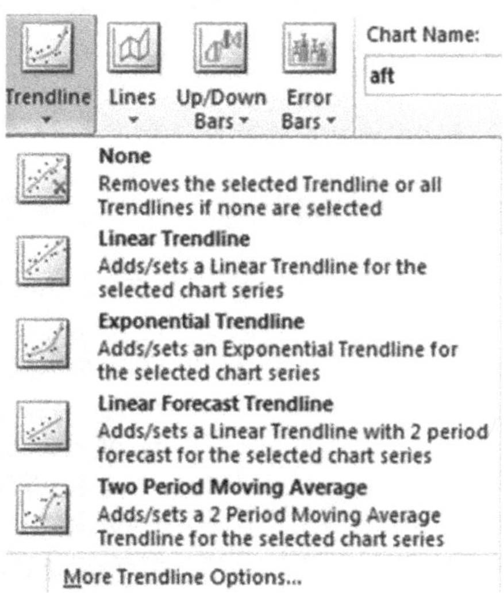

Column Charts

In order to produce a column chart (Figure A.10):

- Select "Insert" on the Ribbon.
- Select "Column."
- Pick one of the many column charts.

You do not have to constantly write these statistics; you can automatically record macros with the Visual Basic (VBA) programming language found in the Developer ribbon.

You do not have to constantly put cell range when completing the arguments when writing formulas. By defining a range of scores, you can replace the reference to a range of cells with a mnemonic name you assign.

FIGURE A.10 Producing a column chart.

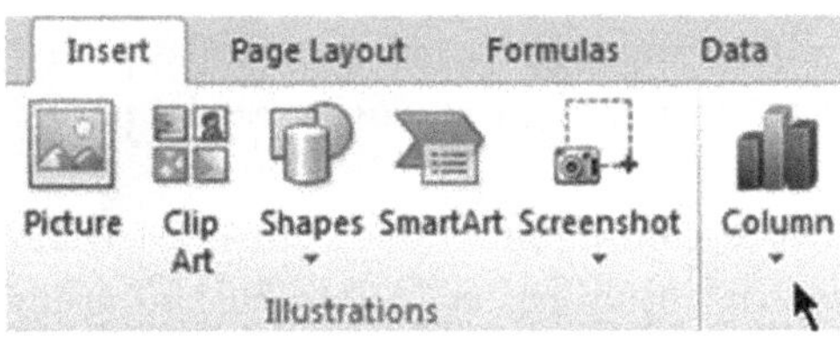

Statistical Functions

Figures A.11 shows the Function Library from the Ribbon found in Excel.

Figure A.12 shows a listing of additional functions. For our purposes, the statistical functions are most beneficial.

FIGURE A.11 This shows some of the commands in the Function Library.

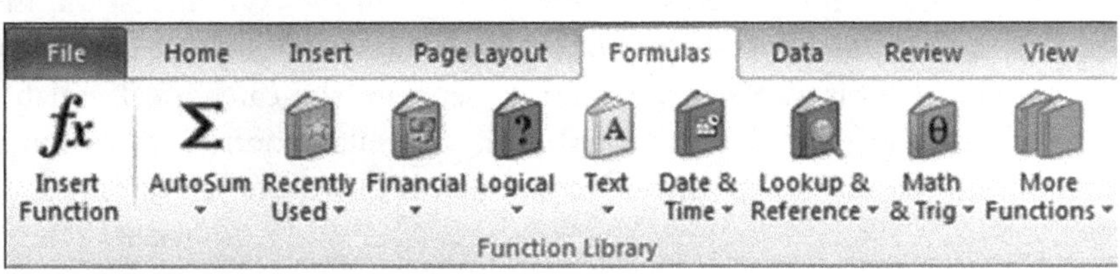

FIGURE A.12 Become familiar with the functions in the Statistical selection.

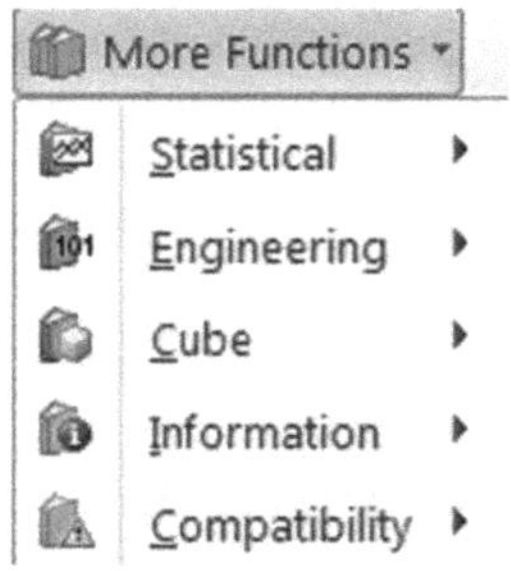

Statistical Counting Functions

COUNTIF
COUNTIFS
SUMIF
SUMIFS

Sum of the 18:00 to midnight sessions > +10 points =
Sum of the 18:00 to midnight sessions < −10 points =

What function will compute this statement?=SUMIF(

Use this abbreviated spreadsheet (Table A.1) to follow along with the formulas for the functions displayed.

=COUNTIF(i2:i1109,">10") is a single criteria statement; it is searching in the price change (PC) column for a price change >10. It does not make a distinction between a bull or bear market.

=COUNTIFS(G2:G1109,">10",I2:I1109,1)

This COUNTIFS function is a multiple criteria statement.

The "S" in the statement indicates that it has the capability of analyzing an assortment of different variables.

This is evaluating the number of evening sessions with a 10+ (">10") point gain when this contract was in a bull market (1).

The "G" column represents the price change for the evening session; the ">10" is asking the program to count those days with a price change of greater than 10 points. Since we want to separate the categorical variable (1 = bull market, 2 = bear market), this formula requires the column representing this categorical distinction, which is down the "I" column.

TABLE A.1 This demonstrates some of the headings in a simple worksheet showing the daily prices of the ES contract, including its PC (price change), spread (range difference between the highest − lowest intraday price), and bull/bear (categorical response designating either a bull (1) or bear (2) market).

	A	B	C	D	E	F	G	H	I
1	**Date**	**Open**	**High**	**Low**	**Close**	**Volume**	**PC**	**Spread**	**Bull/Bear**
2	06/30/11	1,315.25	1,316.25	1,312.50	1,313.75	24,893	1.50	3.75	1
3	06/29/11	1,304.00	1,307.25	1,302.25	1,306.75	35,551	−2.75	5.00	1
4	06/28/11	1,294.50	1,294.50	1,291.50	1,292.00	31,395	2.50	3.00	1
↓	↓	↓	↓	↓	↓	↓	↓	↓	↓
↓	↓	↓	↓	↓	↓	↓	↓	↓	↓
1107	03/15/07	1,400.00	1,401.50	1,397.00	1,400.00	18,129	0.00	4.50	2
1108	03/14/07	1,403.50	1,404.25	1,401.75	1,403.25	11,782	0.25	2.50	2
1109	03/13/07	1,392.00	1,393.00	1,389.50	1,390.50	16,957	1.50	3.50	2

TABLE A.2 Differences in the timing of a 3-day SMA versus a 5-day SMA.

Month	Closing Price	Price Change	3-Month SMA	5-Month SMA	3 to 5 Month Difference
Jan-13	58.80				
Feb-13	58.60	−$0.20			
Mar-13	58.40	−$0.20	58.60		
Apr-13	58.20	−$0.20	58.40		
May-13	58.00	−$0.20	58.20	58.40	−.20
Jun-13	57.80	−$0.20	58.00	58.20	−.20
Jul-13	57.60	−$0.20	57.80	58.00	−.20
Aug-13	57.40	−$0.20	57.60	57.80	−.20
Sep-13	57.20	−$0.20	57.40	57.60	−.20
Oct-13	55.20	−$2.00	56.60	57.04	−.44
Nov-13	55.40	$0.20	55.93	56.56	−.63
Dec-13	55.60	$0.20	55.40	56.16	−.76
Jan-14	55.80	$0.20	55.60	55.84	−.24
Feb-14	56.00	$0.20	55.80	55.60	.20
Mar-14	56.20	$0.20	56.00	55.80	.20
Apr-14	56.40	$0.20	56.20	56.00	.20
May-14	56.60	$0.20	56.40	56.20	.20
Jun-14	56.80	$0.20	56.60	56.40	.20

Moving Averages

A simple moving average is not an accurate yardstick to measure success because the earlier days are given the same computational significance as the more recent days. Taking this into consideration, observe the latest scores to see if they are increasing or decreasing your percentage error score.

Table A.2 provides an ascending monthly assessment between two simple moving averages. It reflects the difference in these two averages as the analysis takes on a new month.

After subtracting the 3-month from the 5-month signal (3 to 5 month difference), the 5-month SMA retains its $0.20 price advantage; that is, until the $2.00 decline. In December 2013, this discrepancy widens, peaking at $0.76, but once this loss no longer impacts the shorter moving average, it falls to $0.24.

When the $2.00 drop is not a burden on either SMA, the 3-month average overtakes its competition by establishing a $0.20 advantage as prices steadily advance by this margin.

If the score you drop is unusually positive or negative in comparison to the newest number, it will disproportionately affect the outcome of the moving average score. The contrast between these two scores greatly influences your trading decision.

Given the $2.00 (October 2013) decline, the differences become apparent as the 3-month signal falls $0.80 ($57.40 to $56.60, the 5-month fall is $0.56 ($57.60 to $57.04); otherwise, the signal returns to its $0.20 advance.

When using this indicator, carefully observe how these excessive scores affect your trading signal. As you would expect, a simple moving average with a shorter time frame is going to react more strongly to the appearance, as well as the absence, of excessive price moves.

Three-Day Moving Average in a Downward Setting

When downloading historical prices, a descending order is customary; therefore, a study with the more recent dates occupies the earlier rows. Table A.3 shows the actual scores for the spiders; the computation uses a 3-day SMA. It reports the trading position, the daily price change (difference in the closing price between two successive days), and the performance results, as well as the respective summary scores for entering into a long or short position.

When taking a short position a negative score is profitable; consequently, its 5-2 record becomes 2 winning trades against 5 losing trades, and its positive summary score turns into a $1.89 loss (Table A.3).

Aggressive trading brought this instrument down slightly. With both positions providing dim results, it appears as if this indicator does not function effectively in a sideways trading market (Figure A.13).

Forecasting in an Uncertain Environment

A moving average is the best-known smoothing technique. With its construction, the time frame can be flexible; however, the more days in your analysis, the less emphasis is given to the more recent performance. Its primary function is to follow emerging patterns of success or failure. Simple moving averages are below the actual price when prices are rising but above this price when they are falling. When rising prices or falling prices reverse direction a moving average is slow to respond to these changes. Since it is a lagging indicator, it is always slow to digest market sentiment.

Despite your trading horizon, developing the reliability of your forecasting model is a requirement for anyone trading the markets. In order to

TABLE A.3 A daily 3-day SMA with the worksheet showing the trading signal for entering into a long or short position.

Date	Closing Price Spiders	3-Day SMA	Trading Position	Price Change	Long Position	Short Position
11/17/2011	122.11	124.09	short	−1.97		
11/16/2011	124.08	125.21	short	−2.00		−1.97
11/15/2011	126.08	126.07	long	0.62	−2.00	
11/14/2011	125.46	125.48	short	−1.20		0.62
11/11/2011	126.66	124.71	long	2.34	−1.20	
11/10/2011	124.32	125.12	short	1.16		2.34
11/09/2011	123.16	125.77	short	−4.72		1.16
11/08/2011	127.88	126.54	long	1.62	−4.72	
11/07/2011	126.26	126.00	long	0.78	1.62	
11/04/2011	125.48	125.24	long	−0.77	0.78	
11/03/2011	126.25	124.08	long	2.26	−0.77	
11/02/2011	123.99	123.83	long	1.99	2.26	
11/01/2011	122.00	125.37	short	−3.50		1.99
10/31/2011	125.50	127.58	short	−3.10		−3.50
10/28/2011	128.60	127.18	long	−0.03	−3.10	
10/27/2011	128.63	125.33	long	4.33	−0.03	
10/26/2011	124.30	124.28	long	1.25	4.33	
10/25/2011	123.05	124.17	short	−2.44		1.25
10/24/2011	125.49	123.71	long	1.52	−2.44	
10/21/2011	123.97	122.25	long	2.31	1.52	
				SUM	−$3.75	$1.89

FIGURE A.13 This oscillating trading pattern, showing the closing price of the spiders, does not make this an attractive investment for a 3-day SMA.

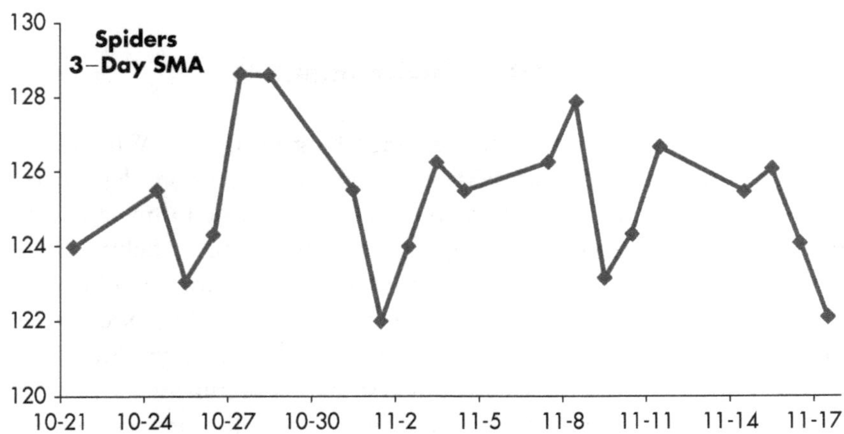

accomplish this difficult task, market participants often look to the past to predict the future. Nevertheless, past scores do not always offer us a reliable glimpse into the future, because predicting market direction is an inexact science—especially when you are trading instruments with unpredictable price swings in a trendless environment.

Measuring Results

My operational definition of reliability can briefly be expressed this way: You have to cut a 32-inch length of wood. You measure once; it is 32 inches long. You measure again and get the same results; therefore, you have confidence in these numbers. Conversely, if you take several measurements and get different results, your findings are not reliable. The validity of your measurement comes from the instrument that you are using; are you using a ruler or your feet to measure the cut?

Of course, your source of downloading historical prices may be different from mine (Interactive Data Corporation); therefore, we will get slightly different numbers. And, depending on our response variable, the precision may differ. There is greater consensus on the closing price, but there has always been more disagreement over the opening price as well as intraday prices of a stock or commodity. This slight inconsistency among data providers is part of the measurement error.

Cross-Validation

Another way to assess the measurement error of an indicator is to run a cross-validation of your analysis. You accomplish this by breaking your study into smaller segments or creating another study using a different time frame. A comparison between these two different trading settings will give you a better reading on the reliability of a rolling average, but the percentage error score is the more meaningful ingredient. Remember, reliability demonstrates consistency. If you get a 30 percent error score in both studies, the indicator is reliable, but with such a high percentage error score, there is room for improvement. In summary, when cross-validating your results, repetition of a percentage error score is an indicator of reliability; however, it is meaningless if your indicator is not a good measure of validity; that is, it is not a good predictor of future price direction.

Solution to the 16 Charts in a Bear Market (from Chapter 1)

Figure A.14 provides the answers to the stock charting question in the opening chapter. Table A.4 provides the price of this stocks at three different dates.

FIGURE A.14 Alongside every line chart is the symbol showing the price movements of this stock, during this bearish market environment. Table A.4 reports the performance scores of these 16 companies.

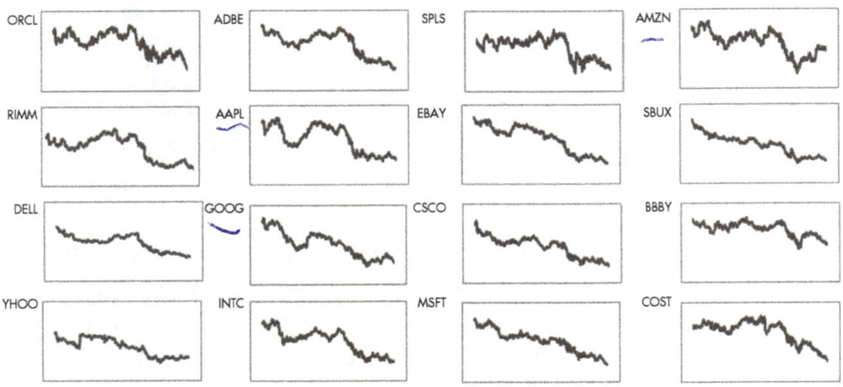

TABLE A.4 Performance scores of the 16 companies.

	10/31/07	03/09/09	05/31/11
ORCL	22.17	13.85	34.22
RIMM	124.51	35.25	42.85
DELL	30.60	8.04	16.08
YHOO	31.10	12.66	16.55
ADBE	47.90	16.78	34.63
AAPL	189.95	83.11	347.83
GOOG	707.00	290.89	529.02
INTC	26.90	12.55	22.51
SPLS	23.34	14.63	16.82
EBAY	36.10	10.27	31.17
CSCO	33.06	13.62	16.80
MSFT	36.81	15.15	25.01
AMZN	89.15	60.49	196.69
SBUX	26.68	8.27	36.79
BBBY	33.94	19.82	53.89
COST	67.26	38.44	82.48

About the Companion Website

This book includes a companion website, which can be found at www.wiley.com/go/trongone. This website includes Excel spreadsheets mostly showing the results of the spiders (ticker: SPY) using intraday numbers. The worksheets show how to perform various Excel functions in which you can produce the statistical findings for a variety of different trading systems.

- Chapter 1: When the closing price of the spiders is within a few pennies of their lowest price of the trading day, does this offer us a trading opportunity?
- Chapter 3: This demonstrates the absolute reference command by selecting the 20 lowest trading days of the spiders (with column chart of results).
- Chapter 4 (a): This is a demonstration on how to run the auto-filter command.
- Chapter 4 (b): This worksheet uses the =IF function. Besides showing this logical function in action, it demonstrates how to construct a column chart showing the daily performance results after the spiders produce a daily loss in excess of one percent.
- Chapter 5: This worksheet shows the user how to monitor the performance of a trading system; it displays running line charts showing the ongoing results of the overnight trading session and the regular trading session in separate performance charts.
- Chapter 6: This worksheet displays the running summary of trading the spiders from 06:00 to 09:00 over 252 trading days (July 1, 2011, to June 30, 2012).
- Chapter 7: This worksheet displays a dot chart showing the results of the overnight session when the closing price of the spiders is within .001 percent of its lowest price.
- Chapter 8: An example of a 3-day SMA (simple moving average), it includes the inner workings of two assessment functions.

- Chapter 8: An example of a 3-day WMA (3 × 2 × 1 weighting of a moving average)
- Chapter 9: An example of a 3-day simulation design of the best performing moving average over the first 125 trading days in 2012.
- Chapter 10: This shows a scatter chart assessing the results of a system when the daily trading volume of the spiders was either above or below 200 million shares.
- Chapter 11: This worksheet reports the performance results of taking a long position after the spiders have a $0.50-plus loss in the 16:30 to 19:30 timeframe.
- Chapter 12: This is a comparison of daily trading volume in the two extremes. Using the =PERCENTILE function, it examines the two outlying percentiles.
- Chapter 13: This study using the spiders as a predictor variable. After the spiders drop $0.60, or more, in the 06:00 to 09:00 setting, does this offer us a buying opportunity in this popular gold fund (GLD)?
- Chapter 14: An illustration of an extremely profitable cross-hedging strategy between the makers of two companies manufacturing smart phones.

About the Author

Dr. Anthony Trongone earned his PhD from NYU in 1987 and is a Certified Financial Planner (1990) as well as a Commodity Trading Advisor (1998). He is one of the Master Educators for eSignal and has written more than 60 articles for various trading publications, including 23 articles for *Technical Analysis of Stocks & Commodities.* Besides his extensive trading experience, which includes trading equity futures in the commodity pits, his 25 years teaching graduate courses in finance, psychology, and quantitative methods in the United States, as well as many cities in China and Taiwan, has given him a dynamic perspective on trading the equity markets. Anthony is an intraday trader who attributes much of his success to consistently playing the percentages, along with making trading decisions without the emotional distractions that often hamper our ability to achieve mastery over the markets.

When not trading, he is passionate about snowboarding and mountain biking on the single-track trails of Sussex County in New Jersey.

Index